ROCK MUSIC AND THE MIDDLE CLASS

ROCK MUSIC AND THE MIDDLE CLASS

DREAMING IN MIDDLETOWN

CHRIS McDONALD

INDIANA UNIVERSITY PRESS
Bloomington and Indianapolis

This book is a publication of

Indiana University Press
601 North Morton Street
Bloomington, IN 47404-3797 USA

www.iupress.indiana.edu

Telephone orders   800-842-6796
Fax orders   812-855-7931
Orders by e-mail   iuporder@indiana.edu

♾ The paper used in this publication
meets the minimum requirements of the
American National Standard for Information Sciences—Permanence of Paper
for Printed Library Materials, ANSI
Z39.48-1992.

Manufactured in the United States of
America

Library of Congress Cataloging-in-
Publication Data

McDonald, Chris, date
    Rush, rock music, and the middle
class : dreaming in Middletown / Chris
McDonald.
      p. cm. — (Profiles in popular music)
    Includes bibliographical references and
index.
    ISBN 978-0-253-35408-2 (cloth : alk.
paper) — ISBN 978-0-253-22149-0 (pbk.
: alk. paper)
    1. Rush (Musical group)—Criticism and
interpretation. 2. Rock music—History
and criticism. I. Title.
    ML421.R87M34 2009
    782.42166092'2—dc22

2009019548

3 4 5   14 13 12 11 10

TO

ROB

CONTENTS

ACKNOWLEDGMENTS

There are many people whose input, time, and generosity helped this project to develop, and I want to acknowledge as many of them here as I can. Thank you to my instructors, mentors, and colleagues, who helped shape the intellectual trajectory of my research. In particular, I thank Rob Bowman, Beverley Diamond, Bob Witmer, Susan Fast, Robert Walser, Daniel Yon, Kip Pegley, Austin Clarkson, and David Lidov for their instruction and counsel. Thank you to my colleagues and friends, with whom I shared, and in many cases continue to share, ideas, advice, and feedback, including Marcia Ostashewski, William Echard, Jonathon Bakan, Sherry Johnson, Jacqueline Warwick, Charity Marsh, Simon Wood, Brad Klump, Geoff Whittall, Durrell Bowman, Colette Simonot, Anna Hoefnagels, and Kim Morris.

Special thanks to those who participated in this research as interviewed consultants and questionnaire respondents. Your time and candid responses made this book so much more than it would have been without the voices of fans. Thanks especially to Cat Ashton, Larry Carter, Dave Crothers, John Crothers, Paul M. Fournier, Alisa Frohlinger, Anthony Guida, Alex Hofstrom, William Johnston, Mark Joseph, Tanya Keenan, Joe Kositsky, Allen Kwan, Tim Smith, Laura Sypien, Kes Theodosiou, and Dave Ward. Thanks to those who helped with questionnaire distribution in various venues, including Ed Stenger at *Rush Is a Band,* Anthony Guida at *The Rush Interactive Network,* and Terry Pidsadny in Toronto.

Many thanks to Alex Lifeson, who agreed to an interview in December 2001, and whose candid and articulate answers to my questions provided valuable primary data for this project. The interview took place during a very busy time in Rush's career, and I very much appreciate Lifeson's willingness to speak to me, even as Rush prepared for a new album and tour.

Thanks to the courteous and helpful staff at Indiana University Press, including Jane Behnken, Katherine Baber, Jeff Magee, and the anonymous peer reviewers for their detailed attention to this book. Thanks to Eric Schramm for a great copyedit. Thanks to Sander Taylor and the research department at Cape Breton University for their help in setting up the research ethics guidelines. Thanks to Rod Nicholls and Richard MacKinnon for their support at Cape Breton U.

Thanks to my family, Jim and Dianne McDonald, for their years of love and support as I became a musician and scholar. They also provided apt models of patience and tolerance during my early years as a Rush fan, when roaring power chords, shrieking vocals, and my attempts to master Neil Peart's drum figures and Lifeson's guitar licks were (I imagine) not always suffered easily.

My heartfelt thanks to my partner, Heather Sparling, who supported this project in more ways than I can count. She listened to my ideas, provided invaluable feedback, kept an eye out for useful resources, and read each of the chapters. I am so fortunate to have a partner who shares my love of music, ideas, and writing, and knows intimately the discipline and profession of an ethnomusicologist.

Some passages of chapters 1 and 2 are reprinted with the kind permission of Taylor and Francis. These passages originally appeared in my article "Open Secrets: Individualism and Middle-Class Identity in the Songs of Rush," *Popular Music and Society* 31, no. 3 (July 2008): 313–328, available from www.informaworld.com.

RUSH

ROCK MUSIC AND THE MIDDLE CLASS

Introduction

Toronto in the 1960s was not a stereotypical rock 'n' roll city. It was a running joke in urbane, clean, and conservative Toronto that the sidewalks retracted at seven o'clock in the evening. Musically, its vibrant folk scene of Yorkville (Toronto's equivalent to Greenwich Village) helped incubate the careers of artists who would soon personify the smooth sounds of the 1970s, including Gordon Lightfoot, Joni Mitchell, and Murray McLaughlin. Until then, Canada's most cutting-edge rock music seemed to come from somewhere else—working-class Winnipeg, for example, produced Neil Young, the Guess Who, and Bachman-Turner Overdrive—and there was no reason to assume that Canada's most prominent hard rock band would emerge from the sprawling, sleepy suburbs surrounding Canada's affluent financial capital. But in 1968, two high school students from Willowdale, part of Toronto's North York suburb, began jamming together and formed a band which would endure for four decades, purveying a loud and distinctive form of progressive heavy metal to millions of fans in North America and Europe. The two students were guitarist Alex Lifeson and bassist/singer Geddy Lee, and the band they formed was Rush.

On the surface, Rush at the start of its recording career scarcely reflected Lifeson's and Lee's suburban Toronto origins. Their densely distorted guitar rock borrowed generously from the acid rock of the late 1960s and the early heavy metal sounds emanating from Britain's declining blue-collar industrial centers. Lee's strident, strained, and nasal tenor voice cut through the musical texture as sharply as that of Led Zeppelin's Robert Plant. On stage, Rush appeared as long-haired, rough-hewn heavy metal rockers, and the band's volume, rebellious stance, shrieking vocals, and guitar solos were anything but models of gentility. But Rush was not all it appeared to be at first glance. It had songs about futuristic societies, swords and sorcery, and interstellar voyages—themes that would appeal to any teenage boy deeply into *Star Trek* or Dungeons and Dragons. The lyrics occasionally quoted Shakespeare, Coleridge, and Hemingway. In between thunderous heavy rock sections were acoustic passages vaguely reminiscent of European classical music. Rush rarely sang about partying on the weekend, preferring instead to play philosophical anthems about individual will and standing out from the crowd. Offstage, the members of Rush surprised some interviewers by appearing as soft-spoken, studious young men who seemed somewhat uncomfortable with the media's attention.

This was the group that I discovered as a pubescent rock fan in the early 1980s. Rush's music spoke vividly to me of the suburban context that I, like many other Rush fans, knew, capturing the in-between-ness that I experienced as a suburban middle-class kid. The band's music drew from the sound of blue-collar rock, yet its lyrics gestured toward highbrow themes. Rush combined the blunt-force power of hard rock with the disciplined complexity of classical music. The musicians made a living performing in the public eye before hundreds of thousands of fans, yet appeared camera-shy, even introverted off-stage. Moreover, Rush spoke directly to the ambivalence of the suburbs. In some songs, the band took listeners far away from the tree-lined residential streets of the present to alternate realities; other times, Rush eloquently confronted the reasons why such flights were necessary. "Any escape might help to smooth the unattractive truth," Geddy Lee sang in "Subdivisions," "but the suburbs have no charms to soothe the restless dreams of youth." "Subdivisions" fed directly into the dystopian myth of the North American suburb, describing the predictability, the cultural bleakness, the uneventful, unchanging landscape that endless residential neighborhoods provided for the North American middle class. This ambivalence seems strange given the comfort and relative affluence suburban postwar America enjoyed, but there remained an uncomfortable in-between-ness here for some young suburbanites who felt both a pull toward the conformity of North American middle-class life and a revulsion from it. Rush's take on these matters hit a nerve and won it a sizable chunk of the suburban rock audience through the 1970s and 1980s.

The group's resonance with such audiences is not surprising, since Rush's Willowdale was scarcely different from any number of suburban communities throughout Canada and the United States. It was a grid of small bungalows, townhouses, and medium-size family homes punctuated by new redbrick schools and strip malls, green belts and power lines, commuter lots and freeways. Its very structure modeled the ideal lifestyle of the modern middle class: it was orderly, carefully engineered, self-disciplined, and a comfortable distance from the social stresses of the urban core. There was a reassuring regularity and consistency in its predictable house designs, similar car models, styles of décor, and well-manicured gardens. In "Subdivisions," Rush's drummer and lyricist, Neil Peart, would describe suburbs like this as an "insulated border," a tidy, comfortable zone between the bright lights, bustle, and pollution of the big city and the sparsely populated rural hinterland. Its inhabitants were the middling sorts, neither rich nor poor, mostly white, mostly educated, and highly sought-after as consumers because they formed the great masses referred to stateside as "Middle America."

Rush, Rock Music, and the Middle Class is about the group and its music, fans, and place in the history of rock. The book centers on Rush's embodiment and representation of North American "middle-classness," looking at the complex relationship between the group's music, fandom, and middle-class subjectivity. Of course, Rush, as a rock band, is not unique in its suburban origins, but the case can be made that Rush is a perfect subject for exploring these themes, given the vividness and acuteness with which it represents and wrestles with its suburban, middle-class identity. Rush provides a rich opportunity to explore many aspects of rock as a "sound track for the suburbs," speaking to the dreams, fantasies, fears, and self-criticisms of a particular slice of the North American middle class. Engaging with Rush's music also provides an opportunity to reflect more broadly about middle-class suburban identity and music, including the many ways in which lyrics, music, performance practices, and fandom articulate specifically middle-class ways of experiencing gender, ethnicity, political orientations, social status, leisure, and lifestyle. My argument is not that Rush's appeal is simply limited to the middle class; nor will I assert that its music encapsulates middle-class life in any complete or comprehensive way. But the band's music and career are a sustained and revealing response to the condition of being *of* the North American middle class during the last three decades of the twentieth century.

But what do the middle class and the suburbs have to do with rock 'n' roll? After all, middle-class life has long been considered the very antithesis of everything rock music stands for. It is rare to find discussions of rock that do not attend to its roots in the working-class and black cultures of the American South. This emphasis is quite justified, since rock's development hinged on the appropriation of styles like the blues by audiences and musicians across the social spectrum. For many journalists and scholars, this emphasis has an enduring appeal because the musical culture of the lower classes, the disenfranchised, and the subaltern seems more exciting and authentic, especially for those who subscribe in some way to the Marxist idea of a revolutionary subject springing up from the underclass. Rock's critique of white, middle-class values and its presentation of alternative cultural ideals remain part of its ethos, rhetoric, and power. But in another sense, rock and the suburbs have always been closely connected, precisely because of the alternative it presents to middle-class norms. From the beginning, it provided stimulating opportunities for middle-class kids to subvert their parents' values and expectations. Indeed, if we take seriously the oft-repeated thesis that postwar teen affluence was essential in fueling rock 'n' roll's explosive popularity, then the suburbs played a crucial role in its history. The suburban life of rock music is an open secret, since huge parts of its audience, some of its musicians, and many of its journalistic tastemakers spring from this class, yet historically there has been little about this discussed.

In exploring this topic, I seek neither to celebrate North American middle-class culture nor reinscribe prejudices about it. I use recent and classic historical and sociological literature on the North American middle class, as well as my own musicological training, to develop a critical understanding of Rush. But this task confronts many challenges, since bad attitudes toward both the suburbs and the middle class in general are part and parcel of the savage treatment these topics suffered in the writings of many twentieth-century intellectuals and cultural critics. It is difficult to discuss the suburbs or the middle class without being pulled by the gravity of many years of pessimistic analysis and negative representation. Even Rush itself has commented in song and interview about the dreary sameness of suburbia, just as surely as it lauds other aspects of middle-class identity. For my purposes, the middle class and suburbia are best approached as sites of conflicted self-perception, and this book examines the sometimes contradictory expressions of middle-class consciousness that are constructed through Rush. Rush's critical gaze upon middle-class life is remarkably similar to that of sociologists and cultural critics such as Theodor Adorno and C. Wright Mills, viewing that lifestyle as limited, parochial, conformist, and over-managed by experts and bureaucrats.[1] Yet

Rush's songs articulate an optimistic, uplifting enthusiasm for ideas deeply rooted in middle-class history, such as individualism, personal autonomy, rationalism, technological progress, capitalist free enterprise, and a respect for high culture, which are positioned in opposition to the constrictions of suburban life. This is symptomatic of a great ambivalence lying close to the heart of many in the North American middle class, a conflict between shame and pride. On the one hand, to belong to the middle strata of society is, for many, to be mediocre, average, another face in the crowd; as Rita Felski observes, the middle class has "nothing to declare," for its identity and lifestyle are written off (even by its own denizens) as banal, uncool, and kitschy.[2] On the other hand, middle-class values emphasize upward mobility and self-improvement; the central belief is that the individual's hard work, innovation, and initiative will lead to material gain, satisfaction in life, and personal distinction.

Rush illustrates these internal conflicts clearly and colorfully. Its appeal to suburban teen audiences throughout the 1970s, 1980s, and 1990s flowed out of its ability to articulate, on many levels, the ambivalence of the "middling" lifestyle—its promises and its problems. The ways Rush did this, however, were often polarizing. Rush's music was a love-or-hate proposition for many rock critics and listeners, not only because of Rush's strident heavy rock sound, but also because its music, lyrics, and style presented a particular suburban point of view that many rock fans did not want to hear. This book addresses several questions related to these themes. Why does Rush celebrate middle-class values while criticizing the very society which carries and sustains those values? Why do Rush and many of its fans feel that those values need to be celebrated, and from whom do they need to be defended? Which middle-class values, mores, and behaviors does Rush embody, and how are they carried through Rush's lyrics, music, performing style, and career history? What do the fans say about all this, and what does their engagement with the band reveal about the values and attitudes which arise in Rush fandom? What does Rush reveal about the interrelationship between suburban middle-class identity and other factors, like gender and ethnicity? What is the relationship between

Rush's reputedly poor critical reception and the issues of social class and middle-class culture that its music raises?

With respect to the last question, there is much to be gained from contemplating Rush's apparent exclusion from most rock canons. Rush does not easily fit into conventional rock histories, in part because the band seemed so out of phase with the direction rock was heading in the late 1970s and early 1980s. After punk blazed its trail in 1977, musical minimalism, working-class bravado, and a cool, arty, ironic distance were hailed by critics as rock's new state of the art. Rush went in the opposite direction on all counts, self-consciously complexifying its songs, singing about the suburbs, philosophy, and individualism, and wearing a patina of seriousness devoid of any apparent irony. The themes that anchor Rush's music are not at all unique to the group, but in the combination and configuration that Rush uses them, they do say something about the male, middle-class, suburban context in which the band operated. The band's members had clear ideological commitments: they wanted to be seen as professional musicians very much in the middle-class model; they performed in a detached, disciplined way which connected with their desire to make music that appeared authentic and serious; and their individualism provided them with a politics and means of addressing vexing questions about white, middle-class identity. Rush's music was sometimes escapist, but it will become clear that even its escapist music faithfully illustrates middle-class values and desires. These are the central themes this book addresses as it places Rush, rock music, and the middle class in mutual contexts. To clarify the book's scope, I introduce each of the three intersecting topics—Rush, rock music, and the middle class—which provide the framework for this study.

Rush

Though this book is not intended as a biography, a general overview of Rush's history is necessary for context. Rush produced very little in the way of hit singles, but its string of gold and platinum albums places the band not far behind the Beatles, the Rolling Stones, and Elvis Presley in this respect. As such, the band should be familiar to anyone who listens to FM classic rock stations or who watched music videos in the 1980s and early 1990s. Nevertheless, Rush's position in rock's emerging historical canon remains highly contestable.[3]

Rush belongs to a generation of rock bands that rose to fame during the early to mid-1970s, when the music industry's corporate culture (following the success of the Beatles and Woodstock) still deferred to the priorities of rock musicians. The band released its first album on its own label, but was fortunate enough to receive airplay from FM DJs who still programmed their own playlists. Thanks to Donna Halper at Cleveland station WMMS, Rush gained favorable exposure in the American Midwest. The group's ensuing popularity in this region led Rush to a contract with Mercury Records at a time when record labels gave artists leeway in building an audience and a stylistic profile. The contract came with a respectable cash advance, and Mercury tolerated the low sales of the band's first three albums while mildly pressing the young group to broaden its appeal. But this gave Rush enough time to develop its musical identity until finally connecting with a large audience with its fourth album, *2112*, released in 1976.

A number of Rush biographies of varying quality have been published over the past twenty-five years,[4] though with few details about the band members' backgrounds. Geddy Lee (born Gary Lee Weinrib) and Alex Lifeson (born Alex Zivojinovich) were sons of immigrants from Eastern Europe, while Neil Peart was raised in a white, Anglo-Saxon, Protestant family. Because the musicians have militantly guarded their personal lives from the public gaze, biographers typically narrate Rush's career as a remarkably steady and stable pattern of alternating albums and tours, with virtually no scandals or episodes of serious in-fighting. The departure of original drummer John Rutsey and his replacement by Peart shortly after the release of the group's first album in 1974 was the only change in personnel.

Rush's commercial success can be represented by a long and gradual arc, with sharp spikes in 1976 following the release of *2112* and again in

1980 after the album *Permanent Waves* and the single "The Spirit of Radio." During the band's peak years of popularity, from 1980 to approximately 1992, Rush consistently attained platinum album sales in the United States and held successful concert tours in both North America and the United Kingdom. Since the early 1990s, new album sales have declined steadily, but Rush has remained a lucrative touring enterprise in North America up to the time of this writing.

Rush's biographers emphasize the group's meteoric rise from obscurity and stalwart career longevity, attributed to the band's professionalism, hard work, and down-to-earth attitude toward rock stardom. The central theme of Rush biographies is generally the music and the evolution of the group's style as a manifestation of artistic growth. As such, Rush's career is presented most often as a set of stylistic periods, an artistic evolution reminiscent of the Beatles' development during the 1960s or even of classical composers. The basic shape of this narrative begins with Rush's eponymously titled first album (1974), featuring original drummer John Rutsey, a fairly generic hard rock style derived from Cream, the Who, and Led Zeppelin. After Rutsey quit the group and was replaced by Peart, Rush's sound immediately became more virtuosic and busy, and Peart's role as principal lyricist introduced philosophical musings and fantasy-oriented storytelling into the band's repertoire. Rush's three studio albums of 1975 and 1976 document the group's fusion of its heavy metal sound with progressive rock, culminating in *2112*, hailed by biographers as the first stylistically definitive Rush album. From here, the group changed, updated, or enlarged its musical style every two to four albums. During the late 1970s, Rush drew even closer to progressive rock with lengthy songs and multi-movement rock compositions; in the early 1980s, the band continued in this style, but shortened its songs considerably. Through the mid-1980s, Rush experimented with influences from new wave rock, including the expanded use of synthesizers and reggae or ska grooves; the group placed less emphasis on distorted guitar sounds at this time. During the 1990s, Rush gradually reduced the role of synthesizers, played with funk-style rhythms, and returned to a guitar-dominated heavy rock style.

The role of Peart's lyrics in the "evolutionary" narrative of Rush is also pivotal. In the early part of Rush's career, Peart's interest in science fiction, Tolkien-style fantasy, and medieval imagery was evident in most of the band's albums, and the lyrics frequently portrayed fictional stories. His shift away from storytelling and toward humanist and libertarian philosophies during the 1980s is considered a key part of Rush's general stylistic evolution. Lyrics from later albums addressing social concerns (war, prejudice, hunger, environmentalism) marked another phase of Peart's lyric writing. In contrast, love, hedonism, and personal confession (all common in pop and rock music) were subjects Peart deliberately avoided throughout Rush's career. He often strove in his lyrics for a high poetic register, borrowing themes, quotations, or allusions from literary sources ranging from Shakespeare and Coleridge to more recent writers such as John Dos Passos and Ayn Rand. The putative intellectualism of the lyrics became one of Rush's identity markers, leading some journalists to use the "paradoxical" label of "the thinking-person's heavy metal band" to refer to Rush. This reputation was a two-edged sword, however, since other rock critics chided the band's lyrics for being pretentious and over the top. In any case, some nonbiographers have focused exclusively on Peart's lyrics, including Carol Price in *Mystic Rhythms: The Philosophical Vision of Rush* and Leonard Roberto in *A Simple Kind of Mirror: The Lyrical Vision of Rush,* both indicating the centrality of the lyrics in Rush's appeal.

Despite selling more than 40 million albums, Rush has often been regarded as a cult band or a band with a limited appeal on the fringes of the mainstream. One fan whom I interviewed recalled that as a teen, being interested in Rush was like being "part of a secret society, instead of just following what everybody else is listening to."[5] As such, Rush belonged to a category of 1970s album-oriented rock (AOR) bands whose appeal was based both upon a mystique and a sense of being "outside" the pop music/entertainment mainstream, a band whose template was formed most notably by Led Zeppelin.[6] The image of Rush as esoteric, outside the mainstream and secret (underexposed in the media), helped the band appear artistically pure and independent of commercial music fashion; it also flattered fans who asserted that their musical tastes were above clichéd, mainstream fare. But it was also not necessarily an accurate image—throughout the 1970s, 1980s, and 1990s, Rush was reasonably well covered in newspapers and music magazines, its music was played regularly on FM or classic rock radio, and during the mid-1980s, at least, its videos were played on MTV and Canada's MuchMusic. It must also be acknowledged that part of Rush's appeal as an esoteric band lies in its elaborate and technocratic musicianship, which is an inspiration to a significant contingent of its fan base who identify as musicians. These are musicians of a very specific kind, defining themselves through a well-displayed knowledge of, and conversance with, music theory and advanced musical techniques. To this part of the fan base, appreciating the finer points of Rush's musicianship is part of belonging to the "secret society" of Rush fandom, in which the recognition of modal patterns, asymmetrical meters, polyrhythms, and bass harmonics are almost musical shibboleths.

This brief description of Rush's history, and the sources of its appeal, reveals a number of critical issues which frame the band. The building of Rush's career profile around certain characteristics—an aura of professionalism, a self-conscious musical and artistic evolution, the group's vocation as musicians who described their work as a "calling," their reticence about being celebrities, their rhetoric of anti-commercialism, and their musical and lyrical virtuosity manifested in many ways—these are among the characteristics explored in this book that emerge from Rush's response (and fans' responses) to its middle-class contexts.

Rock Music

How should the study of a rock band be approached? In recent decades, rock and other forms of popular music have received attention from a number of disciplines, including musicology, ethnomusicology, music theory, sociology, communications, cultural studies, anthropology, folklore, and English. Popular music studies has thus emerged as an interdisciplinary field. It is difficult to offer a succinct summary of the diverse research into rock music over the past twenty-five years, but studies based on textual analysis, sociological analysis, subculture, genre, and reception have predominated. More recently, musicology and music theory have begun to contribute to the field. My own background lies in ethnomusicology, which itself draws from anthropology, musicology, and folklore, although it has borrowed models from literary criticism, linguistics, and diverse areas of postmodern philosophy. Given the sheer breadth of the field, I provide a brief description of how I situate this book in relation to existing studies of rock, and the theories and methods that have informed it.

This book is a contribution to a relatively recent and small body of work focusing on a single popular rock group or artist. Most such studies focus on one artist as a way of accessing larger social and analytical issues, bringing together an intimate study of a particular repertoire, musician(s), and fan base with a broader conceptual and methodological framework. Daniel Cavicchi's *Tramps Like Us: Music and Meaning among Springsteen Fans* is one such study, using in-depth ethnographic interviews with Springsteen fans as a basis for exploring the priorities and taste orientations of a particular rock audience. A similar model of scholar-fan dialogue was used by Susan Fast in her study of Led Zeppelin, but here, fan discourse is used as part of a larger undertaking of musical and textual analysis. Fast examines significant themes in Led Zeppelin's repertoire, including the representations of power, ritual, mysticism, the body, gender, and ethnic difference, and she demonstrates how these themes were essential to the band's social significance. William Echard's *Neil Young and the Poetics of Energy* builds his study of Young's career and repertoire through similar means, with a special emphasis on the use of particular metaphors (such as energy and waywardness) drawn from journalistic and fan discourse. These provide the thematic material for larger questions about the location of meaning in Young's repertoire and style of performance. I am indebted to these path-breaking studies for providing frameworks for using textual and musical analysis together with fan research to build larger studies from engagement with single artists, and I build on many of these frameworks as I look at Rush's relationship to issues of social class.[7]

My first three chapters focus on Rush's music and lyrics, the analysis of which establishes the primary middle-class themes of the book. I begin with textual interpretation of Rush's recorded repertoire to establish the character and tenor of Rush as musicians and songwriters, as well as to study the kinds of messages they present. I also seek to establish the importance of the music itself in representing a middle-class social and cultural identity. When conducting these in-depth musical analyses, I proceed from the assumption that popular music, like all music, should be taken seriously as a historical record and an embodiment of cultural values and practices. This assumption is the basis for a great deal of the musicological and ethnomusicological work upon which this book builds. A number of landmark studies make substantial connections between social and musical details from a position of close familiarity with the relevant cultural contexts. John Chernoff's 1979 book on West African drumming provides an example of moving from closely observed musical details to the discourse surrounding music and finally to an understanding of social values.[8] For example, Chernoff examines African rhythmic polyphony and relays West African musicians' explanations and perceptions, including how a rhythm is abstract and meaningless when it is not in context with other simultaneous rhythms. Chernoff ultimately demonstrates, through his own close familiarity with life in the culture, how West African social sensibilities are profoundly pluralistic: just as rhythms are not valued except in propinquity with other (and very different) rhythms, so one's life and thoughts are believed to be meaningless without contact with others. Chernoff's argument proceeds in a nuanced and detailed way, showing how deeply musical and cultural sensibilities are intertwined.

Other ethnomusicologists have worked to theorize this connection between music, social sentiment, and cultural values. For example, Judith and Alton Becker, in their 1981 study of Javanese Gamelan music, state that the power of a tradition (musical or literary) comes from its status as icon—a cultural metaphor so powerful it ceases to be regarded by cultural insiders as a metaphor and gains the status of truth. Becker and Becker imply that what is considered "natural" or "true" or "beautiful" in musical organization reveals what is considered natural or true in other social, cultural, or intellectual spheres. For example, with regard to the cyclical nature of Javanese music, Becker and Becker point out that "the coherence system of Javanese music is felt to be natural [because] it is iconic with Javanese conceptions of the workings of time."[9] As such, music becomes meaningful for a certain group of people because the music is organized around the same metaphors which articulate those people's values, assumptions, and desires.

The earliest application to popular music of this kind of thinking can be found in Theodor Adorno's work on the sociology of music. Adorno's appraisal of popular music was pessimistic and elitist, but his theoretical bases were of such strength and insight that many scholars concerned with popular music remain strongly influenced by aspects of his approach. Adorno insisted that music's production, form, and reception are indivisible, and that the social relationships and material conditions of a society affected all three aspects of music. Moreover, he theorized that changes in the conditions of production affect musical form, which in turn affects the socialization of listeners.[10] The conclusions that Adorno drew included his admonition that popular music, because it was manufactured by large businesses as a commodity, tended to be standardized and clichéd in its form, and led to a passive acceptance of the status quo by its consumer-audience.[11] In contrast, Adorno held up European avant-garde concert music as promoting progressive, enlightened social consciousness because it was made in contexts autonomous from capitalist production, and eschewed all manner of cliché and banal standardization of form.[12] Though Adorno's conclusions are problematic (popular music is not uniformly standardized; it clearly has presented challenges to the sociopolitical status quo at times; and his approach to reception seems to make caricatures out of audiences rather than revealing concretely their actual uses of music), his linking of musical form and reception with wider social and economic structures and processes has been acknowledged as a substantial contribution to musical scholarship.[13]

Another landmark in the relationship of popular music to society is Christopher Small's *Music of the Common Tongue: Survival and Celebration in African American Music*. Small advocates a change in the conception of musical activity: it should not be viewed as a product, entity, or commodity, but as something people do. Hence, Small proposes the introduction of the term *musicking*. Small argues that musicking is a way of doing identity work, as well as articulating social values: "We are moved by music because musicking creates the public image of our most inwardly desired relationships, not just *showing them to us* as they might be but actually *bringing them into existence* during the duration of the performance";[14] moreover, the act of musicking "teaches us what we really feel about ourselves and about our relationships to other people and the world in general, helping us to structure those feelings and therefore to explore and evolve our own identities."[15] Elsewhere, Small notes that the musical participant is "affirming or celebrating a sense of identity," "taking part in an ideal society which the participants have brought into existence for the duration of the performance," and "modeling, in the relationships between the sounds he or she is making, listening to or dancing to, the relationships of that ideal society."[16] Small argues further that these processes are powerful because this modeling takes place beneath the surface of consciousness. Thus, music provides us with important identity-forming tools, and does so powerfully because it involves communicating with means exceeding the bounds of language.

In the study of popular music, many of the above insights have been put into practice by scholars such as Susan McClary, John Shepherd, Robert Walser, David Brackett, Edward Macan, Harris Berger, Steve Waksman, and Adam Krims, among others. Their work involves the close reading and analysis of musical details, relating them to genre discourses and demonstrating how social meanings, values, and relationships are articulated through the music. For Susan McClary, such activity is important in the project of creating a "critical musicology . . . to examine the ways in which different musics articulate the priorities and values of various communities."[17] Walser's *Running with the Devil* is an example of critical musicology, in which he demonstrates how the sounds of heavy metal enact discourses of power and masculinity that articulate heavy metal participants' attitudes and desires regarding both. These attitudes and desires are discussed in larger social contexts—with respect to politics, ethnicity, gender, and class—which make these discourses possible. Work like this provides the theoretical and methodological background for the analyses that follow, as I show how Rush's songs and music embody and represent the desires, values, and identities emanating from its North American middle-class context.

The latter three chapters of the book shift the focus from the textual interpretation of Rush's music to its performance and reception. Chapter 4 explores the themes of discipline, detachment, excess, and spectacle as important aesthetics evident in the lyrics, music, and performing practices of Rush. In contextualizing these themes and performing practices, I draw on the work of Pillsbury and Bannister, who relate rock's rhetorical gestures of detachment, intellectuality, and seriousness to the white, male subject position;[18] using the work of historian Peter Stearns, I go on to show that these are linked to middle-class norms and behaviors.[19]

In chapter 5, I study representations of Rush's audience, drawing on commentary from fans, the band, and journalists. This chapter is concerned with how fans and fan practices are portrayed by both insiders and outsiders to the audience, and explores how these portrayals are socially positioned. My discussions of the internal aesthetic economies of fandom, as well as various notions of "cult fandom," are informed by several recent collections of fan studies, including Cheryl Harris's *Theorizing Fandom: Fans, Subculture and Identity,* Jonathan Gray et al.'s *Fandom: Identities and Communities in a Mediated World,* and Matt Hills's excellent monograph *Fan Cultures.*[20] Ethnographic data used in this and other chapters were drawn from fan questionnaires, interviews with fans, and observations of internet message boards and discussion groups. The fan surveys were conducted in three phases, in 1996, 2000, and 2008, from which I collected 272 responses in total. I also interviewed eighteen Rush fans, including nine face-to-face in Toronto; the other nine were questionnaire respondents whom I interviewed by phone. I provide further details about the ethnographic component of this research in chapter 5.

The chapter on Rush's critical reception emerged from collecting a large number of articles about Rush and reviews of its music written between 1974 and 2006. In general, journalistic writing in a number of domains (musicians' magazines, music industry trade magazines such as *Billboard*, American and British rock magazines such as *Rolling Stone* and *Melody Maker*) provides important ethnographic sources for discourse on Rush and rock music in general. I refer to these throughout the book as a way of tracking Rush's reception over the past thirty-five years. In analyzing this body of writing, I am indebted to the work of sociologist and former rock critic Simon Frith, whose studies of "rock ideology" as represented in the music press are seminal, and to scholars working in media studies, such as Lisa Lewis, who explore the linkages between rock criticism and gender bias, and Bernard Gendron, whose discussions of how rock fuses together lowbrow and highbrow aesthetics are particularly germane to this study.[21] This chapter also looks outside popular music studies, using work on the reception of middlebrow literature as a way of making sense of Rush's critical reception.[22] Through such models, I am able to relate Rush's critical reception to the book's larger theme of social class, exploring how concepts of populism and elitism are deployed with respect to the judgment of Rush's music.

Popular music's relationship to identity formation has been an important topic in scholarship over the last fifteen years, and it is here that I believe this book's strength lies. Studies have tended to focus on identities related to gender, race, and sexuality, with class being a rare topic, especially in studies looking at rock music in North America.[23] Most North American studies of popular music address class only briefly (if at all) as an ancillary consideration when studying other kinds of identity. Studies of popular music and class are more common in Britain, especially in the discipline of cultural studies, largely because of that country's greater degree of class consciousness and its strong intellectual traditions of engaging with class-related topics. The priority in British cultural studies, however, has been the culture of the working class, and studies of middle class-oriented popular culture remain rare. This book attempts to open up issues in studying the middle class with respect to popular music, focusing particularly on North America. This does not simply arise out of a desire to make this study different. It arises out of some years of difficulty with trying to research and write about Rush in a way that attends to the social context of the band and its fans in the most meaningful and appropriate way possible. My earliest studies of Rush, focusing on gender, simply did not produce satisfying insights about the group, and largely worked over already-trodden and quite generalized ground with respect to rock, gender, fandom, and musicianship.[24] Similarly, my later research, in which I tied Rush's music to issues of ethnicity and whiteness, also seemed generalized and strangely detached from the band. It was not that gender or race were irrelevant to studying Rush, but that these topics, by themselves, did not seem to say anything meaningful about Rush specifically. The issues raised could have been applied almost by rote to any number of other white, male, hard rock bands. Only when I began to think about Rush's music in a middle-class social context as the starting point for inquiry did Rush's position in the history of popular music in North America begin to make sense. As I studied existing work on the North American middle class, I began understanding Rush and its music much better, and started grasping my own subject position and experience of Rush fandom with greater clarity. Rush's music provides excellent opportunities to discuss not simply masculinity or whiteness, but suburban masculinity and middle-class whiteness. I realized that Rush's music spoke to middle-class issues with more directness than any other rock band I have heard. The great contradiction about the experience of social class in North America is that its presence is apparent everywhere, yet almost no one discusses it explicitly. This contradiction holds true for Rush as well: its music primarily addresses middle-class issues, yet almost none of its songs openly mention the word "class." This leads to a problem that I will begin to address below. How can the North American middle class—something taken for granted and so rarely discussed—be theorized for the purposes of this study?

The Middle Class

My emphasis on the North American middle class as the primary contextual frame for Rush was the most challenging theoretical hurdle I faced when writing this book. This is because, as a social and historical formation, the contemporary middle class is notoriously hard to locate and define. This may seem counterintuitive, since its enormous size and pervasiveness in North American society is generally well known, but as some historians and sociologists note, there are many reasons why the middle class remains under-studied and under-theorized. Historian Burton Bledstein notes that studying the middle class, for many intellectuals, involves studying one's own position, making it difficult to claim enough distance from the topic for effective participant-observation.[25] He further notes that the social sciences, because of their general acceptance of Marxist precepts, grant so much historical importance to the upper or capitalist classes and the working classes that the middle strata are not regarded as a historical and cultural formation of any consequence.[26] Marx believed that the middle strata of capitalist societies were unstable and ephemeral, and expected them to sink into the proletariat save for some of the luckier and more industrious who would rise to the upper classes. In America, this failed to materialize; the United States, as described by historian Arno J. Mayer, became an archetypal middle-class nation "whose labor force is preeminently non-manual."[27] Despite this, the social sciences have been slow to give the middle class much analysis, and the sociology and historiography of the middle class remains underdeveloped.[28]

The North American middle class is also an elusive subject because of its own reticence about self-definition. Two tendencies, especially in the United States, are evident. On the one hand, Americans often view the middle class as a catch-all so all-embracing as to be almost meaningless.[29] America's mythic perception of itself as a predominately middle-class nation places its history and sociology outside the Marxist narrative, and this serves obvious ideological and nationalist ends. Furthermore, awareness of social class is repressed—even replaced—by the widespread American ideological belief in individualism. Stuart Blumin notes that the middle class "binds itself together as a social group in part through the common embrace of an ideology of social atomism"; in other words, their widespread commitment to individualism leads to a refusal to acknowledge the existence of social class altogether.[30] The paradox of social cohesion being fostered through individualist ideology makes the middle class invisible to itself, and therein lies one of the challenges in discussing it as a discernible class. For Mayer, the middle class "was never a class *for* itself" but "has been a class *in* itself."[31] Its ideas and values are trumpeted everywhere in American media and culture and thus seem commonsensical and "true"; though middle-class individuals do not possess vast amounts property or capital, as a group they virtually define Middle American social and lifestyle norms. In American culture, the middle class has a kind of hegemony that makes any other segment of society (from inner city to rich to rural and so on) seem like an exotic Other in the gaze of mainstream popular culture. This invisibility, combined with the prevailing middle-class view of society as an aggregate of autonomous individuals, makes it seem as though, when searching for the middle class, there is simply nothing there.

The prevailing views of intellectuals on the middle class present another challenge. While I have found a number of sociological and historical sources that explore the middle class in a critical and balanced way, nearly all of them speak of a long tradition of disrespect among intellectuals for the middle class. Many intellectuals spring from the middle classes, and the ambivalence felt for their origins is readily apparent. As Bledstein observes, the middle classes have often been unflatteringly satirized and caricatured by intellectuals, and the term "middlebrow" has long been a derogatory epithet.[32] Thinkers such as Theodor Adorno, C. Wright Mills, and Herbert Marcuse took very pessimistic views of the cultural content of middle-class lives, which they believed to be filled with the standardized, mass-mediated, and inauthentic pablum of mass culture. From this perspective, popular songs, television, Hollywood movies, and pulp fiction were the mainstays of middle-class entertainment, all pre-packaged, formulaic, and unchallenging. As Rita Felski notes, attempts by the middle class (especially the lower middle class) to engage with high culture and high art were often scorned by scholars, who lambasted the middle class's aesthetic conservatism and inability to appreciate irony.[33] Culturally and aesthetically, the middle class at large has been given little credit among the intelligentsia. Sociologist Peter Bailey insightfully states that it is hard for intellectuals not to relish "putting the boot in on the middle class" because it acts as "an exorcism . . . of the guilty little secret so many of us share as closet petit bourgeois denying our own class origins."[34]

Ironically, these contemptuous attitudes toward the middle class have important implications for this study of Rush, and reveal much about the internal cultural dynamics of the middle class. On the one hand, Rush and many of its fans agree with the gist of the mass culture critique and regard much of popular culture as predigested, insubstantial fare. These fans see the music of Rush, along with other forms of rhetorically non-mainstream rock (e.g., progressive rock, extreme metal, punk), as an enlightened alternative to the commercial mainstream, somewhat outside the domain of mass culture. But on the other hand, it is precisely Rush's attempts, and those of many other prog-rock and metal colleagues, to create this alternative—by merging elements from high and low culture—that has led to sparse critical approval. Critics often described Rush's music as unapologetically middlebrow, vulnerable to the same kind of criticism surveyed in the previous paragraph.

I should also note that my class-focused approach challenges some of the prevailing thinking on the creation and reception of popular music. Popular music scholarship accords surprisingly little importance to social class, especially in the North American context. For example, Lawrence Grossberg, in his pioneering work on rock's reception in America, describes meaning in rock as dependent more on its "temporal rather than sociological" context, particularly its post–World War II historical position, and he doubts that class, race, gender, or nationality has much more than a limited effect on rock's meaning.[35] More recently, Sean Albiez has insisted that static or simple understandings of social class have obscured the complex developments of progressive rock and punk music, and that detailed attention to "personal histories" of musicians like John Lydon would shed better light on this music.[36] While I agree that static and simple models of social class can generate misleading or undynamic pictures of music history and musical meaning, I think that such a dismissal of class-based analysis of musical culture speaks more to its underdevelopment than any problem with its viability. The dynamics of social class and culture are complex, fluid, and changeable in many ways, but at the same time there are abiding patterns and traditions within the cultures of social classes which demonstrate the staying power of many facets of the social structure. Discussing something such as the "middle class" with respect to popular music is a difficult undertaking in both methodological and ontological ways, but this does not mean that class analysis as such should therefore be avoided.

Obviously, a term like middle class is multifaceted, contentious, and problematic. To clarify, I explain how I use this term and also what I do not mean by it. The commonplace, colloquial North American use of the term "middle class" often refers to a broadly conceived "average" position in society, which excludes the extremes of rich and poor. There are a number of social surveys and ethnographies confirming that large numbers of Americans think of themselves as middle class, even if this self-categorization does not always make sense on the basis of income or lifestyle. "Middle-class" as an adjective meaning "average" has little cachet with sociologists, but it is a linguistic habit that has great explanatory potential when looking at why North American popular culture is so often produced with an ideal middle-class audience in mind, and what this means for the reception of popular culture by audiences who are not necessarily middle class. Although I will not be using the term "middle class" in this commonsense way, this definition will be critically addressed as I talk about Rush's lyric themes, audience, and reception.

The Marxian definition of the "middle class" corresponds to America's traditional capitalist class, its elite of investors, captains of industry, and owners of large-scale income-producing property. Neo-Marxist sociologists, such as Cedric Herring, recognize that the Marxian term "middle class" is quite confusing in the North American context, where the propertied capitalist class is not between anything—it is simply the upper crust. Neo-Marxists prefer the term "capitalist" class to the older Marxian "middle class" (or "bourgeois"), while the middle segments of society (called the "middle layers," but not the middle class) are made up of middle management, professionals, small entrepreneurs, and public servants. From a sociological standpoint, this arrangement of social layers is useful, insofar as it makes clear how American society is stratified. But some American historians, like Stuart Blumin, believe that these middle layers should still be considered a class in and of themselves.[37] The American experience of class is difficult to bring into focus through a Marxist lens, partly because class is not understood as the polarizing division in the United States that it is elsewhere. The fact that so many Americans call themselves middle class suggests that other divisions (in race or religion, for example) are seen as far more pronounced. Similarly in Canada, awareness of class divisions is somewhat overshadowed by the historic rivalry between the English and French cultures, as well as the country's wider regional divides. Blumin argues that the middle class in North America is not best approached through theories of class polarization, class consciousness, or overt ideology. Middle-class people in North America are class-aware—that is, middle-class individuals recognize that they have something in common with others who have similar value sets, lifestyles, and habits—but they are not class-conscious, in the sense of seeing (or admitting) that these commonalities arise from class.[38] For these reasons, my use of the term middle class should not be understood as a straightforward invocation of Marxist sociology.

My study is influenced by C. Wright Mills's concept of the "new middle classes" from his classic sociological study *White Collar*. Along with the neo-Marxists, Mills argues that the "old" middle classes (the capitalists and industrialists) are no longer in the middle, but he does not believe that the term middle class should be abandoned. Instead, he suggests that postwar America developed a new structure, and that a new middle class

—one weaned on bourgeois and professional values, but lacking significant property holdings—was now defining America's hallowed middle ground as skilled workers, consumers, and pursuers of leisure. Admittedly, Mills's book unfolds as a pessimistic screed about the new middle class as a mass of uncritical, conformist, cultureless robots. While I agree with many commentators on the unfairness of Mills's relentlessly negative appraisal of contemporary American middle-class life, his articulation of middle-class alienation and cultural anxieties is incisive and reflects many of the same anxieties that Rush and its fans articulate when talking about the group's music (and popular culture generally). Mills's definition of the new middle classes more closely reflects my own understanding of the term.

Even more centrally influential on my use of the term middle class is the detailed archival and ethnographic work that has been conducted by historians. Their focus is often less on defining the structural position of the middle classes in America and more on describing the lifestyles and cultural habits of these middling sorts. For example, Robert Bellah and his colleagues, in *Habits of the Heart: Individualism and Commitment in American Life*, look at the importance of individualism as a central myth in American middle-class self-perceptions and worldviews, using both historical-archival work and ethnographic interviewing. The book examines individualism as a source of the middle class's ideological strength, but also as a potential force eroding the cohesion of American society. Burton Bledstein chronicles the development of the culture of professionalism which was so important in defining the middle-class career and for promoting the perception of middle-class work as prestigious, valuable, and highly skilled. Sociologist Pierre Bourdieu's ethnographic study of taste and aesthetics provides a wide-ranging view of different kinds of middle-class relationships to culture, depending on levels of wealth, cultural capital, educational capital, and family environment. Peter Stearns has written two books looking at the development of the emotional character of the American middle class from Victorian times to the present, showing how values and norms around emotional control and acceptable emotional expression changed and crystallized over time. Attitudes toward the body, comportment, hygiene, self-control, child-rearing, political expression, and consumerism are discussed as aspects of lifestyle learned within the matrix of social class. Studies such as these capture a number of facets of class—values, habits, mindsets, preferences, expectations, behavioral norms—which provide important resources for the present study. Along with ethnicity and gender, social class comprises an important part of how individuals learn to live, speak, work, and play. Following Rita Felski and Adrie Kusserow, I think of class as a social identity that has not only economic and sociological dimensions, but cultural and psychological ones as well. At the same time, social class in North America needs to be understood as fluid and ambivalent, since people may change their class position in partial ways, form political allegiances in ways that contradict their class position, and may consume or participate in cultural expressions that come from all over the sociological spectrum. While this makes it complicated to talk about popular culture and social class, I believe that studying popular music and the middle class has great potential to advance our understanding of music and identity in contemporary North American society.[39]

Finally, I want to qualify my use of words like "suburban" and "suburbia." In concrete terms, Lee, Lifeson, and Peart describe themselves as hailing from Ontario's suburbs, so suburbia is literally the context from which this music emerges. I may appear to presume that Rush's North American audience comes exclusively from the suburbs, which of course it does not. But the suburban constituency for Rush is quite large: in surveys where I asked respondents about Rush's connection to suburban life, 85 percent identified themselves as having grown up in suburbs. Moreover, several respondents who grew up in small-town or urban contexts found that the putatively suburban themes outlined in songs like "Subdivisions" (peer pressure, lifestyle regimentation, the pressure to fit into one of society's "subdivisions" or boxes) were relevant to them, even if they did not grow up in the suburbs. The middling condition is an important theme in this book because the middle class is situated between social strata, between rich and poor, between highbrow and lowbrow. Thus suburbia—a living space between city and country—provides an apt metaphor for this middling theme. Suburbia, which Lorraine Kenny calls "the imagined social core of the nation,"[40] is a concrete living space, but also a mythos, associated with middling social and cultural conditions. In this sense, the suburbs serve as a symbolic Middletown and this book's journey into Rush's world begins there.

1

"Anywhere But Here"

Rush and Suburban Desires for Escape

I n 1982, Rush released "Subdivisions," a song that scathingly depicted the suburbs from which the band's members came as a dull, parochial, and stifling environment in which to grow up. The suburbs grip its inhabitants in conformity, and for many of its young, the song asserts, suburbia is something from which to escape. Rush addressed this anticonformist theme numerous times before and after the song's release, but "Subdivisions" provides a clear and engaging introduction to some of the key mythologies of middle-class identity and the suburbs. In "Subdivisions," Rush portrays the North American suburb as a place where quiet and comfort is privileged in place of stimulation; a place that traps young people in ennui and conformity; a place hostile to "dreamers and misfits."

The bureaucratic rationality and "geometric order" of the suburb hold sway over the chaotic, unpredictable, but ultimately creative character which presumably resides in young people who seek escape. The video dramatizes the song's theme through a narrative involving a young, white, male high school student who is studious, aloof, unable or unwilling to conform to the standards of his peers, pursuing any release he can find from the routines and demands of his environment.

The video alternates images of Rush, performing with an urgent and dour seriousness, and aerial images of the suburbs. Residential subdivisions appear in grid-like patterns of concentric boxes, amplifying the geometric imagery of the lyrics. Ground-level views of middle-class suburban houses drift by, showing street after street of dwellings whose architectural designs are remarkably similar. Even though it is the camera that passes them, it seems as though the houses are rolling by on an assembly line, underscoring the song's description of the suburbs as "the mass production zone." As we approach the first chorus, we meet the "dreamer and misfit" mentioned in the lyrics. The camera pans across a high school cafeteria and focuses on a boy with thick glasses and greasy, uneven hair, sitting by himself and reading. Throughout the video, the boy is always alone, his aloofness contrasting with the packs of high school students who hang out in groups. The other students are much like the suburban houses—similar to each other, predictable, and almost indistinguishable as they walk by the camera. The alienation of the boy who plays the outcast is accented by the taunts, teasing, and laughter of his peers, and by his parents' rules, all of which intrude on his escape from the suburbs through reading and music.

Rush's "Subdivisions" illustrates this theme of suburban conformity and alienation primarily through the high school, but the song and video also gesture toward the consumer marketplace and the workplace. Whether the video shows the halls of a high school or the corridors of a shopping mall, the refrain that Geddy Lee sings is the same—"conform or be cast out." Any escape found by young people, the chorus states, is temporary, for the suburbs were designed with bureaucratic efficiency in mind, not creativity or individuality. In the later verses, crushing masses of adult workers and businesspeople are seen, fleeing the downtown core and escaping to their homes in the subdivisions in a routinized daily ritual shared by people who once—as teenagers—dreamed of leaving the suburbs. For these people, the appeal of the suburbs proves too great to resist: the inexpensive and spacious housing, the safety and calm of the neighborhood, provide respite from the stresses of work, as well as the high rents and the turmoil of the urban social landscape.

"Subdivisions" expounds on widespread postwar American myths about the suburbs. As far back as the mid-1950s, the stereotype of the American suburb as the epitome of middle-class cultural uniformity was becoming well established. Sociologist William H. Whyte's 1956 book *The Organization Man* played a large role in asserting the conformist image of the suburbs, which has become widely known (characterized partly as "harried commuters, their frustrated wives and spoiled children").[1] Folk singer Malvina Reynolds helped to entrench this image in the public imagination when she released "Little Boxes" in 1963, a song which describes the suburbs as cookie-cutter housing mirrored in a cookie-cutter suburban mentality: "And the people in the boxes / All went to the university / Where they were put in boxes / And they came out all the same."[2] Neil Peart captured a similar sentiment in "Subdivisions" when he wrote, "Growing up, it all seems so one-sided / Opinions all provided / The future pre-decided." Alongside conformity, the suburbs were identified with boredom, repose, and inactivity. Symbolically, the suburbs became the feminine counterpart to the myth of the masculine urban center. As Susan Saegert observes, the city became associated with the masculine virtues of assertiveness, adventure, individuality, the intellect, and activity. The suburbs, in contrast, became associated with the traditional feminine stereotypes of domesticity, repose, family, mindless consumption-on-impulse, and safety.[3] Despite the fact that they were supposedly designed for raising a middle-class nuclear family—with parks, schools, and shopping malls conveniently available—the stereotype of the suburb was typically that of the cultural and economic wasteland. Gainful employment, arts, culture, interesting cuisine, and other opportunities were associated with the cities, while the suburbs remained simply a place to sleep and shop. More troubling, the suburbs socially reflected a continued desire for exclusivity among the American white middle class, who used the suburbs to create new pockets of socioeconomic and ethnic homogeneity, while the cities buzzed with diversity and multiculturalism but also grappled with problems like inner-city decay, caused in part by middle-class emigration.[4] A recent Canadian documentary on the suburbs, Radiant City, rearticulates many of the key suburban critiques, showing how the suburbs achieve a "disaggregation" of urban life, a retreat into the isolation of the family home, and the production of monocultures where people are grouped into large pockets of similar age, lifestyle, and income brackets. The retreat into private space, the documentary claims, erodes feelings of community and engaged citizenship, the very things that stave off social alienation.[5] Some sociologists have critiqued such perceptions of the suburbs as oversimple and unfairly stereotyped, noting that various kinds of suburbs (middle-class, working-class, industrial, and so on) currently exist, and new theories of the suburbs as economically lively "edge cities" have entered the sociological literature.[6]

The growth of the suburbs after World War II was expected to herald a more prosperous, halcyon time in American history. The GI Bill in the United States gave veterans access to postsecondary education after the war as well as cheap mortgages, both of which swelled the suburbs and the white-collar middle class.[7] By the 1960s, almost 40 percent of North Americans lived in suburbs, making it the most populous residential category, exceeding even the cities themselves. These kinds of suburbs were an anomaly of the British ex-colonies, springing up primarily in the United States, Canada, Australia, New Zealand, and the United Kingdom itself. Kenneth Jackson suggests that there is a peculiarly British dislike of the cities manifested here, and notes that this residential and socioeconomic pattern is quite unique. In continental Europe, Asia, and Latin America, the cities' fringes are most commonly the home to the most destitute, not to middling and affluent property owners.[8] The idea of moving up the social hierarchy and out of the city was a distinct process in the English-speaking world, making these suburbs a privileged socioeconomic belt.

Nonetheless, the image of the suburbs as the American Dream-turned-nightmare continues to have a lot of cultural power. For Grossberg, rock music arose in large part because the suburbs were dull, and young Americans turned to edgy, exciting forms of popular culture to alleviate boredom. Grossberg invokes the myth of suburbia's failure, stressing its detachment and isolation: "The result was a generation of children that was not only bored (the American Dream turned out to be boring) and afraid, but lonely and isolated from each other and the adult world as well. The more the adult world emphasized their uniqueness and promised them paradise, the angrier, more frustrated and more insecure they grew."[9] In the imagination of some, the picture of the postwar suburb was painted in harsh and dismissive terms: it was no place to live, no place to work, and no place to dream. This is a remarkably grim way to aestheticize privileged lifestyles, but as Lorraine Kenny argues, middle-class suburbanites seek ways to "in-fill" their lives with exaggerated dramas and stories that make mountains out of molehills.[10] Imagining the suburbs as restrictive, pathological, tragic, or desolate provides a suitably dystopian starting point for fantasizing about escapist journeys.

This chapter explores the desire for escape from the suburban context and the means Rush provided for such escape. I consider a representative selection of Rush's repertoire from 1974 to 1981 which can be seen as "escapist," and discuss how the kinds of escapism Rush provides reflect middle-class values, priorities, and experience. In the latter part of the chapter, I look at how the different forms of Rush's escapism are implicated in the middle-class aesthetic disposition itself, drawing from the work of Pierre Bourdieu. The central themes of the suburban myth which Rush emphasizes—conformity and isolation—present an intriguing contradiction, juxtaposing regimented sameness with loneliness and isolation as some of the most urgent problems with the suburban context; and this chapter looks at how Rush mediates these themes as it critiques the suburbs. Though I discuss the theme of escape with respect to the suburbs and middle-class youth, this theme obviously applies broadly across the social spectrum. The idea that rock, pop, rap, disco, or rave music provides escape for young people from a variety of social milieus is a truism that need not be rehearsed here. But I show how the kinds of escapism Rush provides are situated in the values, desires, and anxieties of a predominately middle-class, male, and suburban audience.

The desire for escape was established on Rush's first album, prior to the arrival of Neil Peart. One of the most popular tracks on *Rush* was called "Working Man," an ominous, lumbering, heavy rock piece in which the band, ironically, takes on a blue-collar viewpoint. The song centers on the repetitious drudgery of working a day job and describes how work gets in the way of living. The traditional working-class separation of labor from life is dramatized: work is an economic necessity but a personally meaningless, alienating activity, while leisure provides meaningful personal space. The end of each verse makes clear the desire for escape from the workaday lifestyle, when Geddy Lee sings, "It seems to me I could live my life / A lot better than I think I am," delivered during the song's most intense dynamic build-up. The song presents hope for upward mobility or a more personally satisfying way of spending one's time, though without a great deal of certainty or expectation. Isolation is a key theme in the song as well, as the "I" persona comes home, pours himself a beer, and wonders "why there's nothing goin' down here." The home context seems removed from life as well; working is not living in this song, and leisure time at home is an inadequate respite, empty and inactive.

Rush's sympathy with the working class on its first album is interesting given the group's strong middle-class identification on nearly all its later records. To some degree, Rush's discarded proletarian posture on its first album might itself be understood as something of an escapist gesture, revealing a desire to identify with working-class others. Simon Frith notes that the "middle-class use of rock . . . has been [seen] as a way into working-class adolescence. What is on offer is the fantasy community of risk."[11] Dressing down, slumming, taking on a bohemian identity—these are all well-known strategies that have been used by some in the middle class as a way of escaping, critiquing, or negating their class origins. This had been done by middle-class jazz fans in the 1930s, the "beatniks" of the 1950s, the folk revivalists of the early 1960s, and the hippies of the late 1960s. In each example, middle-class youth take on the jargon, music, aspects of lifestyle, and sometimes the appearance of underclass groups as a way of placing a claim on a rebellious identity, and articulating a separation from parental standards and expectations. Hard rock and heavy metal in North America provided one such avenue of escape through marginality for middle-class youth. Studies of heavy metal found that the genre's appeal was difficult to map along class lines—its audience was not clearly dominated by working-class or middle-class fans—but this does not mean that the uses made of this genre for the formation of identity were identical across class lines.[12] The potential of hard rock's working-class defiance and machismo for use in reclaiming—if only vicariously and temporarily—a sense of masculine and rebellious vitality for middle-class, suburban boys is certainly part of the genre's appeal.

The musical-stylistic transition Rush made between 1974 and 1976 on its first four albums reveals a shift both in what kind of class identity the band was putting forward, as well as a shift in what kinds of escapism it chose to offer its audience. Rush's early style construction was keyed to an understanding of hard rock as rough, streetwise, and decidedly blue collar, yet the band gradually drew away from this conception toward the end of the 1970s. This is especially apparent in the changes that developed in Geddy Lee's vocals. On *Rush* and *Fly by Night,* Lee's pronunciation tended roughly toward a working-class and southern American dialect. This included, for example, the tendency to truncate "ing" suffixes to "in'" (e.g., "workin' man"), to leave off /r/s from the ends of words or after vowels ("bee-uh" for "beer"), and the tendency to replace /ai/ diphthongs with /a/ ("Ah" in place of "I"). In his study of the sociolinguistics of pop song pronunciation, Peter Trudgill discusses the tendency among postwar popular singers to imitate southern and working-class American linguistic tendencies even when they are not part of the singer's regional and class background. Trudgill notes that singers may use different pronunciation habits when singing, as opposed to speaking, in an attempt to identify themselves musically with a different social group.[13] Rock drew from southern, black, and working-class roots, and it followed that many singers in this genre would modify their vocal style to sound closer to the perceived social, regional, and ethnic roots of this music. But Lee's vocal pronunciation changed following the arrival of Neil Peart as drummer and lyricist. The band's growing efforts on its second, third, and fourth records to move toward a progressive rock style (discussed in detail in chapter 3), as well as Peart's tendency to write in a less conversational and more formal poetic register, conflicted with Lee's previous vocal style, propelling Lee's pronunciation toward an urban, northern U.S./central Canadian, middle-class dialect by the time of *2112* (1976).

These vocal and musical-stylistic changes also coincided with the shift in thematic material that Peart's lyric writing brought to Rush, as fantasy, swords and sorcery, and science fiction tales replaced working-class angst. Between 1975 and 1978, Rush established its reputation as a high-concept, storytelling rock band, and song suites, rock operas, and extended song forms lasting beyond ten minutes were now a noted part of the group's repertoire. Rush's *oeuvre* was never dedicated exclusively to epic science-fiction and fantasy songs, but these stood out to the point that rock critics frequently remarked upon this aspect of the group's repertoire, even after the early 1980s when it abandoned such themes. I discuss three representative examples from Rush's escapist repertoire, the fantasy-based song suite "The Fountain of Lamneth" (1975), the science-fiction-based epic "Cygnus X-1" (1977), and Rush's unusual, futuristic take on the archetypal rock 'n' roll theme of fast cars, "Red Barchetta" (1981). There are certain commonalities among these pieces: all three take the form of quests and describe wanderlust, and in each case the journey is undertaken in an imaginary world usually set in the remote past or future. However, each piece illustrates different strategies for providing escape and raises different analytical issues. Moreover, each provides an opportunity to discuss different facets of middle-class and masculinist values.

"The Fountain of Lamneth," from Rush's third album, *Caress of Steel,* comprises six songs that cover the entire second side of the original LP. The suite narrates in first person the journey of an unnamed protagonist who lives in a paradisiacal valley, and has an obsessive fascination with a majestic mountain in the east, upon which sits a fabled fountain. The first piece, "In the Valley," characterizes the fountain exclusively as an object of desire and mystery, and we never learn anything more about it, or why it fascinates the protagonist. Yet the protagonist—young, naïve, and inexperienced—must leave his valley/home that "soothes and feeds" because it is a "blur" without depth or meaning. The protagonist's sense of purpose is completely bound up in the desire to find the fountain, and the rest of the suite narrates the journey which the protagonist is compelled to undertake. The narrative is fairly loose and open to interpretation, and the songs come across as moods, impressions, or reflections that the protagonist experiences during each stage of the journey. The lyrics also leave the temporal context of the story somewhat open, though Rush hints that this story takes place in a mythical past time. The imagery of the story—a mountain, a valley paradise, a journey partly on a sailing ship, a mystical fountain—has mythical and archaic undertones, and the idyllic and pastoral setting is reminiscent of Tolkien fantasy or medieval romances. Rush's musical choices support this impression: the entire suite is book-ended by a twelve-string acoustic guitar introduction and coda, setting up a quiet, pastoral mood; the fourth song, "Panacea," features classical guitar and English Renaissance motifs which, in the introduction, recall the chord sequence from "Greensleeves." These suggestive impressions of the archaic come mostly through the music; nothing in the suite's lyrics insist upon an ancient, medieval, or Tolkienesque setting for the story.

This ambiguity leaves open the possibility for interpreting "The Fountain of Lamneth" as both an escapist fantasy and as a somewhat abstract, symbolic story of growing up and departing from the family or the suburbs. The valley where all needs are met could easily be the suburban home, the domestic setting that soothes but does not stimulate; the mountain in the east and the fountain could represent anything worth escaping to—the city, a challenge, a career, an adventure. The second and third songs in the suite present obstacles that the protagonist must overcome on the journey. The second song, "Didacts and Narpets," is mostly a chaotic drum solo, featuring vocal and guitar interjections that sound a bit like sudden, marauding attacks and a bit like the barking of orders. Of the odd title, Peart explained in a 1990 edition of the *Rush Backstage Newsletter* that "Didacts" are teachers while "Narpets" is an anagram for parents, and the song could be read as dramatizing a struggle between the protagonist and the two primary authority figures in the teen's life.[14] The third song, "No One at the Bridge," presents the protagonist on a sailing ship, abandoned by the crew and tied to the ship's mast. This part of the journey is a reflection on loneliness, isolation, and despair, and its bleakness and pathos are underscored by Geddy Lee's painfully strained vocal performance and Alex Lifeson's slowly rolling triplet guitar arpeggios, moving in a poignant tritone relationship between an E minor chord with an added 9th and B-flat major 7 with an added 6th. For the journey to continue, the abandonment and even betrayal by friends are trials that must be endured, and these represent another degree of separation from the home.

Having braved these tests, the next two songs feature the protagonist ascending the mountain and meeting with better fortune. In the fourth song, "Panacea," the protagonist finds shelter, comfort, and an erotic interlude. The musical texture is dominated by a classical guitar and low-tension vocals, producing a mollifying effect. Rush's shift from electric rock to an acoustic texture here works in tandem with the entry of a feminine character into the story. As explained by Edward Macan in *Rocking the Classics,* the metaphorical or archetypal gendering of musical textures in progressive rock was typically organized around the idea that "feminine" musical sections were marked by the use of acoustic instruments, the absence of the rhythm section (bass and drums), slower rhythmic motion, lyrical melodies, and open textures; sections signifying as "masculine" generally featured electric instrumentation, the presence of the full rhythm section, faster rhythmic motion, thematic or motivic melodies, and denser textures.[15] This paradigm provides a useful touchstone for characterizing the deployment of musical texture in rock, but should not be applied mechanically to the analysis of that music. "Panacea" is the track in the suite that conforms most closely to Macan's feminine paradigm, featuring classical guitar from beginning to end, and withholding the rhythm section from all but the choruses. Though the electric guitar is featured as a secondary guitar line, the timbre is clean and it is played using the volume pedal, creating warm, gentle "swells" of sound without any audible pick attack. All this amplifies the imagery of the lyrics which describe the protagonist's feelings of comfort and security, as well as Panacea's gentle grace, allure, and promise to give the protagonist's life meaning. There is a strong temptation for the protagonist to stay here with Panacea, to settle down and enjoy the comforts of a domestic life. Despite the protagonist's grief at leaving, this interlude is understood as another test of resolve, in which he eschews comfort in favor of continuing on to his goal.

In the fifth song, "Bacchus Plateau," the protagonist nears the summit of the mountain and grapples with mixed emotions. Jubilation and celebration alternate with doubt, weariness, and a hint of nostalgia for what was left behind. The conclusion of the journey is reached on the final track, "The Fountain," where the protagonist finds the attainment of the goal banal and unsatisfying. The fountain itself turns out to be neither magical nor mystical, and there is a sense of having come all this way to end up nowhere; the music reinforces this by simply recapitulating the themes of the first track. However, the protagonist does reach an insight from this disappointing moment: "Many journeys end here / But the secret's told the same / Life is just a candle and a dream / Must give it flame." Life, the protagonist realizes, is not about reaching a destination so much as it is about the journey. To live is to follow a dream, to chase an ambition, to seek progress and reject complacency. The fountain, the protagonist concludes, is not really the end of the voyage, but merely a stop on an ongoing journey.

"The Fountain of Lamneth" is escapist insofar as it takes the listener into a mythical space, an unspecified setting that seems to be of another time and place. The Grail-like quest superficially resembles Arthurian legend, and some of the musical motifs, as I discussed above, provide an archaic aura, evoking a sentimental nostalgia for premodern times. Of course, this nostalgia feeds not on historical reality, but on an idealized, fairy-tale image of the medieval period, drawn from Romantic nineteenth-century artistic depictions of the Middle Ages and still found in contemporary popular culture such as Disney-style movies, cartoons, and fantasy novels. This romanticized medievalism is well described by Kim Selling, who observes that "the 'Romantic' view that developed during [the nineteenth century] promoted an idealized vision of the Middle Ages as a kind of mythical, primitivist 'Golden Age' of harmony, simplicity, joy, order, faith and creativity, which was contrasted to the tumult and squalor of the modern world. This Romantic construction of the Middle Ages as iconic Other is one of the lasting myths of modernity, which has retained its deep symbolic and cultural value as a medium for social critique to this day."[16] Indeed, there are many ways in which this kind of medievalism lives on in popular culture. As Walser observes, the evocation of a decontextualized pre-industrial past in popular music holds a great deal of appeal because of its strong association with mystery and power, providing an imaginary time and space into which escape is both pleasurable and affirming.[17] For Walser, the historical accuracy and linear coherence of the symbols, stories, and images drawn from medieval, ancient, or pre-industrial sources are not necessarily important in the creation and reception of such popular culture; and, in the heavy metal songs he cites (as from Iron Maiden, Megadeth, and Led Zeppelin), the disjunct and anachronistic uses of historical, occultist, mystical, religious, and fantasy symbolism represent something of the postmodern condition of "decenteredness."[18] Susan Fast explores the evocation of a premodern imaginary in her study of Led Zeppelin and discusses how the referencing of archaic and folk styles in rock is often understood as an invocation of mythic time. In "Stairway to Heaven," she notes, the song begins by musically evoking the past and the pastoral through vaguely sixteenth-century motifs, acoustic guitars, and recorders; but through the addition of electric instruments and gradually shifting into a "modern" rock texture, the song draws the past into the present, the mythical into the urban or contemporary.[19] "The Fountain of Lamneth" draws upon similar musical strategies in this regard, using elements of acoustic folk music, archaic musical codes, and hard-hitting electric rock to merge the contemporary and the mythical.

Some of the Rush fans I interviewed discussed this idea of being placed in "mythical" time as one of the appealing features of Rush's 1970s repertoire. For Paul Fournier, Rush's fantasy-based songs are interesting because they are difficult to place in time: "They seem medieval, yet futuristic—they have that distant, middle-of-nowhere sense to them."[20] William Johnston observed that Rush's 1970s fantasy-based repertoire

> has a kind of a Tolkienesque feel to it, or at least what you would think Tolkien would sound like. Also, there's an overture to Elizabethan music, except it's not being done on mandolin, it's being done on keyboards. And Alex has his bits with the classical guitar. Then there's that whole affectation that prog-rockers had going with their long hair and flowing robes, that whole "sixteenth-century guys" thing, the Romanticization of times past when we weren't so besot by technology, radio waves going though the air, electricity. . . . Like the middle ages without the plague. It's a Romanticization of a time period intermixed with fantasy elements. The middle ages didn't really have dragons or wizards. They did have alchemists, but they never did find gold. Hero's quests, proving one's mettle, like King Arthur's adventures as a young boy, pulling Excalibur out of the stone—that affirmation is really appealing to young people especially, because you come up with this secret knowledge of yourself, and the self you don't reveal to other people is in fact your "real" self. It's virtuous, it's different from others you see around you. Deeper, more profound, more in touch with the essence of the universe. [They] weave that in with a Tolkienesque, medieval quest for secret pleasures.[21]

Johnston's incisive comments get at some of the important aspects of literary fantasy as escapism. The idea of discovering your "real" self and finding empowerment through dwelling in an imaginary world is something which J.R.R. Tolkien himself described. For Tolkien, people become invested in fantasy and imaginary worlds because "in constructing the fantasy world, we become 'sub-creators'; we realize the image of the creator-God in us, and thus narrative fantasy is able to bring us *evangelium*, the good news that there is more to life and reality than the deadening, technocratized world of ordinary modernist experience."[22] Given the reputation of the suburbs as being precisely this—a deadening, technocratized world—the role of escapist fantasy in providing a kind of spiritual nourishment, a way of being situated in a preferable reality, is easy to see. The insight that the protagonist reaches in "The Fountain of Lamneth" is quite similar to the *evangelium* which Tolkien describes, and the whole suite centers on the theme of finding "more to life" than is provided by the home and everyday routine.

Johnston also points out that the escapism which Rush provided for him had a profoundly private nature. The pleasures of Rush's escapist repertoire were secret pleasures that helped express a part of the self not revealed to others; a self that is more "real" than the self one shows in public. Such a private self, existing only in the mind of the individual, may be argued to be the "real" self, and yet its interiority makes its existence paradoxically immaterial and mythical. Indeed, as Johnston suggests, this private "real" self may be actuated, not through concrete interactions with other people, but through fantasy or myth, through the narration of a story set in an alternate world. George Aichele discusses this apparent contradiction in "Literary Fantasy and Postmodern Theology," observing that modernist metaphysics draw sharp boundaries between reality and fantasy, and teach that fantasy worlds are simply impossible: "For modernism, the fantastic belongs to the realm of the non-real, to which non-belief is the appropriate response. The exclusion of the fantastic (the dream, the fiction, the lie) makes modernist truth possible."[23] Though modernist metaphysics insist on a fantasy world as being false and trivial, "nonetheless, we find that [fantasy] world to be truer and more real than the world of ordinary experience."[24]

What fantasy and escapism provide, then, is a particular experience of interiority that is rooted in middle-class and modernist ideas about individuality. The establishment and maintenance of an opposition between the public and private is very important in actuating middle-class individualism. A belief in the realness and authenticity of the individual subject is the foundation on which modernism, the Enlightenment, and capitalism are based, harkening back to John Locke's idea of the individual as something that arises prior to society.[25] Robert Walser observes that notions of authentic individualism originate in myths of interiority: "They produce an individualized image of the self, an 'inside' not only defined against the outside, but imagined as somehow autonomous from it. They ask us to accept an intangible inner life as the essence of a person: truer than behavior, deeper than one's closest relationships. . . . They paint the social world as a shallow backdrop to the mysterious wellsprings of subjectivity."[26] For many fans, Rush's music produces "deep" experiences because it provides a vehicle for escaping into worlds of interiority, and it enriches the experience of a private, even isolated, imagination. This kind of escapism offers a mythic affirmation of individualism, a confirmation that the private world is indeed unique, rich, and deep and may be shaped by the freedom of our imagination. I elaborate on the relationship between individualism and the middle class in the next chapter, but it is important to establish here the relationship between fantasy, escapism, and individualism in this part of Rush's repertoire.

"The Fountain of Lamneth" is not simply a vehicle for escapism; it also has an overarching message. This parable-like quality is found in a number of Rush's other fantasy epics (e.g., "2112," "Xanadu," "Hemispheres"), but the group also composed works of fantasy that do not have any particular message (e.g., "By-Tor and the Snowdog," "The Necromancer," and "Cygnus X-1," discussed further below). In any case, pure fantasy is an anomaly in Rush's repertoire, as Peart's lyric writing is most frequently oriented toward the presentation of moral, philosophical, or ideological content, whether the song is a narrative or not. The inclusion of a moral or message in the band's songs, even in otherwise escapist songs, is one aspect of Rush's middle-class approach and appeal. Middle-class or middlebrow art or entertainment has long been marked by an insistence on providing a moral or educational component. As Simon Frith observes, middle-class cultural consumers generally expect that art or entertainment should "teach" or have some kind of moral. Referring to surveys of middle-class filmgoers in the mid-twentieth century, Frith notes how food metaphors were often used by these consumers, describing light, message-less films as "empty calories"; the same consumers praised films that offered something more morally substantial as "good for you."[27] Cultural critic Rita Felski, reflecting on her own lower-middle-class background, recalls similar expectations among her family and peers regarding the edifying purposes of culture, an affirmation of "the vital importance of education and the improving value of culture. . . . The purpose of culture was not to dwell on the unpleasant or distasteful aspects of life but to be positive, educational and morally uplifting."[28] This reveals much about the middling cultural position of much of the middle class. On the one hand, there is a desire for something more than entertainment perceived as empty (or without "improving value," as Felski states); rather, the desire is for entertainment perceived as having substance or cultural capital, which provides an affirmation of bourgeois morality. Middlebrow audiences commonly receive the escapism of mass culture (e.g., action films, reality TV, romance novels) as empty, acceptable for a bit of diversion but mostly mindless. At the same time, most of the middlebrow audience does not well understand contemporary elite culture, as represented by the experimental avant-garde, viewing it as subversive, unnecessarily ugly or obscurantist, and even fraudulent.[29] Consuming mass culture with a message is one example of how middlebrow audiences find a compromise between high-culture aspirations and lowbrow cultural forms. Middlebrow culture has historically been an integral part of North American popular culture, and it is here that Rush's escapist repertoire can be mapped onto the middle-class cultural landscape.

The moral provided by "The Fountain of Lamneth" is itself emblematic of several middle-class-derived values. Quite saliently, the suite's narrative supports the value of deferred gratification. The first track, dealing with the start of the protagonist's journey, speaks of the home as soothing, feeding, and providing for a "way of life that's easy" and the fulfillment of "simple needs." The protagonist expresses dissatisfaction with this easy, simple life, and sets off to fulfill a larger, more ambitious agenda. He seems to have no choice; fulfilled needs are not really "living," and the abandonment of this easy-living context is presented as a necessity. As discussed above, the next two tracks describe the endurance of difficulties and trials, and tracks four and five deal with the resistance of pleasant temptations which would divert the protagonist from achieving the goal. The wisdom attained by reaching the fountain is gained only through difficulty and tests of resolve; even then, the wisdom earned turns out to be a bitter pill for the protagonist to swallow. At every turn, gratification is withheld, and even the achievement of the goal frustrates the expectation of a triumphant arrival. On the one hand, this plot is bourgeois Romanticism encapsulated; on the other hand, the song suite presents exactly what is expected of anyone entering a middle-class career. The culture of professionalism, as Burton Bledstein notes, contains built-in initiation rituals which deliberately test the individual's ability to defer gratification. Bledstein uses the examples of the legal and medical professions, in which bar exams and medical boards test not just knowledge but the ability to endure stress; in academia, Ph.D. dissertations are not just about demonstrating skill in scholarly methods, but about showing the endurance needed to be a dedicated scholar.[30] Careers in popular music might be added to the list, since many critics and fans accord more respect to musicians who have clearly paid their dues—struggling to start a career, doggedly honing their craft, slowly rising through the ranks—than to artists who appear to have attained instant success. "The Fountain of Lamneth" narrates such an initiation ritual mythically, presenting the idea that hard work is necessary for advancement and a fulfilling life.

"The Fountain of Lamneth" is also a mythical affirmation of individualism. The protagonist consistently turns away from others in this narrative, diligently and irascibly pursuing his own path. Abandoned by his friends and companions in "No One at the Bridge," the protagonist endures betrayal and continues, "going it alone." In "Panacea," he turns away from the offer of domestic and romantic companionship and affirms the necessity of achieving his goal unassisted and unaccompanied. The quest depicted in the suite is for the affirmation of the protagonist as a self-made individual, an identity affirmed by climbing a proverbial mountain through sheer force of will. As described by Robert Bellah and his colleagues, this quest represents the quintessential American middle-class myth of the self, where "success is thought of in terms of personal choice" with respect to lifestyle, career, and economic independence. Freedom, for the American middle class, is partly the freedom to be "left alone" and not to have views and lifestyles forced upon you.[31] The authors describe how American middle-class myths privilege a radical form of individuality and self-reliance. Family and community traditions, they point out, have declined as openly acknowledged landmarks for lifestyle choice; one is expected to "leave home" in order to find oneself, and one is expected to "leave church" and have one's own conversion experience.[32] Somehow, in this radical version of individualism, the self is "found" through separating from community and kinship. Again, mythically, "The Fountain of Lamneth" articulates this middle-class value of radical individualism, since the protagonist everywhere secedes from, or avoids, social connections.

It is apparent that this "escapist" suite of songs is actually quite entrenched in the myths and values of its middle-class context, particularly easy to see because of a moral within the fantasy narrative. I turn now to Rush songs that present different challenges for analysis, since the escapism they provide is markedly different from "The Fountain of Lamneth." "Cygnus X-1," from Rush's 1977 album *A Farewell to Kings,* is another extended escapist narrative but without a moral; it belongs to the category of science fiction, narrating a story of the distant future in which a space traveler flies a spaceship into a black hole. "Cygnus X-1," although it breaks into clear sections, is not a suite of songs, but ten and a half minutes of continuous music. It should be noted that the "Cygnus X-1" story is a cliffhanger—the piece ends with the space traveler spiraling into the black hole, his fate unknown (the album's liner notes state that the tale is "to be continued"). The story continues on Rush's succeeding album, *Hemispheres* (1978), though it is a highly eccentric continuation. Peart presents the world on the other side of the black hole as the mythological Greek world of gods and goddesses. Science fiction is supplanted by myth, and this sequel epic, "Hemispheres," is a symbolic work with a larger social theme. I focus on "Cygnus X-1" as a discrete science-fiction song and narrative, however, since it reveals a number of aspects of progressive-rock and science-fiction escapism that are quite different from "The Fountain of Lamneth" (as well as "Hemispheres").

Whereas Rush's handling of a fantasy narrative in "The Fountain of Lamneth" makes use of well-established codes that reference the archaic and pastoral, Rush's musical and lyrical setting of "Cygnus X-1" places an emphasis on strangeness, otherness, distance, and spatiality. The first minute and a half establishes these themes aurally, entirely without groove, bass, drums, or any familiar Rush guitar sounds. Building on the experiments of Pink Floyd and similar progressive rock groups, Rush constructs a soundscape through electronic studio manipulation. Peart's tubular bells are heard, but they are muffled, heavily reverbed, and treated with echo until they sound like an eerie, distant, repeating electronic signal. A variety of sound effects are treated with the same kind of digital echo in the song's opening, establishing a sense of massive open space. The ringing, sustained sound of controlled guitar feedback is subtly mixed into the texture, providing another eerie, otherworldly effect. The voice of Rush's producer, Terry Brown, enters about thirty seconds into the soundscape, electronically garbled and tuned down in pitch until it scarcely sounds human. Brown's voice acts as an omniscient narrator, telling us of the "mysterious, invisible force" that comprises the black hole. The first sign of Rush playing in a more familiar rock style comes in the form of Geddy Lee's bass, which gradually fades in as the outer-space soundscape continues to echo and chime away.

The song's lyrical narrative is extremely thin; we are provided with the description of the black hole by an omniscient narrator, as well as two segments of first-person description of the journey into the black hole. The vocal narrative takes about two minutes and fifteen seconds of the piece; the remaining eight minutes are given over to instrumental passages. The lead character is not named or developed, and no reason is presented for the character's interest in the journey and the black hole. The lyrics and vocals function mostly to suggest the scenery, mood, and action on which the instrumental music itself elaborates. Put simply, the instrumental music is the journey. "Cygnus X-1" invites the listener to imagine the action and scenery of the story. Guidelines are given through the lyrics, but the interaction between the music and the listener's imaginations fills in the descriptive and narrative gaps. The music functions somewhat like a film sound track, with all the specifics of the scenes left to the listener's imagination. The music changes in cinematic fashion, shifting abruptly into new keys, tempos, and textures, with each section suggesting different moods and kinds of motion. For example, as the astronaut begins his journey ("I set a course just east of Lyra / And northwest of Pegasus . . . " [at 6:00]), the accompanying music is conventional, major-key rock in 4/4 time; as he approaches the black hole (6:48), a suddenly quiet and static set of pendular octaves from the guitar is heard, making use of a common musical convention for evoking suspense. The repeated octaves are the eerie calm before the storm, and although sudden, sputtering interjections from the bass and drums startle the listener, these are a false alarm. Finally, the octaves descend chromatically and, at 8:35, Rush launches into a swirling, spiraling hard-rock pattern in rolling triplets. The guitar mostly plays parallel minor chords in third relations (C♯ minor–E minor–G♯, then C♯ minor–E minor–C minor) which swirl about without clearly establishing tonal or modal identity, while the drummer plays frantically busy figures on the ride cymbal. Into this musical vortex, the spaceship descends.

"Cygnus X-1," an extended, mostly instrumental form, is a derivation of the long, psychedelic jam of the late 1960s from which progressive rock partly sprang. The science-fiction narrative simply provides a guiding frame to which the instrumental musical themes can be related. Pink Floyd experimented with similar concepts on tracks like "Set the Controls for the Heart of the Sun" and "Careful with That Axe, Eugene" (both 1968), the latter of which John Cotner describes as a "quasi-instrumental fantasy."[33] In both cases, a science-fiction or macabre title provides the frame of reference for extended instrumental exploration, creating a style of rock which Cotner describes as "music for listening and contemplation, deeply pre-occupied with the formal and material aspects of sound."[34] Edward Macan states that such psychedelic forms were wedded by progressive rock groups to certain Western art/music resources (especially nineteenth-century Ro-mantic symphonic forms) in order to attain a more satisfying degree of organization to their songs. This combination worked, according to Ma-can, because Romantic and psychedelic music shared "the same cosmic outlook, the same preoccupation with the infinite and otherworldly, the same fondness for the monumental statement, and the same concern with expressing epic conflicts."[35] Moreover, both styles shared an interest in bringing a programmatic element to instrumental passages. Rush's "Cyg-nus X-1" (along with the band's other largely instrumental works) clearly draws from psychedelia and progressive rock, but with some important revisions. Unlike Pink Floyd, Rush's instrumental playing makes little use of open-ended improvisation, but instead places a much greater emphasis on precisely orchestrated arrangements. Unlike many British progressive rock groups, Rush's knowledge of, and influence from, nineteenth-century symphonic forms is more limited. Nearly all the instrumental passages in "Cygnus X-1" make use of the hard-rock convention of riff or pattern repetition, and the group only rarely attempted the kind of motivic devel-opment or through-composed passages that Yes, Genesis, or King Crim-son practiced. In fact, in spite of Rush's interest in periodically employing classical music resources, a certain distinction emerges between Rush (as well as similar North American progressive rock groups, such as Kansas or Dream Theater) and British bands in this regard. British middle-class children of the postwar decades typically had a greater familiarity with classical music than their North American counterparts. While classi-cal concert attendance has had a fairly long history among the European middle classes, in North America a mass-mediated middlebrow culture took root instead.[36] Thus, although a number of North American rock musicians have appropriated classical influences, they have done so with a certain distance from the classical tradition, a superficiality, that contrasts with the relative depth of classical influence on the music of Yes, Genesis, King Crimson, and other British progressive bands.

But what Rush clearly shares with its progressive rock antecedents is the creation of a type of rock that could be called "headphone" music, or what Cotner describes as "music for listening and contemplation." There is an important congruence between the story of "Cygnus X-1" (the solitary space traveler, cocooned in a rocket ship, embarking on a fantastic adventure) and the way in which this music was often consumed. Headphone listening is solitary, isolating the listener in his or her own sound world, whether alone in the bedroom or listening on a crowded bus. The rocket ship and the headphones are both mechanical apparatuses, conduits for a journey into a very different space than the bedroom, the home, the school, or the suburb. The music, which contains many aspects of narrative (changes of key, texture, intensity, loudness, and emotional states, like the changing of scenes), carries the listener through a variety of soundscapes. As with "The Fountain of Lamneth," the journey depicted in "Cygnus X-1" is individualistic and solitary. Because of the way Rush ties the soundscapes of this song to particular images drawn from science fiction, the escape is not into a different and better society, but into an environment of stars, gravity, speed, vortices, and cosmic rays. The imagery associated with the song's passages is, in this way, abstract and asocial. The song probes and explores a world without other people, where the song's protagonist experiences, alone, the excitement and mystery of distant and remote places.

When thinking about "headphone" music and the kind of stories often tethered to it, it is tempting to suggest that predominantly instrumental progressive rock pieces provide an escape, not just into an otherworldly landscape, but into a kind of musical formalism. Formalist aesthetics, according to Carl Dahlhaus, arises out of a sort of contemplative listening that provides an opportunity to lose oneself and forsake all worldly distractions through the experience of music, becoming completely immersed in an autonomous musical world.[37] Though "Cygnus X-1" was certainly not made to be "absolute music" of the kind Dahlhaus describes, there is evidence that certain fans (particularly musicians) hear Rush's music as interesting principally because of its form, composition, and technical execution; the longer epics, with their extended instrumental passages, are often the most rewarding part of the band's repertoire for such listening. The band itself has self-consciously played toward this segment of its audience periodically, producing rock instrumentals with witty or humorous titles—"YYZ" (1981), "Where's My Thing?" (1991), "Limbo" (1996), "The Main Monkey Business" (2007)—but that dispense with any sense of a program and simply explore musical themes and display the band's musicianship. Some fans whom I interviewed about Rush's more escapist epics were more interested in describing their all-consuming interest in the musical details of the songs than the lyrics; in some cases, the themes or programs in the songs were completely irrelevant to them. For example, Mark Joseph, a long-time Rush fan and professional drummer, described each song we listened to together in terms of learning to play the musical parts himself, and commented on how seamlessly the divergent parts of the songs were put together. Listening to the fantasy epic "Xanadu" (1977), I asked Joseph if he paid any attention to the song's story. "No," he replied, "it's mostly about instrumentation and compositional form for me." When listening to the piece, he noted,

> I'd go into my room, right after I came home from school, I'd listen to [Rush] a lot. I wouldn't even put it through a speaker. I'd put it through my walkman, sit on my bed, and have the headphones on and I'd chill. I'd just try to absorb as much of it as I could. It was always an experience. It's funny, because I remember an interview with Geddy Lee where he said an ideal concert experience for him would be through headphones, that it would be the ideal way for him to listen to music. 'Cause that's how I like to listen to Rush. I like to sit down and put the headphones on and not have anything else get in the way. I like to hear *everything*, even in the background. Like on *Moving Pictures*, there's a lot of studio noise from where they do breaks, you can hear space, and that added depth for me. It was like being there, like, "Oh, I'm in the studio and this is really happening, right now."[38]

Another fan, Allen Kwan, similarly noted that listening to the story in the lyrics was not of interest to him: "For me, it's just music." But while listening to Rush's escapist epics, he responded to the unfolding of the musical changes and instrumental playing as if it were a narrative:

> Ah, those chords—I don't know what it is, but I just love them. I love the way they play different things over those same chords I've heard them do this elsewhere in different ways, like in "La Villa Strangiato" [1978, an all-instrumental track] where it's Geddy going A to F and Alex is doing all the varying stuff. Awesome—it's like they've got an intro, a middle, and a conclusion, it's like a story.[39]

To a fair degree, these fans locate the value of Rush's music in its composition and technical musical features, and their appreciation is made possible, in part, through their own expertise as amateur or professional musicians. This is suggestive of the possibility that something at least resembling formalist aesthetics can exist among some popular music audiences. Formalism is defined by Bohdan Dziemidok as "a theory according to which the value of a work of art *qua* artwork—its artistic value—is constituted *exclusively* (radical version) or *primarily* (moderate version) by its formal aspects. Its 'meaning' or its (conceptual, cognitive, material, etc.) 'content' has no important consequences for its value."[40] Using this definition, one could argue that the fans cited above listen to Rush in a formalist manner, especially if we assume that "form" embraces the details of musicianship (drum fills, riffs, etc.) as well as compositional form, and that "content" refers to the semantic dimension of the lyrics.

In any case, some have argued that formalism (or quasi-formalism) is a kind of escapism itself, and considered this to be a criticism. Leo Treitler, for example, charged formalist understandings of musical aesthetics with being "transcendentalist" and "internalist," emphasizing that the concern with "the music itself" and music's formal systems created an imaginary, private world of aesthetic objectivity, isolated and disconnected from the social.[41] Another way of expressing this is to suggest that the world created by an all-consuming interest in musical form, musicianship, and composition is a kind of escapism through transcendence. All the earthy realities of human relationships, current events, history, the social ambivalence of race, class, gender, and so on (the very things which impact our lives most directly) are swept away by an intensely interior and technical focus on the music itself. Even if "Cygnus X-1" is not listened to in a quasi-formalistic way, there remains a potential for transcendence through the fantasy the story provides. All worldly concerns are made to seem small, unimportant, and mundane when set against more cosmic themes, and we are given license to transcend our day-to-day lives when inhabiting the world that songs like "Cygnus X-1" construct.

From the description up to this point, it may seem as though Rush's escapist repertoire offered listeners only the most abstract and even solipsistic kinds of journeys. As its musicians matured, Rush seemed to grow out of these explorations of inner space: by the early 1980s, the group was turning away from extended songs and escapist fantasy in favor of shorter songs and lyrics that delved into social commentary, current events, and philosophy. But the band did not simply abandon storytelling. A prominent song from this period, "Red Barchetta" (*Moving Pictures*, 1981), was a rare throwback to the escapist science-fiction narrative, but its story was set up in such a way that it folded suburban iconography into an escapist narrative, as I discuss further below. The term "barchetta" means "little boat" in Italian, but the term refers more specifically to a body shape used for European sports cars such as a Porsche or Ferrari. The song is set in the near future (approximately fifty years ahead) when gasoline-fueled motors have been outlawed. The protagonist escapes every weekend to his uncle's farm in the country, where he finds an old automobile that has long since gone out of use. The setting appears to be an overregulated Orwellian society, as the protagonist describes how "on Sundays, I elude the 'Eyes' / And hop the turbine freight / To far outside the wire / Where my white-haired uncle waits." The middle part of the song describes the protagonist's "weekly crime," a joy ride and the sensations it brings—the thrill of extreme speed and control of a high-powered machine, as well as the sunshine, wind, and scented country air—all of which arouse dizzying, elated feelings of suppressed freedom. The final third of the song describes a car chase, as police officers in large "air cars" pursue the protagonist. He manages to avoid capture by finding a narrow bridge which the Barchetta is just small enough to cross, leaving the larger air cars stranded on the river bank. The protagonist finally returns to the safety of the farm and joins his uncle in a fireside reverie.

By fantasizing about the car as a symbol of transgression and freedom, Rush taps into a well-established theme in male teenage culture. Moreover, it centers the story on the very tool that makes suburbia possible. The expansion of highways and the proliferation of the automobile allowed the suburbs to grow, and the car is so ingrained in suburban lifestyles that it is required for just about any activity that takes place outside the home. Indeed, subdivisions are often planned with the car foremost in mind, with few sidewalks for pedestrians, little mass transit, and many amenities beyond walking distance. As a teenage rite of passage, learning to drive is associated with freedom because it reduces parental dependence and releases the teenager from a claustrophobic restriction to his neighborhood. Rush's romanticization of the car, then, plays well to the experience of many suburban youths who made up a significant portion of its audience.

Of course, Rush does not romanticize just any car, and there is much to consider about what is symbolized through the Barchetta. Most salient is the car's gendering. When the song was written, there were a number of vehicles oriented toward families—station wagons, minivans, and family-size sedans—but these certainly were not the preferred vehicles for indulging masculine fantasies of freedom. Like the suburbs themselves, the familial orientation of such vehicles led them to be associated more with the feminine. Sports cars or "muscle cars," all-terrain vehicles and motorcycles, are all associated more with the masculine virtues of power, risk, and transgression, and the fact that they lack a practical application in the suburban environment makes them all the more appropriate as symbols of escape from the suburban context. Many high-end sports cars clearly epitomize independence and individualism, given their compact size and lack of a back seat. With room for only a single passenger, these cars serve an individual as a solitary symbol of status and power, a private vehicle that is nonetheless meant to be displayed publicly. Moreover, the sports car is designed to transgress, to break the law in its ability to exceed normal and safe speed limits by a considerable margin. Through affording and then being able to handle the car, the driver is made to feel exceptional, not bound to the normal limits of society. By setting "Red Barchetta" in the future and making driving of any kind a crime, Rush amplifies these themes and the general fantasy representation of fast sports cars. Again, transcendence through escapist fantasy is achieved: the protagonist experiences the thrill of velocity and the exceeding of normal limits, and the transgression of his society's laws symbolizes his nonconformity and affirms his individuality.

In addition to the fantasy of transgressing social norms, Rush incorporates some other important escapist themes into this narrative. There is a "pastoral" element woven into the song, insofar as the protagonist's escape involves leaving the city or suburb and traveling into the country. The coveted sensations of the driver's escape is not simply tied to speed and risk, but to enjoying the sunshine, the "scented country air," the mountain scenery, and, at the end, a campfire at his uncle's farm. The action takes place in a setting removed from both city and suburb, where the protagonist communes simultaneously with empowering technology and with nature, almost like a trip to a cottage, but with the added overlay of science fiction, adventure, and risk. Complementing this pastoral element is a sense of nostalgia, for the Barchetta is described as a shining relic from "a better, vanished time." The driver's brief flirtation with freedom is also a communing with the past, the reliving of a nobler era before stifling restrictions came into being.

With respect to affect, the music itself amplifies the two thematic areas that are established in the lyrics (the pastoral, dreamlike, and nostalgic on the one hand; the transgressive communing with technology on the other). Although Alex Lifeson uses only electric guitars on this track, a symbolic timbral contrast is established which is similar to the acoustic-electric dyad in "The Fountain of Lamneth." Lifeson uses a clean, chorused guitar sound during the introduction and conclusion and plays figures using "harmonics," a guitar technique that produces bell-like tones. He also uses a clean timbre to play arpeggiated figures during some verses. In other parts of the song, various riffs and segments are played with power chords using a heavily distorted timbre. The predominant modality of "Red Barchetta" is A Mixolydian, and Lifeson's choices of timbre and figuration interact with this modality to produce two distinct affects. His clean-toned arpeggiation, especially during the first verse ("My uncle has a country place . . ."), creates a sense of wistfulness and nostalgia, setting the mood for a daydream about driving in the country. Lifeson's repeating arpeggiated figure outlining an A-major chord with an added 11th is set against different bass notes from the Mixolydian scale (A, F$\sharp$, G$\natural$) which recall accompaniment patterns from folk guitar styles. In contrast, the use of A Mixolydian during the verses where the rhythm is more propulsive and the timbre is distorted produces a more aggressive affect, where excitement and optimism are merged with hardness (for example, in the second verse where Lee sings, "Jump to the ground as the turbo slows . . ."). Walser discusses the use of the Mixolydian mode in hard rock in similar terms, noting that the upbeat "major key" feel is merged with the "hard semiotic value" of the mode's minor seventh.[42] Although the musical contrasts do not always occur in phase with the relaying of the images in the lyrics, the pastoral/nostalgic and mechanical/aggressive themes are present in both the lyrics and music.

Ultimately, what is striking about the narrative of "Red Barchetta" is the way it takes fairly common middle-class scenarios—borrowing a relative's "pleasure" or "vanity" car, going to a cottage or camping—and adds play or fantasy that is consonant with the imaginations of suburban teenagers, especially boys. Unlike "The Fountain of Lamneth" or "Cygnus X-1," "Red Barchetta" draws directly from the suburban landscape in setting up its escapism, but all three of these selections share individualism and the "identity journey" (discussed further below) as important parts of their narratives. These selections could also be considered part of a wider category in rock known as the "road song," where existential journeys are taken or the freedom of the road is celebrated. Such songs have taken the form of blue-collar arena rock anthems (e.g., Judas Priest's "Freewheel Burning," Rainbow's "Stargazer," Steppenwolf's "Born to Be Wild," Metallica's "Wherever I May Roam") as well as more literary or epic journeys from progressive-leaning bands (Led Zeppelin's "Kashmir," Genesis's "Supper's Ready," Kansas's "Carry On My Wayward Son"). Rush's music typically falls toward the latter, but its appeal to fans across the gamut of metal, progressive rock, and classic rock derives partly from the fact that the group provided quest-like "road songs," a narrative category common in a number of rock genres, appealing to both middle- and working-class fans.

Though Rush's escapist narratives fall into a broader, class-ambiguous category of rock song, this chapter has suggested a number of ways in which it expresses values and priorities linked to the middle class. I conclude this chapter by considering more broadly how Rush's escapist strategies have been embedded in the aesthetic and cultural dimensions of social class. To begin, consider how Rush's escapist repertoire articulates distance, in a variety of ways, from the social and the material. "The Fountain of Lamneth" provides a symbolic narrative taking place outside conventional time and history; "Cygnus X-1" is fantasy about privately traversing wide distances and exploring mysterious otherworldly phenomena; "Red Barchetta," though it dresses up familiar suburban themes, nonetheless lifts those themes out of, and away from, everyday life; finally, the quasi-formalist engagement with any of Rush's songs provides entry into a technical and aesthetic domain of an esoteric kind. In all cases, a solitary, distanced subject is privileged.

Much of what I discuss here is theorized as part of a middle-class aesthetic disposition by sociologist Pierre Bourdieu, whose *Distinction* is a classic critique of aesthetics and taste as they are inflected by social class and occupation. For Bourdieu, the middle-class aesthetic disposition is characterized by "a generalized capacity to neutralize ordinary urgencies and to bracket off practical ends. . . . [It] presupposes the distance from the world which is the basis of the bourgeois experience of the world."[43] The aesthetic distance Bourdieu discusses is linked directly to the middle class's economic status, which fosters a mentality that arises from having disposable income and not being concerned with, or anxious about, material necessities: "economic power is first and foremost a power to keep economic necessity at arm's length. . . . Objective distance from necessity and from those trapped within it combines with a conscious distance which doubles freedom by exhibiting it."[44] Bourdieu suggests that the more distant one is from economic scarcity, the more one's taste swings toward more symbolic, formal, or abstract aesthetic preferences. When closer to economic necessity, one's taste swings more toward the realist, practical, and pragmatic.[45] These statements are clearly broad generalizations, and the reader should be aware that Bourdieu's theory of the aesthetic dispositions of classes was based on detailed research and relayed through detailed analysis of the fine gradations of preferences that arise out of the complex interactions of class, occupation, educational background, generation, and gender. However, these statements reveal the broader patterns of class and aesthetic leanings, and they help to explain, to some degree, why Rush's escapist repertoire is marked by the kinds of narratives and strategies outlined in this chapter.

The kind of distance which Rush's escapism articulates is a more general trait of progressive rock, but it stands in marked contrast to the strategies for escaping or transcending one's social context that are often found in working-class subcultures. Scholars working in the domain of cultural studies have looked at how working-class subcultures (e.g., the Mods, the Teddy boys, punk) provide relief or escape from the social positions of their members.[46] Rather than distance, these coping strategies speak suggestively of a closeness to the material dimensions of social class. For the Mods, class angst is temporarily transcended through the consumption of clothing that represents an imaginary capacity for upward mobility. For the punks or the Teds, working-class marginality is emphasized, exaggerated, and turned into an aesthetic style that proudly flouts middle-class standards. Furthermore, cultural theorist Dick Hebdige notes of the punk subculture, "We can say that the early punk ensembles gestured towards the signified's 'modernity' and 'working-classness.' The safety pins and bin liners signified a relative material poverty which was either directly experienced and exaggerated or sympathetically assumed, and which in turn was made to stand for the spiritual paucity of everyday life."[47] In subcultures such as this, the material conditions of social class are quite visible and pivotal in forming the aesthetic and symbolic dimensions of their expressive cultures. But in looking at Rush's repertoire, the issue of class is present but mostly unspoken. In fact, the emphasis on fantasy, individualism, and solitary quests in Rush's escapist songs seems to remove any reference to contemporary society, and although middle-class values and myths predominate, their implication in social identities of any kind is sidestepped. The ubiquity, hegemony, and averageness of middle-class identity is such that, like whiteness, it is left unmarked and unmentioned. The middle-class context is simply assumed as a given, and thus expressive culture arising from that context is not acknowledged as tethered to that context and is free to articulate distance from it.

Rush's choice of escapist genres (Romantic medievalist fantasy and science fiction) are, to some degree, implicated in social class as well. Historically, these genres and their nineteenth-century predecessors were in the domain of bourgeois fiction, and their themes and characters reflected middle-class mores and dilemmas in a variety of ways. In science fiction, for example, the privileging of the scientist places a middle-class professional and specialist in the forefront, as evidenced in works from as far back as Mary Shelley's *Frankenstein* (a precursor of both horror and science fiction), through the fiction of H. G. Wells (*The Time Machine, The Island of Dr. Moreau,* and others), and forward to the works of writers such as Isaac Asimov (for example, his *Foundation* series). The often-imitated "social" template provided by the ever-popular *Star Trek* series is emphatically middle class: the main characters are of the professional-managerial class (the ship's captain, the scientist, the doctor, the engineer), the secondary recurring characters represent lower-middle-class occupations with some prospects for upward mobility (the junior officers), while the working class is represented by the nameless, nonrecurring characters (generic crewmen, security guards) who are expendable and are the most frequently killed off. Though contemporary science fiction films have developed a number of blue-collar-oriented narratives (the *Star Wars* and *Alien* film series, for example, privilege mostly working-class characters), the genre's larger history testifies to a long-term emphasis on the enterprising, middle-class-identified character, and this tells us something about which audiences, historically, the genre has addressed.

With regard to medieval fantasy, I discussed above the use in popular culture of a medieval imaginary, a selective, unspecific, and fanciful reconstruction of medieval times, of which Rush made use in suites like "The Fountain of Lamneth" and "The Necromancer." Although medievalist fantasy as both a Romantic and contemporary phenomenon has a complex history surrounding its use for a number of socially motivated reasons, some of the most common narratives (especially that of the knight on a quest) symbolically flatter a middle-class sensibility. As one of the most common characters in medieval fantasy, the knight or equestrian—higher in status than a peasant, but lower than senior nobility—is decidedly "middling." The archetypal quest corresponds to the bourgeois notion of starting an enterprise or "following one's dreams," and the successful fulfillment of the quest (after some deferral of gratification) leads directly to upward mobility or social elevation. Although it is placed in a setting far outside the bounds of modernity, the medievalist fantasy can easily be used (and is used, as we saw with Rush) to represent archetypally significant and modern middle-class myths about individual initiative, upward mobility, and deferred gratification.

But what is at stake with this kind of escapism? What accounts for the desire to embark on quests of these kinds? A large part of their appeal lies in the way they help fans answer questions of identity. I began this chapter with Rush's pessimistic evaluation of the suburbs and middle-class lifestyles in "Subdivisions," and the song lays out clearly the view that the suburbs do not offer much opportunity for young people, as they grow up, to feel challenged or fulfilled. Rush addresses the spiritual emptiness of the suburbs through symbolic quests to find something "more" to life and something more to the self. Most of the escapist pieces discussed in this chapter—insofar as they are "quests"—are quite similar to what Orrin Klapp calls "identity journeys." Klapp discusses the notion of the identity journey as a contemporary middle-class practice, a response to the erosion of clear, traditional identity markers in an increasingly pluralistic postwar America.[48] Klapp would probably see the quests Rush provides as mostly male-oriented as well, because of the tendency to couch them in risk-based adventures. The undertaking of journeys involving risky or dangerous pursuits, as a way of proving oneself and one's merit, became an important mythic narrative in male-oriented popular culture because, Klapp notes, it provides an affirmation of individuation—a "rite of passage"—that is otherwise unavailable to most middle-class American men.[49] There are particular anxieties and ambivalences about masculinity that arise in the middle-class suburban context, and which these identity journeys address. As Rita Felski observes, values and attitudes exemplified by the suburban lower middle class "are also identified with women: domesticity, prudery, aspirations toward refinement."[50] Peter Bailey points out that many middle-class occupations—the office clerk, the sales representative—are seen as routine, unmanly, and unheroic jobs, perhaps better suited to a feminine demeanor; middle-class men therefore feel the need to reclaim masculinity through leisure pursuits.[51] The working class, for Felski, "is represented through images of a virile proletariat in left rhetoric, [but] the middle class is often gendered female, associated with the triumph of suburban values and the symbolic castration of men."[52] In Felski's article, the suburb seems to connote the womb or the cocoon, a place of repose and of family, where the masculine, rugged individual is neither actualized nor needed. The family itself is a model of dependence and interdependence, but not *in*dependence, and achieving individuality is often linked during the teen years with an almost ritual separation from the family. Male identity quests require "leaving" the family unit, the middle-class career, and the suburb, and insofar as Rush's songs provide vicarious male journeys, they take the listener to places far from the family and far from the suburbs. This may partly explain the attraction of other kinds of popular culture with science-fiction and fantasy themes for their predominately

young, suburban, male demographics, and the predominance of male fandom among progressive and heavy metal bands like Rush, Genesis, Iron
Maiden, and Metallica.

Kim Liv Selling has characterized works of fantasy and science fiction
as a critique of modernity, observing that medievalism "can be viewed
ideologically as part of a broader societal reaction against the rationalistic, anti-heroic, materialist and empiricist discourses upon which modern
Western culture and society are founded—in other words, it perpetuates
and revitalizes the Romantic worldview in the contemporary world."[53]
Rush's characterization of the suburbs along these lines—as bureaucrati-
cally rationalistic, anti-heroic, deadening—situates Rush's escapism in
the neo-Romantic and anti-modernist discourse of which Selling writes.
But over time, this discourse was perpetuated by Rush through broader
means than the escapist narrative. After 1980, escapist fiction ceased to be
a prominent part of its new repertoire, and Rush began writing songs that
articulate more directly the desire to be "anywhere but here" (to borrow a
phrase from "Double Agent" [1993]), the need to break the physical and psychological chains of suburban life. Apart from "Subdivisions," this theme
was revisited frequently during the 1980s. In "The Analog Kid" (1982), a
boy's suburban reverie of busy urban streets, autumn woods, and winter
skies (visions interrupted as his mother's voice calls him back to reality)
dramatizes directly the desire to flee suburbs; "Middletown Dreams" (1985)
traces the routine lifestyles of a businessman, a housewife, and a teenager,
contrasting their daily habits with the more exciting, fulfilling lives they
fantasize about. These songs may lack the fantasy or science-fiction overlay
of Rush's music from the 1970s, but the Romanticism remains, especially in
the way Rush contrasts untethered individualism with conformist myths
about the suburbs. As Neil Peart himself noted,

> Conformity was an enormous power in the community. It was felt from
> pre-school right up to maturity—a very difficult environment to grow up
> in and preserve your balance, self-esteem and creativity. It was difficult
> to be anything other than what everybody else was. That transition—

between adolescence and maturity, innocence and experience, dreams and disillusionment—is a major theme in our lyrics because that particular passage is *the* crucial bridge you cross in your whole life. In our song "Subdivisions," the background that all three of us grew up in is the common denominator . . . and I see our audiences being congruent with us through many of these phases. There's certainly that commonality—it's a question of background, and of needing certain things to alleviate that background.[54]

As we have seen, alleviating this background involved telling stories which emphasized a kind of nonconformity—private, independent journeys and transgressions of socially enforced boundaries—and reinforced the ideology of individualism. The importance of individualism in Rush's music (and in rock music more generally) is a larger issue which goes beyond the theme of escapism, and it is to this issue I turn in the next chapter.

2

"Swimming Against the Stream"

Individualism and Middle-Class Subjectivity in Rush

When Neil Peart joined Rush in 1974, "Anthem" was the first song produced by the new trio. It established Rush's working arrangement—with Lee and Lifeson composing the music and Peart providing the lyrics—and it prefigured several hallmarks of Rush's mature style, including the use of asymmetrical meters ($\frac{7}{8}$ for the song's intro), contrapuntal separation between the bass and guitar, and elaborate drum fills. Most important, it introduced the theme for which Rush would become most renowned—individualism. "Anthem" shares its title with a short novella by Russian American writer Ayn Rand, an author Peart very much admired during the mid-1970s, and whom Rush would acknowledge two years later as the inspiration for "2112." Rand, a Soviet defector, came to the United States in 1926 with boundless enthusiasm for some of the key pillars of American identity—liberty, individualism, capitalism, and certain constitutional rights—which stood in marked contrast to the political climate she fled in the USSR. Her enthusiasm, expressed in novels such as *Atlas Shrugged* and *The Fountainhead,* rubbed off on a young Neil Peart, who used her ideas as a springboard for the lyrics of his first Rush song. "Anthem" merged heavy metal with individualist philosophy, and Lee—who once sang his own lyrics in songs like "Working Man," "Take a Friend," and "Need Some Love" (from *Rush,* 1974)—was now delivering individualist slogans enjoining the listener to "live for yourself," "hold your head above the crowd," and celebrate the virtue of self-interest. Rush was never a one-issue band, but individualism recurred frequently in the group's repertoire, and, as evident in the previous chapter, it was an issue that lay beneath the surface of even Rush's most escapist compositions. Sometimes urgent and other times uplifting, Rush used individualism as a wellspring for optimistic, inspiring messages, as well as a framework for making social and political critiques.

"Anthem" could well be seen as a paean to the 1970s, which became known as the "Me Decade." The song urges listeners to pursue their own interests and forget about what others think. Drawing on Rand's ethic called the "virtue of selfishness," the song tells listeners to take ownership of their lives and never let anyone tell them "that you owe it all to me." Durrell Bowman argues that Rush typifies rock music's shift away from the activist and collectivist ethos that permeated the counterculture, and toward more individualistic and solitary interests.[1] A new focus on the self, self-improvement, and the private lifestyle enclave lay at the end of the social innovations of the 1960s; the hippie counterculture had itself drawn away from collective agitation for social change and began emphasizing personal growth and private revelation even before the end of the 1960s. As a generational rallying cry, "change the world" gradually transformed into "if you can't change the world, change yourself." Not surprisingly, rock in the 1970s evolved to reflect a more self-absorbed era. But Rush did not echo the hedonistic, self-indulgent abandon that is sometimes associated with the 1970s. Rush's individualism reflected more traditional notions of working hard, standing out, fostering self-confidence and being self-reliant, drawing on aspects of the Protestant work ethic. This kind of individualism is very important to the identity of the American middle class and forms the base of its subjectivity. In many ways, the increasingly individualistic turn of popular culture through the 1970s and beyond reflects more than just the decline of the countercultural and activist spirit of the 1960s; it reflects a resurgence in politics and popular culture of more traditional middle-class priorities, a resurgence that coincided with the end of the long postwar economic boom. By the early 1970s, the oil crisis, stagnating wages, and inflation—together with the very beginnings of the neoliberal restructuring of the American manufacturing base—were ratcheting up the cost of middle-class lifestyles and pushing down the number of families who could call themselves middle class. According to a particular body of journalistic social analysis from the last decades of the twentieth century, the middle class found itself suddenly on the defensive in the mid-1970s, anxious about its status and feeling threatened by powerful interests that challenged its beliefs in individual agency, self-reliance, and opportunities in a free market.[2] There was some disagreement about which powerful interests were posing this threat, but the usual suspects included large corporations, bloated government bureaucracies, labor unions, and so-called special-interest groups. Individualism resurgent seemed like an answer to these challenges, reaffirming to many in the middle class that their values remained valid and that the individual needed to be championed politically against the forces threatening to steal its autonomy. Rush's individualistic songs—as well as a plethora of inspirational arena-rock anthems from Styx, Triumph, Queen, and Journey—resonated with a certain constituency in the suburbs during these years because they strongly and evocatively reasserted the values of independence, liberty, and self-realization which formed the moral basis of American culture from a white, middle-class perspective.

Just as the suburbs became associated with conformity, the term "middle class" has become synonymous in the language of white Americans with "the average." In this context, just as escapism answered a desire to be "anywhere but here," individualism answers the desire to be "someone," not just anyone. In this chapter, I explore the significance of Rush's use of individualism, as an expression of middle-class identity, as social critique, and as a political stance. Individualism is a fascinating and revealing source of ambivalence in Rush's music and its reception. It invests Rush's songs with a critical and rebellious edge, presenting independence as defiance, even though the message, for middle-class American audiences, is fairly hegemonic. As lyricist, Peart spent Rush's early years passionately arguing for individualism, but as he reached mid-career, he seemed to struggle with its contradictions and limitations. Individualism was also at the heart of the only major controversy to hit the band. In 1978, British journalist Barry Miles published a high-profile article on Rush in the *New Musical Express* in which he concluded that Rush's individualistic, Ayn Rand–inspired songs made the band socialist-bashing proto-fascists. The article went far over the top in branding Rush as extremists, but the antipathy between Peart and Miles provides a rich opportunity to explore the differences between North American and British perspectives on the middle class and the political meanings individualism embraces.

This chapter casts a critical eye on individualism as an ideology, and for that reason I should explain to the reader my position. I grew up in a politically conservative, secular, middle-class family with a generations-long tradition of small-business ownership, and I picked up a wide range of individualistic biases as a youth, some of which I carry to this day. I am sure that my upbringing as an only child who learned to work and play in abundant solitude only made Rush's (and to some degree, Rand's) individualism more compatible with my teenage worldview. However, as an adult, my training as a musician in the arts and as an academic ethnomusicologist forced me to contend with culture and society in ways that strongly challenged the assumptions that came with my upbringing. By learning how ideologies of many kinds can be deconstructed, I found myself questioning many things that once seemed like the concrete bases of my identity and the society in which I lived. I have come to understand individualism not as a natural, universal, or commonsense truth, but as an important, historically and socially grounded European idea that has led to a variety of both progressive and repressive outcomes in various places and times. My agenda is neither to discredit individualism and Rush's uses of it, nor to defend or glorify them. I want to uncover the social and historical backgrounds that make individualism important to Rush and many of its audience members, and I want to see how it fits into the story of rock music and the middle class.

I begin by discussing the role Rush's individualism plays for fans as a part of the band's appeal and an inspirational aspect of its repertoire. The importance of individualism in Rush's music was aptly illustrated in responses to my internet survey of Rush fans, conducted in 1996, 2000, and 2008. The survey's seventh question asked, "What overall message(s) do you think Rush has tried to communicate through their music and lyrics?" Individualism or issues relating to individualism were far and away the most common responses, though not the only ones. Below are a dozen representative survey responses.

- That each individual should celebrate their uniqueness, strive to be the best they can be, and maintain an open mind and sense of responsibility

- The fact that we are responsible for our own lives and happiness, and we don't need big government to guide us; also, the future will be what we make it.

- I feel the strength of the individual has always been the focus of Rush lyrics. Neil has pointed out time and again how we as individuals create the promise of the future and the "masses" or collective unconscious are something to be feared. Philosophically speaking, Rand and Nietzsche would both agree with Neil that the true strength of man lies within each one of us [the übermensch] and the voice of the masses should always be sought after from the individual's point of view; not from a Gallup poll.

- Rush has proven that a rock band does not have to cater to the taste of the masses and strive first and foremost to be successful. A band can make the music they want to make and say the things they want to say, and if they are doing what's in their heart, the success will come.

- There are two things that have been important to me. Firstly the emphasis on personal responsibility. Secondly the idea that we don't have to feel alone. "Subdivisions" is a good example of that. While we are growing up we are often in situations which are new and unusual. These are not always life threatening or earth shattering, but nonetheless are part of all our development. Neil Peart can encapsulate this feeling in some of his words in a way that offers reassurance that you are not the only person going through this, but that you will come to terms with it and that it's not as big a deal as it seems at the time.

- They are big into the "heroic," literally and figuratively. I would say they try to impart a sense of strength to the listener, to challenge barriers, create your own destiny, and to change into something great. The ultimate thinking man's "pep rally."

- Be yourself. Stand up for what you believe in.

- That you must stand or fail by your own merits. This runs through all of their work. However, the earlier work would emphasize that failure is either the result of your acceptance of the rule of others (read inferiors) or your circumstances that "need not be," while their latter work would emphasize that "failure" comes from a lack of awareness and inability to relate to your surroundings, to change AND adapt to them. That is an important distinction, and shows a maturation on the part of the band's philosophy. Awareness of my surroundings may spark the wish to drive away the "flies that cloud" the eyes of child in a far-away land [reference to the song "Scars" (1989)], or "feel the strength in the hand" of another [reference to "Hand Over Fist" (1989)]. Awareness is far more demanding, and more complex of an outlook than egoism. It requires an effort of Will AND an ability to bend that is harder to sustain than satisfying the drive for self-fulfillment. Take that, Ayn Rand. I can track my own personal development from teen to adult in the Rush albums.

- Ironically, the music is always a seamless blend of three incredible individuals, whereas the most popular theme in the lyrics (although not dominating) is that of individualism (esp. Randian). I don't think that the lyrics intend to be as isolationist as I feel Rand was (by the way, I have only read *Anthem* and a short biography, so I shouldn't really try to sum up her thoughts). Ultimately, I think the lyrics call each person not only to be themselves and fight for what they find important ("Subdivisions," "Mission," "Dreamline," "Closer to the Heart"), but to work with others for a better world for everyone ("Hemispheres," "Red Tide," "Nobody's Hero," "Presto").

—Individual rights & responsibilities
—Self actualization & the right to achieve unfettered personal greatness
—The importance of a small government that does not interfere in the personal liberties of individuals or businesses
—The relationship of humans to one another and to the Earth-Beauty
—A Spirituality that comes from the wonder of our existence, not requiring a supreme being in the equation to appreciate the greatness of Humanity or Ourselves

. I think Rush has been trying to express the challenges of living in this postmodern culture while trying to maintain a sense of self (or learning to release that sense of self in order to change it). They challenge the listener to think for her/himself. Perhaps that is the overriding theme: to always remember to think for yourself, be aware of the influences around you, be aware of the world. But ultimately, you are responsible for how you turn out, because we all have brains. Some of us choose to use ours more than others. Their lyrics AND their music challenge us to do that. Remember, they are also the band who chose to follow the experimental drive that led them to *Signals*. They are their own band. They have taken full responsibility for their musical and lyrical expression. I can only have immense respect for that.

1) Think for yourself, get off your ass, and
   stand up for what you believe in.
2) Be a leader, not a follower.
3) The future can either be wonderful, or dismal,
   depending on the choices we make today.

Many of these responses highlight key aspects of individualism. At the most basic level, the belief in the autonomous self—which arose historically with the European Enlightenment and the rise of capitalism—appeared in many responses, since individualism's very existence depends on such a belief. The exercise of agency—thinking independently and critically, making choices and daring to do so publicly—stands out in several responses. Though no one used the term "free will" (as against determinism) as such, what surfaced periodically was the idea that the outcome of our lives or the future is "what we choose to make of it," not something predetermined by fate or circumstance. Leadership as an individualistic quality is highlighted, not just in terms of Rush's reputed injunctions to "be a leader," but also in the description fans offer of Rush as musicians who took ownership of their career and did not follow trends or bow to the wishes of others. The themes of nonconformity, uniqueness, and difference emerge in some responses. Self-reliance is emphasized as a key individualistic virtue, as is the self-confidence and belief in oneself needed to attain such independence. Finally, some responses emphasize a political aspect to self-reliance—for example, the belief that individualism can only flourish if "big government" does not interfere with our private lives—which is situated historically in important ways in American liberalism, and was recast in the second half of the twentieth century as a pillar of American neoconservatism.

The phrase one respondent used—likening Rush's music to a "pep rally" —captures the uplifting, optimistic ethos that unfolds in a number of the band's individualistic songs. There are also a number of examples of Rush compositions that present individualism through the framework of tragedy—"The Fountain of Lamneth," "2112," "Xanadu," and "Circumstances" all present the theme through narratives of failure or hardship— but nevertheless, these stories usually contain a heroic, romantic dimension. The rhetoric in the majority of Rush's shorter, non-narrative songs which address individualism is motivational or illustrative. One such song, "Tom Sawyer" (from *Moving Pictures* [1981]), quite concisely encapsulates a number of the aspects of individualism noted above, and stands as one of Rush's most popular and recognized songs. Rush adapts Mark Twain's iconic character—a willful, mischievous boy—as a vehicle to convey the characteristics of an ideal, modern individualist. Since the song is a kind of character study, Rush uses the affective content of the music to personify the character and his attitude, as well as the mix of optimism and urgency that Rush invests in individualist ideology. Rush begins by characterizing Tom Sawyer as confident, proud, and purposeful, to the point of seeming arrogant. The music supports the development of the character in a number of ways, beginning with the crisp, metronomically precise groove set up by the drums, which is fairly slow but made vigorously active by the 16th-note feel on the hi-hat cymbals. The bodily gait suggested by the groove is taut and spry, not panicked or hurried. The drum groove is set against a single synthesizer sound, a drone on E but with a highly phased, distinctive downward attack, almost like a sound effect from a science-fiction film, situating the character in an environment of ultra-modernity. Geddy Lee speaks the lyrics of the first verse rather than singing, introducing Tom Sawyer's "mean pride" and "mean stride" in a tough and streetwise manner. This is followed by the dramatic entry of the guitar and bass, delivering the song's thunderous central riff, a powerful rising-octave motif placed in a rhythm that makes it sound like a fanfare announcing the arrival of the heroic character.

Similar to the protagonists in the "Subdivisions" video, "The Fountain of Lamneth," and "Red Barchetta," Rush positions Tom Sawyer antagonistically against the larger society. Tom is described as a warrior, thus positioning him as a fighter, a rebel, and a symbol of strength. The character is also aloof—he is reserved, which is said to be his defense against unwanted outside influences. His aloofness from society is further reinforced by the claim that "His mind is not for rent / To any God or government." Much can be inferred from this couplet. First, he is depicted as beyond the control of the morality of religion or the laws of the state, and is assertively a non-participant in these pillars of society. Moreover, he rejects both sacred and secular authority and their hierarchies. Finally, his aloofness underscores his self-reliance; he needs no sustenance from sacred or secular sources. The band portrays the character as a romantic, larger-than-life figure, since Rush describes him as myth, as mystery, and as emerging from the mist. The song is a vision of a radical individualist—a self-made person, willful, inner-directed, a formidable force in and of himself, and an outsider. Moreover, "Tom Sawyer" aestheticizes the individual as expansive; the fourth and eighth verses describe his life, his world, and his love as "deep," his horizons as "wide."

Although performing collectively as a group, there are many musical gestures in this song—and in many of Rush's songs—which point toward heroic individualism. Foremost among them is Rush's practice of allowing each instrument to lead. Rush has long been acknowledged as a model of a musicians' meritocracy, and individual technical virtuosity is standard on most tracks of a Rush album. In "Tom Sawyer," Geddy Lee weaves bass lines into the texture that are independent of the guitar, and through the song's instrumental middle section, he executes a busy, angular, and asymmetrical groove, providing a complex counterpoint to the guitar solo. Alex Lifeson's guitar work vacillates between power-chorded riffs, arpeggios, and single-note lines, and he executes a variety of flashy guitar pyrotechnics during his solo. Following the middle section, the group plays the main riff in stop-time, allowing drummer Neil Peart to fill the space with elaborate drum fills; he continues to rupture the groove with fills and accents for the rest of the song. In "Tom Sawyer," musicianship is deployed aggressively, with each instrumentalist grabbing at the listener's attention, displaying a kind of musician's heroism and larger-than-life virtuosity, demonstrating that the three musicians can work together and yet turn the music to their own individual purposes.

Although it may not be obvious, Rush's approach to musicianship and musical texture, a kind of competitive collaboration, has deep roots in middle-class society and music. Parallels can be found in Adorno's reading of the sociology of chamber music (especially of the nineteenth century), where he notes that "the players are so evidently in a sort of competition that the thought of the competitive mechanism of bourgeois society cannot be dismissed: the very gestures of the purely musical performance are like the visible social ones."[3] In essence, Adorno argues that ideal middle-class social relations involve some competition and some collaboration, and that chamber music—once the private music of the middle-class home—reflects these relations through the interaction of the musicians' parts. Adorno likens the texture of the string quartet to a kind of ideal "fair-play" version of sports, where an agonistic relationship exists between the different parts, yet an almost "gentlemanly" politeness mediates the contest. This celebration of mutually rewarding competition speaks both to a valuing of individualism and of ideal bourgeois social relations; for Adorno, "the spiritualization of competition, its transposition into the realm of imagination, anticipates the state of things in which competition would be cured of aggression and evil."[4] Rush's musical interplay displays many of these same structures and meanings, and its embrace of middle-class individualism is enacted, almost homologically, in the way songs like "Tom Sawyer" are musically constructed. This aspect of Rush is certainly not unique in rock—for example, Robert Walser discusses the role of guitar virtuosity in heavy metal in actualizing masculine competitive individualism[5]—but Rush's application of this concept to the entire band's musicianship is unusual.

Another important example of individualism as a motivational theme can be found in "Something for Nothing" (1976), written mostly in the second person and urging critical self-examination. The opening verses set a scene in which "you" wait quietly for "the winds of change" to blow misfortune away, for "someone to call" and bring purpose back to your life. But, the chorus states, nothing is free, we only have freedom to choose if we exercise it, and wisdom cannot be attained without experience. The values of self-reliance and responsibility for the self are urgently expounded and laziness is criticized. The song shifts to a more uplifting tenor at the bridge, as the rewards of pro-activity and self-reliance are described. The material rewards of effort and productivity are described as "your kingdom," your work as "your glory," what you love as your source of "power," your life as your "story." Rush magnifies the individual in a number of ways here. The lyrics' echo of the Lord's Prayer (the kingdom, power, and glory motif) makes the bridge seem like a secular prayer to the self, a sanctifying of individualism. This same choice of words is hyperbolic, encouraging the listener to view possessions as a "kingdom," one's career as a pathway to "glory." The song deliberately inflates the self, fostering self-esteem and, to a fair degree, self-importance. The song finally advises the listener to look within for guidance and inspiration because, as the song's opening suggests, other people cannot be counted upon.

Although I have stressed individualism as a distinctly middle-class value, many questions arise from the "inspirational" individualism described in "Tom Sawyer" and "Something for Nothing." First, do these songs simply reflect individualism writ large, or are there *types* of individualism that particularly emerge from Rush? Also, the association of middle-class identity with individualism has been a simple, one-to-one equation so far. How can this be made less simplistic and account for the more complicated social reality of class and ideology? Rush's inspirational and defiant presentations of self-reliance point toward certain kinds of individualism, and the work of anthropologists and sociologists can provide further context for this. Anthropologist Adrie Kusserow, for example, has worked on de-homogenizing the concept of individualism in the American context, and her ethnographic work in various New York neighborhoods revealed three major variants of individualism, keyed to social class. The most commonly discussed form of individualism, she suggests, is one specific to the American upper middle class, and this gets framed too broadly by scholars as an overarching Western ideal. Kusserow paid particular attention to child-rearing and teaching practices in the areas she studied. In the poorest neighborhoods, where crime was high and many families struggled on weak single incomes or welfare, Kusserow found behaviors and dialogue that formed a pattern of "hard defensive" individualism, viewing the self as a lone individual struggling to get by in a hostile world. The individualism taught to children here (the kind of self-reliance they were expected to learn) involved standing up oneself, learning how to resist being pushed around, minding one's own business, and persevering through difficulty.[6] In a more stable working-class and lower-middle-class Queens neighborhood, Kusserow described the pattern as "hard offensive" individualism, emphasizing upward mobility and a more aggressive, assertive expression of self-reliance. Children were taught to be assertive, to go after what they wanted, not merely to defend themselves. Phrases like "go for it," "put your best foot forward," "go after your goals," and "give that little extra" were typical platitudes of parents and teachers.[7] The individualistic pattern found in a professional, white-collar, upper-middle-class Manhattan neighborhood coheres around the concept of "uniqueness," with school activities and lessons designed to puff up children's self-esteem, self-confidence, and sense of self-autonomy. Willfulness and self-assertiveness remain attractive characteristics for children to exhibit, but these were tempered by the belief that children should also learn to display charming, polite, and diplomatic behavior. Children here were typically given greater privacy (both physical and psychological) to cultivate feelings of independence, yet at the same time encouraged to openly express their thoughts and feelings and take ownership of them. Rather than aggressive descriptors, terms like growing, blossoming, and flowering were used to describe the children's progress in this neighborhood. Kusserow identified this pattern as "soft offensive" individualism.[8]

Using Kusserow's paradigm, neither the Rush songs discussed here nor the commentary cited from fans suggest a defensive form of individualism. "Anthem" and "Something for Nothing" contain inspirational, slogan-like lyrics that read like Kusserow's hard-offensive individualistic phrases, and "Tom Sawyer" certainly contains hard images (warrior, invader, arrogance, energy, friction). A brash if optimistic expression of individualism is hardly surprising given Rush's hard rock orientation, where aggression is conspicuously embedded in the musical style; such a hard-offensive approach to individualism suggests that Rush speaks of middle-class aspiration from a lower-middle-class or even working-class point of view. As discussed in later chapters, there are many elements of Rush's music and career that are expressed in a lower-middle-class register, and the band's approach to its career as a small business underscores this petit-bourgeois conception.

Kusserow's discussion of how individualism operates across class lines in America reveals how hegemonic the ideology is: all classes adapt it, in some way, to their own social needs and conditions. Simon Frith makes the observation that "American class experience is mediated through histori cal images of individual achievement and failure; workers remember their past in terms of mobility rather than solidarity, self-sufficiency rather than socialism. Rock 'n' roll accounts of loneliness and rebellion *celebrated* the conditions that produced them."[9] Rush's "hard" individualism, then, resonates across class lines in America, where slogans about self-sufficiency can be adapted to working- and middle-class sensibilities.

At the same time, elements of Kusserow's soft-offensive individualism appeared as the band continued releasing albums in the mid-1980s. "Grand Designs" (1985) articulates the myth of personal uniqueness and "Mission" (1987) deals with individualistic artistic expression, while "Open Secrets" (1987) and "Hand Over Fist" (1989) switch the emphasis from self-reliance to interdependence. This shift in register may reflect Peart's advancing intellectual maturity as well as the band's confidence following what had been more than a decade as a successful band. I suspect that Kusserow's hard-offensive and soft-offensive individualism may be not only an effect of class but also of age; younger people seeking to prove themselves might adopt a relatively hard sort of individualism; more mature, established people might adopt a more nuanced, interdependent, and softer form.

Robert Bellah has also theorized about different kinds of middle-class individualism, particularly "expressive" and "utilitarian" individualism. Expressive individualism is outlined as part of the individual's engagement with culture, leisure, and family. According to expressive individualism, the ideal middle-class life should be rich in experience, in interactions with other people, and in cultural, intellectual, and sensual stimuli.[10] In contrast, Bellah describes utilitarian individualism as overwhelmingly concerned with material success and attainment of career goals.[11] The pursuit of self-improvement is a key aspect here, and Bellah describes psychotherapy as an important twentieth-century invention that seeks to help individuals adjust to the utilitarian demands of the late capitalist economy.[12] In this regard, the Rush songs discussed so far support utilitarian individualism, as they are principally about striking out on one's own and aggressively seeking goals. "Something for Nothing," in particular, provides a motivational message for self-improvement, urging the listener on to pro-active self-reliance. Kusserow's description of hard-offensive individualism correlates with the goals of Bellah's utilitarian version and provides further context for Rush's inspirational repertoire.

At a still deeper level, the individualism Rush puts forward in these songs reveals some important aspects of middle-class subjectivity, especially if we examine how the songs construct and address their ideal listener. Carol Selby Price, in *Mystic Rhythms: The Philosophical Vision of Rush,* hints at this when she interprets "Tom Sawyer" as a song meant to "recruit": the song presents an inner-directed, self-reliant, authentically individualistic character and implicitly asks its listeners, "Could this be *you?*"[13] The listener is tacitly invited to identify with the character, to recognize oneself in Sawyer's attitude, virtues, and outlook. Price is correct, but her point is even more broadly true, in that just about any kind of expressive culture (not just this song, and not just music) hails people as socially and historically positioned subjects.[14] "Tom Sawyer" and other individualistic songs like "Something for Nothing," "Anthem," or "Grand Designs" may take on a didactic, proverb-like tone, but the effect is not necessarily one of teaching or persuasion but of recognition. Music reveals and concretizes one's already-held beliefs about oneself, and this is a key part of music's role in the formation of identity. Or, as Mark Booth explains, we may experience songs as more than simply addressed to us: "We may live the song and adopt it as 'our' testimony."[15] But what are the social and historical connections between the individualism Rush expressed and the mostly white, middle-class audience that it successfully hailed?

To open this issue up, I want to return briefly to the video for "Subdivisions" discussed at the beginning of chapter 1. The boy at the focus of the video is presented, tragically, as an individual alienated by his suburban environment. He is perhaps a pitiable character, and through his greasy hair and studious but awkward demeanor he is recognizable to the audience as a nerd. But he is a dreamer and a misfit, the lyrics tell us, and he—alone and aloof like Tom Sawyer—stands in contrast with his peers who collect in groups, the ones who conform to avoid being cast out. What is at stake in the video is not just self-reliance but *difference*, and it is used here as a marker of nobility and honesty. However difficult difference is to bear, it is a badge of honor; the conformists who are held up as the Others to the "dreamer and misfit" are the ones we are invited to define ourselves against: they are the compromised, the dishonest, the cowardly. But what is this difference which the video sets up—whose difference, and what kind of difference? As a white middle-class male, the boy is already positioned well within the mainstream of American or Canadian society, and he scarcely contrasts with the teenagers around him in dress or comportment. But it is clearly important to the song's and video's rhetoric that he be marked off as different. Why?

Many have argued that individualism is the central myth around which white and middle-class American identity revolves precisely because it provides a desperately desired sense of difference. As a number of sociological studies reveal, because whites are the largest and most hegemonic group in America, they experience a lack of cultural and ethnic identity. The hegemony of white, Anglo-Saxon-based ethnicity becomes invisible, perceived as "normal" or as unmarked American-ness or Anglo-Canadian-ness. Ethnicity becomes an empty category for whites, leading to a gap that must be filled through other means. For example, in the late 1970s, Jennifer Hurtsfield explored identity among high school students in Southern California and discovered that while race and ethnicity were frequently key identity markers for black and Latino students, white students were far more likely to use "existential self-references" such as "I'm unique," "I'm an individual," or "I'm just me."[16] In fact, she found a prevalent bias among these white students against identities that were grounded in anything but the most universal, abstract terms (i.e., identifying myself simply as a human being; a person). Adding class to race, Pamela Perry's more recent ethnographic study of American whiteness, *Shades of White*, compares

self-perceptions of middle-class white students at a white-majority suburban high school to those of predominately working-class white students at
an inner-city high school where blacks were in the majority. Perry found
that the suburban kids had almost no concept whatsoever of themselves as
having ethnicity or culture; their self-conception seemed to lack any kind
of aggregation apart from circles of family or friends. Their habits, musical
tastes, and clothing preferences were couched in terms of either "normality" or "personal choice." In their linguistic repertoire, they seemed to
have nothing else on which to hang their identities; ethnicity, for them,
was an empty category which Perry described as a "cognitive gap."[17] A different picture emerged at the inner-city school, where the white students
understood their identity in highly relative terms to the black majority;
they understood that their rock and country music, their jeans and T-
shirts, were a function of belonging to a social and socioeconomic group
to at least some degree. Though hegemony did function in their lives in
important ways (for example, one student described the home of his white
family as "normal" and school as a "foreign country"), these students were
not baffled as were their suburban counterparts when asked to describe
their ethnicity.[18]

Bellah comments insightfully on the contrast in identity self-perception
among different classes in the United States: "It is in the lower class that
ethnicity, as a specific pattern of cultural life, survives in America, and as
individuals enter the middle class, ethnicity loses distinctive social content
even when it is symbolically emphasized."[19] Bellah further describes how
the middle class enviously fantasizes about "more 'meaningful community'
among lower-class racial and ethnic groups or among (usually European)
aristocracies."[20] Ethnomusicologist Tim Taylor describes how the white
middle-class envy of ethnic difference figures into the marketing of world
music, and may explain the wave of popularity Celtic music enjoyed in the
1990s.[21] The desire for difference among the North American middle class
has played itself out in a number of ways, including racial or ethnic cross-
dressing and escapes into bohemian or socially marginal artistic cultures,
all of which provide ways to stand out. In many ways, middle-class indi-

vidualism serves this purpose as well, because it fills the cognitive gap that Perry describes and affirmatively answers the anxious question, "Is there anything special about me?" Rush's individualist songs indeed address this question, creating a discourse in which the individual is always contrasted with the crowd, the masses, or the status quo. For example, in the coda of "Vital Signs" (1981), the band fades out with repeated exhortations to "deviate" or "elevate from the norm." In "Grand Designs" (1985), a dichotomy is set up between "style without substance" and the "real thing," and between "the run of the mill" and "a diamond in the waste." This song also provides this chapter with its title, since Rush urges us to "swim against the stream" and live our lives according to our own rules. If we don't, then we are just playing a part in a "mass production scheme." Similar rhetoric has already been discussed with respect to "Anthem" (with its admonition to "hold your head above the crowd"). The nonconformist, authentic identity Rush advocates is set against an imagined hegemony of sameness, fakery, and mediocrity.

The dichotomy Rush sets up is one that has a significant history in modern Western philosophy. It resembles Nietzsche's dichotomy of master and slave moralities, where the heroic, assertive will is set against the herd mentality, but it also reflects the European Enlightenment ideal of a critical, individualistic consciousness that is deemed necessary for full, active participation in a liberal democracy. Price's *Mystic Rhythms* provides some insight into the ways in which Rush's lyric themes are embedded in various strains of Western philosophy. For my purposes, her book also provides a useful foil for discussing how these ideas are positioned with respect to social class because she strongly buys into Rush's individualism and throws the individualism/conformity dichotomy into vivid relief: "Neil Peart's prescription for conformity is courage. The assumption is that there are no natural herd members, that every individual can and should embrace the glory, the destiny, the risk of individuality. It takes courage to be what you really are: an individual with a destiny revealed to you by your own dreams."[22] She compares the lyric theme of "Grand Designs" (a critique of conformity) to Martin Heidegger's description of "inauthentic existence."

Using Peart and Heidegger as reference points, Price elaborates on what is at stake with individualism:

> What have we fallen into? *Conformity.* And the evil of conforming is *abdication.* We are happy to be absolved of the duty to forge our own values, to make our own decisions, to bear the responsibility for their consequences. Who will blame us, who will trouble us, if we take refuge in the mass-existence of the herd. . . ? Public opinion, inherited values, political slogans and religious dogmas substitute for our own critical thinking. And we, lazy slugs, are only too happy to surrender. We loyally march in lock-step conformity with the mass, the collectivity, what Heidegger calls *das Mann,* more or less the idea of the faceless "John Q. Public." Such existence is inauthentic, it is copping out; we were intended for better things.
>
> Rush says the real thing is buried, like gold ore or a diamond beneath a ton of rock. That means two things: first, it's worth finding; second, it's not going to be easy. Start digging. In practical terms, this means a lot of listening to a lot of useless talk. . . . You have to hear enough of it to know why it is so useless. And that is because you are listening to *others*—other sold-out conformists, other cookie-cutter compromisers, other happy herd-members. The talk that will be useful, useful for liberation, is the talk you can hear, if you listen hard enough, *from within.*[23]

This dichotomy which sets "the courageous individual against cowardly conformists" is generously applied throughout Price's book, and for those who are hailed by individualism, it is certainly powerful rhetoric. At times, the argument assumes both an unremitting force and a Manichean absoluteness that, in my opinion, crosses well into overstatement. It must be admitted that Price's intended readers, as she relates in her introduction, are adolescents in the grip of one of the most important identity-forming periods of their lives. It is also fair to say that the force of peer-group conformity (especially among North American adolescents) is a major issue that has well-documented negative psychological consequences. In this regard, the lessons she relays through Rush may have instructive and inspirational value for such an audience. But what is revealing is how her rhetoric sets up a straw man onto whom all sorts of vices are projected: conformity, cowardice, compromise, sheep-like docility, facelessness, laziness, indoctrination, and inauthenticity. Getting branded with such characteristics is the individualist's greatest nightmare, for it indicates a total lack of difference and therefore a lack of identity—and this, as discussed above, is a great anxiety in the white middle class. Her straw man constructs an Other to whom the white middle class feels superior; but it is also a manifestation of what the white middle class fears about itself.

Price's dramatization of the individual-against-the-masses myth reveals the central goal of middle-class identity: to stand out. The white middle class in North America not only belongs to the largest ethnic group, the largest social class, and the largest targeted market; it also belongs to the class most dedicated to competition.[24] Individual achievement and distinction is sought in both material and symbolic/cultural terms. The inspiration, the stoking of self-esteem, the "belief in the self" rhetoric provided by individualistic ideology pushes middle-class individuals to attain these things, to compete faithfully and vigorously. It is the very nature of American individualism to create a discourse of winners and losers, leaders and sheep, individuals and masses. Popular culture has a long history of reflecting this discourse: for example, rock music itself is used to evoke feelings of an enlightened, hip minority who have risen above the duped, faceless masses. Lawrence Grossberg explains it well: "This mark of difference is not . . . a simple boundary between inside and outside, hegemony and revolution. Rock and roll locates its fans as different even while they exist in the same hegemony. The boundary is inscribed in the dominant culture. Rock and roll is an insider's culture which functions to position its fans as outsiders."[25] This certainly speaks to the experience of some Rush fans I interviewed. Allen Kwan, for example, notes that Rush fandom introduced him to a sense of individual identity and difference he had not experienced before:

> I wasn't a very confident person growing up. Not to say that I was a nerd or anything, but I wasn't exactly secure in myself or my personality. Like

every high school kid is, right? [laughs] But as soon as I started listening
to Rush and had something to identify with, it was just stages from there.
I have something and I don't care if anybody else likes this. I believe in
what I believe in, and those lyrics were a very good foundation for growing as a person. I want to express myself just like they express themselves.
You know, be yourself. I think I've kept that throughout my social life,
my professional life, my working life. I think that has been a big factor in
my personal development.[26]

William Johnston recounts a similar experience of Rush fandom, and recognizes that the sense of difference it provided assuaged social anxieties
through a feeling of superiority:

> As a Rush fan, you're part of a secret society instead of just following
> along with what everyone else is listening to. That was part of the appeal
> back when I was 14. My friends didn't listen to them. Here were these
> great musicians with these thoughtful lyrics and it opened up a whole
> new avenue toward prog-rock—Yes, King Crimson—and that reinforces
> the teen's longing for a sense of their own place in the world, as well as a
> *dire* need to feel superior. [laughs] Especially when you're a sort of book-
> ish kid with bad skin and glasses. . . . I went through a phase of being the
> only person I knew who listened to Rush. So you kind of cultivate that on
> your own. It's funny, because it reinforces a kind of a reclusive, exclusive
> superiority complex of a very fragile kind.[27]

These descriptions resonate with my own experience. The fact that my peer
group included very few Rush fans did much to make Rush fandom feel like
a mark of difference, and feelings of superiority were certainly not irrelevant. Preferring the high-register language of Rush's lyrics, the "brainy"
philosophical themes and the complicated musicianship, affirmed that I
was not a member of the masses Price writes about; Rush seemed to offer
so much more than faceless, uncritical music. Rush fandom seemed to
fulfill the lyrics' rhetoric: by listening to Rush, I was "swimming against
the stream" and "elevating from the norm." But I was also partaking in a
hegemonic myth, taking my place in an almost traditional ritual of grow-

ing up with a middle-class identity. As Bellah describes it, "The meaning of one's life for most [middle-class] Americans is to become one's own person, almost to give birth to oneself. Much of this process . . . involves breaking free from family, community and inherited ideas."[28] But Bellah points out that individualism is itself a dominant idea in our culture: "The American understanding of the autonomy of the self places the burden of one's own deepest self-definitions on one's own individual choice. . . . The irony is that here too, just where we think we are most free, we are most coerced by the dominant beliefs of our own culture. For it is a powerful cultural fiction that we not only can, but must, make up our deepest beliefs in the isolation of our private selves."[29] Radical individualism, he further notes, "is a rhetoric that educated middle-class Americans, and, through the medium of television and other mass communications, increasingly all Americans cannot avoid."[30] For many Americans, and for many Canadians inundated with American culture, individualism may *feel* like defiance, but it is actually a well-ingrained, hegemonic idea.

By critically examining individualism, I am not denying that each of us has an individual consciousness and the agency to make choices. I was recently reminded poignantly of the power of the individual's agency to choose while reading Viktor Frankl's *Man's Search for Meaning,* in which Frankl, a Jewish psychoanalyst who once believed firmly in determinism, chronicles his experiences as an inmate in Nazi concentration camps. As his captors tortured him, Frankl discovered to his surprise that he retained his identity and the ability to choose his response to his environment: "Everything can be taken from a man but one thing: the last of human freedoms—to choose one's attitude in any given set of circumstances, to choose one's way."[31] And I am also not suggesting that there is something necessarily wrong with various values (self-reliance, pro-activity, a rigorous work ethic) associated with middle-class individualism, or for that matter with Rush's lyrics. But I am concerned that individualist ideology (and Rush's use of it) be understood as part and parcel of a particular social and historical context. Though Price above insisted that "there are no natural herd members," it is equally true that the individual she describes is not natural either: it is a post-Lockean, modern, Western idea, difficult to conceive of outside the history that gave rise to Protestantism, the Enlightenment, the industrial revolution, and modern states. Moreover, Bellah's comments strongly suggest that the individualism under discussion is inflected in a distinctly American way. And as Kusserow, Perry, and Hurtsfield revealed, it is embedded in middle-class and white American identity in important ways.

Now that the social context of individualism in Rush's music has been established, I want to explore more directly its political context. Individualism provided Rush with a framework for making social critiques, and from 1975 to about 1985 individualism was one of the most important underpinnings for the critical, protest-oriented facet of Rush's repertoire. This led Rush, inevitably, to criticize just about anything threatening individuality, especially those ideas, social institutions, and circumstances that "massify" people. There are many levels to this: we saw in "Subdivisions" how conformity and peer pressure were depicted as blights on suburban life; Rush critiqued commerce and the mass media in various songs (including "The Spirit of Radio," "Natural Science" [both 1980], "The Big Money" [1985], and "Superconductor" [1989]) for their capacity to homogenize and cheapen expressive culture; Rush cast political collectivism of various kinds (socialism in "2112" [1976] and "The Trees" [1978], vigilantism in "Witch Hunt" [1981], nationalism in "Territories" [1985]) as potentially dehumanizing. Rush also devoted a number of songs to problematizing the role of high technology in Western society, assessing its potential to empower, serve, control, distract, desensitize, and dehumanize. The album *Grace Under Pressure* (1984) was marked almost throughout by ambivalent references to technology in the age of Cold War tension, industrial pollution, and electronic surveillance, and other songs like "Natural Science" (again), "Countdown," "Digital Man," and "The Weapon" (all 1982) explored narratives where technology sometimes serves people, but other times is used to oppress them.

Rush's individualist critiques extend from several strands of thought which are critical of modernity. As discussed in the first chapter, Rush drew upon an existing tradition of criticizing the suburbs for producing a homogenous, conformist, and undynamic social environment. Similarly, Rush's critique of commerce and the mass media is a prime example of how the logic of the "mass culture critique," formulated initially by the Frankfurt School of Critical Theory and further popularized by American essayist Dwight Macdonald, has become a set of beliefs that circulate *within* mass culture itself. Commonly associated in academic music studies with Theodor Adorno's writing, the mass-culture critique advanced a number of scathing ideas about the anti-individualistic nature of popular song. For Adorno, popular music is circumscribed to formulas and simple, repetitive forms that are so easy to understand that they require no effort on the part of the listener. Popular music reduces music's purpose to a commercial or economic one, prostituting talent and destroying music's profundity and authenticity. Popular music is fundamentally deceptive, tricking audiences into buying similar music over and over again by making novelty masquerade as originality.[32] Moreover, popular music had some very undesirable effects on audiences themselves, and Adorno compared what he saw as regimented dancing in jazz and swing (the popular music of his day), as well as people's obsession with celebrity singers and bandleaders, to herd-like conformity and mimicry. While expressive culture should provoke thought and stoke the imagination, Adorno insisted that popular music did the reverse: it pacified, depoliticized, and distracted its listeners, not because of any deficiency on the part of the audience, but because of the commercial, mass-produced, predigested nature of the music itself. Adorno felt that mass culture stole individuality away from its consumers and enculturated them into a symbolic world of sameness and repetition. With millions of people now consuming the same limited repertoire of hit songs and recordings, individualized aesthetic sensibilities were replaced by regularized, routinized mass tastes, made predictable by demographic models and market research. Intriguingly, these ideas have become familiar to a public that may never have heard of Adorno. Moreover, the popularization of these ideas denuded them of their original Marxist content, though much of the highbrow elitism remained intact. These ideas became, in a sense, pop culture platitudes during the late 1960s and 1970s, with rock musicians and folk aficionados differentiating themselves from routinized "pop" music by claiming that their music was different, thought provoking, and either experimental or steeped in authentic traditions. Adornian logic lay behind the elevation of rock above pop, as critics made the argument that rock music was more artistic and less commercial than popular song of the old Tin Pan Alley model. The idea of formerly authentic rock artists "selling out" and "going commercial" reflected the same concern about the corrupting potential of commerce about which Adorno wrote.

Rush's "The Spirit of Radio" addresses exactly these kinds of anxieties. The song waxes rhapsodic about the "magic" of music, its "timelessness," its humanizing power as it gives us "emotional feedback," and describes music as a gift "beyond price" yet "almost free." The latter half of the song, however, describes how the "freedom of music" can be jeopardized by "glittering prizes and endless compromises." The regimentation of music into charts and categories is described as "cold." Music and the radio, the song suggests, have great humanizing potential, but the priorities of salesmen and profits often thwart this potential. The song "Superconductor," from *Presto* (1989), expands on a similar theme, but more directly portrays the entertainment industry as deceptive. The song describes pop celebrities as "packaged" and "targeted" to certain segments of the market; their aim is to "orchestrate illusions" and "manipulate reactions." The chorus captures the distraction and mesmerization that mass culture putatively engenders, as we are invited to "watch [the pop star's] every move" and the pop star stares back, "hoping you'll believe / designing to deceive." I have found no evidence that Peart ever read Adorno (and he would not have to, since the basic points of the mass-culture critique have circulated so widely), but I found it intriguing that Rush mentions dancing as part of the deception ("A strong and simple beat / That you can dance to"), echoing Adorno's equation of social conformity with dancing to popular song's repetitive rhythms.

Of course, Rush's participation in the mass-culture critique is itself open to the challenge that the band criticizes entertainment while being entertainers and criticizes the commercialization, commodification, and massification of music while releasing albums commercially, playing to an audience which, at Rush's peak, swelled into the millions. Many Rush fans agree with the mass-culture critique; as one respondent above stated, "Rush has proven that a rock band does not have to cater to the taste of the masses." The quote demonstrates the belief that Rush is somehow in but not of mass culture; their integrity and individuality as musicians somehow remain intact. But does this mean that Rush, as commercially successful rock stars, have "orchestrated an illusion" themselves? As discussed earlier, individualism plays an important role in creating a feeling of difference in a "mass" social context where very little difference is otherwise experienced. This is partly a flattering and self-serving illusion. But the apparent contradiction of entertainers criticizing mass entertainment is also another manifestation of the larger theme of this book: the ambivalent, "middling" aspect of middle-class identity. Rush quite deliberately tries to articulate an intermediate position between commercial entertainment and a more idealized, autonomous position as artists. To put it another way, Rush, like a number of rock bands, carves a niche in modernity's commercialized cultural landscape by being self-consciously critical of it. Pink Floyd, especially in "Welcome to the Machine" (1975), makes similarly pointed critiques of mass culture while selling millions of albums. I make no argument here about how well Rush or Pink Floyd negotiate this in-between status (some find it very unconvincing, while others have responded affirmatively).

This in-between-ness that Rush articulates is very much apparent in the music itself for both "The Spirit of Radio" and "Superconductor." "The Spirit of Radio," in one sense, is exactly what Adorno describes: at the most general level, the song has a formulaic verse-chorus form with a bridge occurring in the expected place. The chord progressions and tonal structures mostly outline conventional diatonic patterns. Riff repetition underlies almost every section of the song. The rhyming schemes and poetic meters of the song's lyrics correspond mostly to established patterns that can be traced back to the earliest rock and pop songs. The principal roles played by the vocals (melody), guitar (harmony and figuration), bass (harmonic ground and rhythm), and drums (groove, accent, and punctuation) are entirely conventional for rock. However, "The Spirit of Radio" also gestures away from popular song convention in a variety of ways, individuating itself in a sense. In the first place, the song contains an unconventionally high number of musical themes (the introduction alone iterates three separate themes before the vocals enter), and the verse-chorus pattern is broken after the bridge, with the chorus never recapitulating. A number of surprises are interjected into the song, including a fast, virtuosic ensemble passage that cuts off the return of the verse progression after the bridge. The band also includes an extra pair of stanzas in the final minute of the song with a reggae feel, which jarringly contrasts with the heavy rock of the rest of the piece. "Superconductor" is less formally adventurous than "The Spirit of Radio," but the pop song convention mentioned in the lyrics (the strong, simple, danceable beat) is exactly what Rush avoids. The main riff, which accompanies the verses, is set in $\frac{7}{4}$ time, and the pre-chorus sections move into a half-time $\frac{4}{4}$ feel, creating an illusion of tempo change; the chorus is in regular $\frac{4}{4}$ time. Asymmetrical meters are associated in rock with complexity and mental rather than bodily responses; such changes diminish the sense of repetition at the formal level as well as the rhythmic flow. Although the song does have the expected forward momentum of hard rock and can be said to have a memorable hook, it also deviates from popular convention. Through these means, Rush articulates an ambivalent, in-between position, making the claim that mass culture can be routine, predigested, and cynical, but the group also doesn't believe that mass mediation must equal mediocrity (a claim often made in middlebrow culture).

As a political critique, Rush's use of individualism is well represented in the short rock opera "2112," a story about a future dystopian society, based somewhat on Ayn Rand's 1938 novel *Anthem*, and a comparison of the two works is revealing. *Anthem* was an alarmist work of fiction, best understood as part of the red scare of the 1930s, when socialism was gaining political favor in the midst of the Great Depression. It portrays a communist society of the future in which individual identity is so completely suppressed that even the word "I" is outlawed. The protagonist of the story is called Equality 7-2521, a name that encapsulates the society's ideological collectivism and bureaucratic facelessness. The protagonist narrates his growing alienation from this egalitarian society as he becomes aware that he stands apart from the people around him. He is taller and smarter than his fellow citizens, and he is continually punished for it. Rand's imagined society has regressed technologically and relies on candles and beasts of burden rather than electricity and machines. Equality 7-2521 rediscovers electricity, but his discovery is denounced by the Council of Scholars, who lambaste his presumptuous taking of initiative. Eventually, he flees into the woods with a woman who shares his prodigious physical and intellectual characteristics, and they rediscover individuality.

Rand's polemic was clearly aimed at communism; "2112," in contrast, casts a wider critical net. Peart's society of the future is also collectivist, but the central control of the society is held through an elite body called the Priests, adding a theocratic element to the narrative. Their control of society is maintained through high technology (housed in the Temples of Syrinx), with their computers maintaining surveillance over the population and providing all aspects of culture, including literature, music, and art. Unlike Equality 7-2521, the protagonist in "2112" is not distinguished from his peers in any particular way; in fact, in the extra narrative provided in the liner notes, he is portrayed as an average citizen who is happy with the status quo. Things change for the protagonist when he discovers an ancient artifact, a guitar, preserved in a cave behind a waterfall. He learns how to tune and play the instrument, and after a lifetime of having music provided for him by the Priests' computers, he discovers musical self-expression. Believing that he has made an important discovery, he takes the instrument to the Priests and expects praise for uncovering something that he thinks will enrich everyone's lives. The Priests respond angrily, telling him that "toys" like this "helped destroy the elder race of man," and crush the guitar beneath their feet. Dejected, the protagonist returns home and falls asleep, dreaming vividly of a different (perhaps ancient) world without the Priests, where creativity flourishes and people's lives are not so regimented. The narrative ends with the protagonist taking his own life, hoping that death will deliver him into the world of his dream.

In contrast to *Anthem*, "2112" is not simply an anticommunist or antisocialist polemic; Peart brings together in his dystopian future three things that have the capacity to massify: religion, technology, and ideology. But from another standpoint, "2112," in spite of its political overtones, symbolically provides another critique of mass culture. In the second section of the suite, "The Temples of Syrinx," the Priests declare that they "have taken care of everything / The words you read / The songs you sing / The pictures that give pleasure to your eye." Their computers electronically generate "all the gifts of life." To a fair degree, the Priests provide what is already available to us today through television and other mass communications. Their technology provides culture and entertainment which the society's average citizens simply consume. The protagonist's sin in "2112" is simply that he makes his own music; he becomes an unwanted producer instead of a loyal, passive consumer. In "Presentation," where the protagonist brings the guitar to the Priests, his rejection is like a failed audition; his music is refused because it is "nothing new." The protagonist appeals to the Priests to see all the common people as potential artists ("Let them all make their own music!"), but the Priests spurn the suggestion. Like the mass-culture industries, the Priests are gatekeepers, and their rejection of the protagonist affirms that he is nothing more than part of the mass audience. By naming them Priests, Peart captures the cult-like aspect of mass culture, since rock bands, movies, and television shows spawn cult followings, and by producing celebrities the industry tries to create "false gods." The Priests' culture factory is thus a Temple, and the mass audience congregates (at their computer terminals or televisions) to worship their creations; they surrender their will with religiosity and cede their creativity by proxy to the producers of mass culture. In 1976, Peart himself made this connection to the culture industry: "I just re-read Ayn Rand's [novels] for the first time in years, and I'm relating it to the music business. It deals with corruption of the spirit. . . . I like to feel that we're doing our part to change that through our music. And so far, we've managed to justify our ideals to the people in the music business—and they're the ones that count, because they're the ones in a position to hurt us."[33]

This line of interpretation, of course, does not exhaust the political criticism articulated by "2112." The piece also treats political ideology as part of the massification of the society. In "The Temples of Syrinx," the Priests declare equality their "stock in trade" and their society "the brotherhood of man." The presumption that all the citizens are the same—that the same ideas and culture will suit everyone—is what makes the society so deadening and bleak. Thus, the piece retains the antisocialism that Peart drew from his Randian inspiration, and the red star emblem that adorns *2112*'s album cover (with an individual man facing and resisting it with defiantly outstretched arms) is no doubt the red star of communism. The power of the Priests' collectivity is symbolized in their dialogue with the protagonist by their loud, distorted dynamic level; in contrast, the protagonist's solitary voice is marked by a quiet, undistorted dynamic. Musically, the Priests overwhelm and oppress with volume and the shrillness of Lee's vocal, while the protagonist speaks softly, rationally, and even meekly over gentle chords and arpeggios. Just as *Anthem* reflects its 1930s red scare context, "2112" updates the anxiety about communism for the late Cold War period by merging political collectivism with an ominous, threatening technology (a reflection of the fact that the Soviet Union had beaten the United States in the first round of the space race, and had kept pace technologically with the capitalist West, at least until the 1980s). Peart's collectivist state, with its priestly elite and malevolent, all-seeing technology, is a perfectly menacing threat, penetrating the physical, mental, and spiritual world of its subjects.

"2112" and other Rush songs ("The Trees," "Anthem," "Bastille Day," "A Farewell to Kings," "Witch Hunt") that made political cases against collectivism and in favor of individualism are challenging to contextualize, because they intersect with both broad and specific contexts. On the one hand, such political statements resonate with the rising tensions of the Cold War during the 1970s and 1980s, which climaxed during the Reagan presidency. The economic crisis of the mid-1970s and the erosion of faith in the welfare state, Keynesian economics, and other progressive government programs are also certainly part of this political turn. But on the other hand, the explicit connections Rush made to Ayn Rand in "Anthem" and "2112"—and the implicit links apparent in numerous other songs from 1975 to 1981—associated the band with a specific marginal political movement forged by Rand and her followers, known as Objectivism. Locating Rush between these two guideposts is tricky. Neil Peart's much-publicized interest in Rand during those years left an indelible mark on Rush's repertoire and became a frequent journalistic touchstone in articles about the band, especially in the British press. This singular focus on Rand's ideas, however, exaggerates her importance and fails to account for the precipitous decline in her influence on Rush's lyrics after 1981.

The choice of Rand as a literary and philosophical lodestar in Rush's early years cast the band's individualism as symptomatic of an extremely conservative political position. By referencing Rand, Rush seemed to align itself with a politics that emphasized laissez-faire capitalism, individualism, and a decidedly pro-business posture, often associated with libertarianism, neoliberalism, and secular neoconservatism. Rand's novels and nonfiction provide one of the best known expressions of this philosophy in popular culture, also represented in the writings of philosopher Robert Nozick, economists Milton Friedman and Friedrich von Hayek, novelist Robert A. Heinlein, and television journalist John Stossel. The philosophical and economic basis of this political movement was highly influential on mainstream neoconservatism, with many of its tenets adopted by Ronald Reagan's Republican government in the early 1980s and Margaret Thatcher's Conservatives after 1979. Ironically, its influence was weaker on the politics of Rush's home country, Canada, but Brian Mulroney's Conservatives (1984–1993) and Jean Chretien's Liberals (1993–2003) certainly bore marks of its influence. The impact of resurgent individualism in mainstream politics was nowhere more apparent than in Thatcher's famous October 1987 statement that "there is no such thing as society. There are individual men and women, and there are families."[34]

Rush's evocation of Rand in its early albums garnered relatively little attention in the American press, but in 1978 an article in the Canadian magazine *MacLean's* positioned Rush at the vanguard of a new, more conservative, self-centered generation of rock fans. Entitled "To Hell with Bob Dylan—Meet Rush: They're In It for the Money," the article probed the band's affirmative posture toward Rand, her version of capitalism, and the band's self-congratulatory assessment of its perseverance and hard work ethic. As reported by Roy MacGregor, Rush

> held no kindred love for the social conscience of a Bob Dylan or Phil Ochs, for that matter not even the street justice of a Mick Jagger. Rush was, on the average, a full decade younger than the ruling class of modern pop music. They found themselves speaking for a large group of young rockers without spokesmen—a group who, despite their love of loud, violent music, were themselves non-revolutionary, highly conservative and certainly self-centered.[35]

The British press also remarked on Rush's conservative bent, but in even starker terms. Barry Miles, a writer for the *New Musical Express,* wrote the most infamous article in Rush lore in which he engaged Neil Peart in a debate about the merits of laissez-faire capitalism. Miles's transcription of the debate was riddled with after-the-fact annotations, comparing Peart's comments with Nazi slogans and painting Rush as right-wing extremists. Miles concluded:

> These guys are advocating this stuff on stage and on record and no one even questions it. No one is on their case. All the classic hallmarks of the right wing are there: the pseudo-religious language. . . . The use of a quasi-mystical symbol—the naked man confronting the red star of socialism (at least I suppose that's what it's supposed to be). It's all there. They are actually very nice guys. They don't sit there in jack boots pulling the wings off flies. They are polite, charming even, naive—roaming the concert circuits preaching what to me seems like proto-fascism like a leper without a bell.[36]

One can only presume that Miles was unaware, when he drafted his accusation of fascism, that Geddy Lee's Jewish parents had been imprisoned at Auschwitz. On rereading the article, I agree that Peart comes across as rather extreme regarding Rand, capitalism, and individualism, but he seems more like a naive, excited young man who has just discovered a miraculous ideology that seems to explain away all the world's problems than a proto-fascist. He advanced nothing so suggestive of fascism as racism or authoritarianism.[37]

Miles's article might have been little more than an eccentric, ugly episode in Rush's critical reception, except that the "proto-fascist" or "crypto-fascist" epithet was repeated often in the British press. Brian Harrigan, one of Rush's staunchest supporters there and the first of Rush's biographers, did not think Miles was trying to insult the band—he "wrote it as he saw it"—but the "crypto-fascist" phrase stuck, and Harrigan notes that the Miles article "established" Rush in the British rock market with a particular reputation.[38] Although the fascist trope was most virulent between 1978 and 1982, British rock critic Paul Stump, in his 1998 history of progressive rock, *The Music's All That Matters*, revived the accusation, calling Rush's songs "a social prescription of great toxicity."[39] Stump contextualized Rush's rise to fame in the UK during the late 1970s by stating, "This was perhaps the logical outcome of an era of accelerating individualism of the haves but [also] the increased defensiveness and parochialism of Western society's blue-collar have-nots in the face of recession."[40] Rush's songs, Stump claimed, were "Thatcherite/Reaganite politics made music."[41]

The alarming reception Rush received in Britain had almost no counterpart in America.[42] In the American context, the lower-middle-class form of individualism Rush delivered invoked dominant American ideas about politics and the self, and so its individualism and decidedly middle-class sensibility rocked few boats. In Britain, however, with its more pronounced and hardened class structure, Rush's apparent political stance was sometimes associated not with liberation but with an unapologetic and brash defense of class privilege.[43] Unlike in America, where individualism is part of the national myth about social mobility and the fluidity of social class, in Britain its meaning is far more politically divisive.[44] In their analysis of middle-class political activism in the United Kingdom during the 1970s, Roger King and Neill Nugent underscore the decidedly anti-collectivist nature of many political campaigns initiated by groups representing lower-middle-class interests. In many cases, feelings of being squeezed between corporate/upper-class power and working-class unionism led to ardent declarations that the British political system had failed to protect the rights and well-being of individual (read: middle-class) citizens.[45] These political movements tended to find allies on the right side of the British political spectrum, and thus middle-class politics, especially when it flirted with libertarian-style rhetoric, was seen broadly as arch-conservative, which the left painted as proto-fascist.

Moreover, the connection between fascism and an individualistic, lower-middle-class ethos has, in fact, been an obsession of British and other European scholars, as noted by Rita Felski:

> Much scholarly writing about the lower middle class is devoted to analyzing its role in the emergence of fascism and Hitler's rise to power. Theories of lower-middle-class status anxiety were applied to the United States in the 1950s to explain right-wing political movements and McCarthyism. More recently, commentators have attributed the success of Thatcherism to the gradual embourgeoisement of the British working class, which abandoned its traditional values and embraced an individualistic and consumer-oriented ethos.[46]

Historian Sven Beckert offers a similar summary of scholarly opinion:

> The political proclivities of the lower middle class have stood at the center of historians' attention, with interest in the pronounced radicalism of the petit bourgeoisie, as in the case of nineteenth-century France, and its affinity to fascist politics. . . . Most historians have seen the lower middle class as providing the foot soldiers for the Nazi ascendancy to power, and the petit-bourgeois embrace of *völkisch* and anti-Semitic ideas have motivated historians to give them a central role in their research.[47]

Both Felski and Beckert rightly point out that the blame placed on the lower middle class for the rise of Hitler is prejudiced and unfair; upper-class industrialists (British and American as well as German) were initially all too happy to do business with Germany's Nazi regime, and they expressed some admiration for Hitler's and Mussolini's exercise of executive-style authority in reforming their countries' economies into greater organization and efficiency; some upper-middle-class intellectuals and artists (such as philosopher Martin Heidegger, painter Salvador Dali, and composer Anton Webern) were also publicly supportive of these regimes. But prejudices about the lower middle class's historical role in the rise of hard-right politics (from Hitler's fascism to Thatcher's neoconservatism) may partly explain Miles's seemingly arbitrary leap from Rush's individualism to fascism.

All things considered, the individualist theme helped Rush define its identity as a band and gave it a cause around which to rally, serving it quite well with North American audiences. But its public dabbling with Rand's influence became an unexpected political bomb which blew up in the band's face, thanks to the British rock press. In one interview, Peart remembers feeling "shocked, stunned and wounded that people could equate adherence to individualism, self-reliance and liberty with fascism or dictatorship," but admits that he became too loose-lipped in the press in the mid-1970s about political ideas with which he was only just becoming acquainted.[48] By the early 1990s, Peart felt that his interest in Rand had been grossly overemphasized:

> [I was] like many people getting labeled with an influence like that; I was just reading Camille Paglia last year, and she said that anytime she mentions Freud, people automatically think she buys into every word that Freud ever said, which is far from the case for almost anybody with regard to their mentors or exemplars or early heroes. . . . Most of us are independent enough to take a selection of different people's ideas and meld them together into something of our own. It was just simplistic labeling at the time, and thankfully it's died out.[49]

Geddy Lee pointed out in some interviews that the interest in Rand he shared with Peart mostly involved drawing on her inspirational themes of self-esteem, unlocking of creativity, and moral integrity: "I found Ayn Rand's work at a certain time in my life—this is going back to '76–'77—to be a great liberator and a great relief because her artistic manifesto was so strong and inspiring. Her views on art and the sanctity of individuals were very inspiring to young musicians in a band, fighting for their own identity."[50] In the long run, it seemed that their interest had little to do with Rand's hard-line capitalist economics and politics per se, and Rush's repeated forays into the mass-culture critique suggested a great deal of suspicion toward music as big business, a suspicion Rand likely would never have endorsed. Rush's individualism, to the extent that it was conservative, sought to uphold and defend an old, entrepreneurial model of the individual, what David Riesman called the "inner-directed person." For Riesman, the inner-directed person learned to follow abstract principles and apply them in any given situation; her core identity was based on her own chosen values. This stood in contrast to the "tradition-directed person," a paradigmatic model from pre-industrial societies, whose life course and behavior were guided by custom, family, ethnicity, and community; it also stood in contrast to the "other-directed person," who arises in the more recent phase of corporate capitalism or socialism; her behavior is guided and regulated through careful observance and imitation of others.[51] Thus, the kind of individualism Rush and similar rock bands espoused looked back to a romantic, nineteenth-century entrepreneurial model, sustained as an alternative to a more postmodern, ideologically flexible, and other-directed self.

Through the 1980s and 1990s, Peart's explorations of individualism became less Randian and idealistic, and more pragmatic and critical. As early as 1980, Rush came out with a song, "Natural Science," that criticized the blind, solipsistic pursuit of individual agendas. Using tidal pools as a metaphor, the song describes people becoming so narrowly focused on themselves (their pool) that they forget that they are part of a bigger picture (the sea). "Time after time we lose sight of the way / Our causes can't see their effects," Lee sings, in a song that markedly contrasts the "live only for yourself" ethos of "Anthem." In "Open Secrets" (1987), Peart deals with a similar theme, only in the context of a personal relationship. The song describes the inwardness and isolation that results from hiding feelings and keeping private secrets from one's intimate circle; the relationship described is full of miscommunication and irritation, because the parties are distracted by their own concerns, even as they try to open up to each other: "I was looking out the window," Lee sings; "I should have looked at your face instead." The things we keep inside are barriers, Peart writes; the things we conceal "will never let us grow." Bringing these barriers down, learning to empathize, learning to be vulnerable to another person takes real courage.

Another interesting contrast lies between "Something for Nothing" and "Chain Lightning" (1989). While the former puts forward the claim that "what you do is your own glory," Peart observes in the latter that sometimes the ideas and feelings that pass between people are what really matter. Energy is contagious, the song suggests, laughter is infectious, enthusiasm spreads: the responses and feedback between people give life its momentum. The song also acknowledges the dark side of this, since "bitterness breeds irritation" and "ignorance breeds imitation." The profundity and consequence of an idea, experience, or insight may not always be apparent to the person having it, but it may be for the person who responds to it, for the "spark still flies," Peart writes, "reflected in another pair of eyes." Finally, in contrast to the larger-than-life, individualistic character of "Tom Sawyer," "Nobody's Hero" (1993) revises Rush's past views on heroism. "Nobody's Hero" includes personal anecdotes about people Peart had known and who had passed away; he realized that they were not heroes in the conventional sense, yet their lives had more influence on him than he imagined. Peart told journalist Ula Gehret,

> "Nobody's Hero," as it existed in my notebook and in my thoughts, was really just about, "what is a hero, what is the Western idea of a hero, and is

it good?" And ultimately I decided that our idea of a hero is a superhuman being, whether it's an athlete or an entertainer or a politician or whatever. . . . And I decided no, it isn't a good thing. It's not good for people to think they are trying to measure themselves against perfect superhuman deities. Much better they should measure themselves against role models or the type of heroes that I outlined in the chorus, which are ordinary people doing extraordinary things. . . . And then I thought, "Who are the other people who have that impact on somebody's life?" And in my own life, too—for instance, the first verse about the first gay person that I knew and what a great example he set for me for what a gay person is, and prevented me from ever becoming homophobic. And in the second verse I happened to know this family that this terrible tragedy had happened to, and I thought of what a hole in their lives the girl had left behind. These were people who had more impact [on me] than any hero, but at the same time in our Western way, they were nobody's hero.[52]

When viewed in the context of Rush's nearly thirty-five-year career, individualism stands as an important theme in its repertoire, but other themes and concerns became dominant as the band's career progressed. Moreover, when the Canadian government awarded the members of Rush the Order of Canada in 1996, the dedication credited the band not with embodying Rand's "virtue of selfishness," but quite the opposite: "these veterans of the stage have raised over a million dollars for charities such as food banks and the United Way. Their efforts have enhanced an awareness of the plight faced by society's less fortunate, inspiring and awakening the social consciousness of an entire generation."[53] This strongly suggests that, in public perceptions of the band, Rush had managed to balance its ideology of individualistic self-interest with one of civic duty and responsibility.

Although it was not a frequent pattern in the ethnographic data I gathered, it should be noted that some Rush fans thought the individualist theme was one of the less attractive aspects of the band. For example, Cat Ashton, though initially quite intrigued by Peart's lyrics, read Ayn Rand and remembered, "I was fine with [Rush's lyrics] until I actually went out and read Ayn Rand. It was one of those throwing-the-book-across-the-room type of things. It sort of cast everything Neil said in a whole new light, and I just didn't agree with it as readily as I would have before." Another fan, after reading a draft of this chapter, agreed with the general tenor of my discussion of "Tom Sawyer," but wondered what Rush was really saying about this kind of individualism. "I don't know if I'd want to meet Tom Sawyer. I don't think I like the guy," he told me. "He's arrogant, he's devious." He quoted the lyric from the fifth stanza, "The space he invades he gets by on you," and notes, "It sounds like they're talking about the worst traits of the United States. Is Rush praising him or criticizing him?" Although I still hear the song mostly as a celebration of Tom Sawyer's character, which is consistent with Peart's comments on individualism,[54] it remains, of course, open to interpretation.

3

"The Work of Gifted Hands"

Professionalism and Virtuosity in Rush's Style

As a teenage Rush fan in the 1980s, I had a voracious appetite for reading newspaper and magazine interviews with the band members. In retrospect, I am struck by how odd this obsession seems now, given that these pieces were fairly dull, at least by rock 'n' roll standards. Led Zeppelin fans could revel in the mythology and mystique of their favorite band, centering on group's reputed excesses of sex, drugs, and the occult. Fans of Guns 'N Roses and Mötley Crüe could trade sensational stories about all sorts of band misbehavior and controversy. Bruce Springsteen, for whatever reason, brought out the best in rock critics, serving as the subject of some of the most celebrated essays in the field. Pop artists like Madonna kept their fans guessing about their next moves and their motivations. In

contrast, articles and interviews with Rush centered—fairly unglamor-
ously—on the band's processes of composition, the rigors of touring, the
routines of rehearsal and practice, as well as the delicate matter of balanc-
ing career and family. There was no question that Rush was living the rock
'n' roll dream—platinum albums, successful tours, video and radio air
play—but based on what the band members told journalists in countless
interviews over the decades, they lived it in an oddly straight-laced, low-
key manner.[1] As Neil Peart told Sylvie Simmons of *Sounds* magazine, "We
like to get away from the panoply and glitter that surrounds this business.
When you're driving down the highways of America every day you can't
help but get the pulse of the streets and keep in touch with reality. We're
a pretty low-key bunch."[2] Rush's manager, Ray Danniels, once quipped,
"These guys are pure boring to most music people."[3] The band members
consistently emphasized the work involved in being rock musicians, rather
than the frills and glamour, in their interviews. There was no innuendo,
biographical or psychological undressing, or controversy discussed. Nevertheless, like most Rush fans I interviewed, I was riveted by the band
members' explanations of their musicianship and career. Why were we
drawn to this?

A plausible preliminary answer may lie in the "everyman" persona that
the members of Rush project. In many discussions with fans, I found that
Rush's appeal was linked to the down-to-earth way the band stood apart
from the image-obsessed ethos of the 1980s. One of Rush's most celebrated
songs, "Limelight" (1981), a reflection on being a professional performer
and grappling with fame, speaks of a need to remain grounded and "in
touch with reality," lest one become absorbed into the fantasy and artifice
of stage performance. Neil Peart has echoed this sentiment in a number of
interviews; for example, in 1988, he told *Metal Hammer*'s Malcolm Dome,
"I never wanted to be famous and people just don't seem to understand
that. All I wanted was to be a musician, to be good at playing my chosen
instrument."[4] In 1984, he told *Off the Record*'s Mary Turner, "I don't enjoy
fame in any of its manifestations. I enjoy, of course, being respected for the
work, anyone would, and that to me is where it begins and ends."[5] As this

latter quote suggests, Peart is ambivalent about fame, valuing recognition for his work as a musician, but expressing discomfort with being recognized as a celebrity. For years, Rush's desire for privacy was a dominant theme in interviews—especially with Peart—and it figures into discussions of Rush's creative process as well. Peart once stated, "No one has the right to exert any pressure on us. We've never allowed anyone else in the studio. No record company people are running around offering opinions and no one hears our demos but us. It's very much a closed shop."[6] This closed-door policy is clearly part of Rush's claim on artistic freedom and the privileged distance the band members maintain from their record companies.

Eschewing artifice, cultivating a down-to-earth persona, claiming to make music for the sake of art rather than fame, and declaring artistic autonomy from the music industry—all these mobilize a number of well-discussed discourses surrounding rock music and authenticity. Several excellent studies have probed why commercially successful popular artists assume anti-celebrity postures and claim artistic rather than commercial motives. Jon Stratton, for example, notes that the Romanticism of the nineteenth century—which introduced notions of artists as bohemian misfits or recluses, making art for its own sake, being autonomous from the marketplace, being indifferent to their art's reception—lives on in popular music, acting as an appealing selling angle. Indeed, says Stratton, the music industry needs its Romantic Other to drive the production and sale of new music and celebrities who appear authentic to their audiences.[7] Lisa Lewis and Kembrew MacLeod show that the distinctions that rock artists and critics make between rock and pop align with a series of binary oppositions (rock/pop, authentic/inauthentic, artistic/commercial, innovative/derivative, real/fake, and, in terms of the artists and fans most often grouped under these categorical oppositions, male/female).[8] Simon Frith theorizes that value-laden distinctions between "art," "popular," and "folk" do not simply align with large-scale sociological categories, but are also distinctions that get made *within* subcultures and taste publics related to certain musical genres.[9] Thus, in rock music itself, particular songs or albums are valued as "works of art," others dismissed as "corporate rock fodder," and still others authenticated as "music from the street" or "direct from the underground."

I want to add to this larger discussion of rock's authenticating discourses by addressing an important aspect of Rush's appeal to authenticity: its salient concern with a particular model of professionalism. This chapter explores both Rush's musical style and the band's rhetoric as it unfolds in journalistic interviews as key components in creating an image of the group as professionals. Professionalism is an important facet of middle-class identity to explore, for, as William Weber observes, middle-class people identify themselves less as a class and more through their professions.[10] Rush draws from what Burton Bledstein calls "the culture of professionalism," a set of attitudes toward work, working relationships, skill, and prestige that emerged in North America during the late nineteenth and early twentieth centuries and has become an important part of how middle-class careers are shaped and understood.[11] Discussing professionalism in rock musicianship provides an interesting angle for exploring the construction of musical authenticity, because it adds complexity to the kinds of folk, popular, or art discourses that Frith and others discuss. It also provides an opening to discuss neglected aspects of the popular musician's place in the history of work, especially as it relates to social class. I argue that Rush musicians actively constructed their careers through a model of middle-class professionalism, using musical virtuosity of many kinds, eclecticism, and the idea of creative autonomy as the main pillars of their professional identity. Rush was aided in this endeavor by the climate of the music industry and rock culture in the 1970s and 1980s. Also playing a role was a body of journalism known as "musician's magazines" (e.g., *Guitar Player, Bass Player, Modern Drummer*), which encouraged and provided a discursive framework in which Rush, along with a number of other select rock musicians, could present its music, career pattern, and motivations in terms consonant with the middle-class professional. My overarching concern is to discuss why Rush sought to construct this professional aura around itself—and why it is so important to many of its fans—when rock music typically requires no formal qualifications whatsoever.

The significance of Rush's successful interpolation of middle-class professional values into its career becomes clearer if we start by discussing the ways that occupations in popular music are generally incompatible with such values. It is a truism that popular music, and entertainment more generally, is a highly volatile industry, and despite potentially high economic payoffs, performers are typically regarded as having low prestige. This is especially well illustrated in North America by the fact that social groups that were marginalized at various points in history (Irish, African Americans, and later Jews) have worked in the entertainment industry in disproportionately high numbers. The volatility of the popular music industry means that for every long-term, stable career achieved by blue-chip artists, there are countless market failures, one-hit wonders, and artists of precarious sales figures. Ever-shifting trends in the marketplace and the whims of record company executives threaten to wipe out careers. Career patterns are highly unpredictable and irregular, and success can seem more akin to winning the lottery than rising through the ranks in the way of white-collar professionals. For musicians especially, there is often a frustrating ambiguity between career and hobby, since the majority of musicians never attain enough success to quit their day jobs, even after spending years in practice and small-venue performance. And for others in the music industry, whether it is the sound engineers, roadies, A&R representatives, or producers, the industry has been notoriously difficult to professionalize. Since World War II, the authority and effectiveness of professional organizations (including unions and trade schools) have been undermined by unexpectedly successful self-trained mavericks, independent operators, hobbyists, and dabblers who demonstrate time and again that success in the music industry does not require formal professional training. Moreover, in rock, some careers (e.g., those of the Sex Pistols or Bob Dylan) flourish through a deliberate flouting of professional standards or by shunning the aura of professionalism entirely. Indeed, eschewing anything resembling middle-class professionalism is sometimes a component of successful youth-oriented music because it upholds the expected separation of leisure from work, or the kids' world from their parents' world.

Given the instability of performing careers in the music industry, as well as the romantic fictions that persist about how artists should be creatively free and autonomous from the pressures of the marketplace, it is not surprising that many musicians express ambivalence about the music business and claim to resist its strictures. The very idea of selling out is based on the idea that commercial pressures are a hindrance, even damaging, to musical creativity. Rock critics themselves have earned a reputation for championing obscure, commercially unsuccessful artists ("semi-popular popular music" is how Robert Christgau once described his preferences), and turning against those same artists if commercial success accrues. All this demonstrates how the romantic and modernist idea of artistic merit varying inversely with commercial popularity has endured and infiltrated the sphere of popular culture.

The members of Rush place creative autonomy among their highest priorities when characterizing their careers. In interviews, the band members assert nothing more vehemently than their hard-won creative independence. As early as 1977, Geddy Lee told *Circus*'s Scott Cohen Frost:

> The worst thing in the world is to have to answer to somebody. For us, the most frustrating thing in the world is being told what to do. We feel we know what we're doing. We know our music and how it should be presented to the world. We know who we're trying to appeal to and we know us—and there's no one who knows us better than us. That's why we have an excellent manager—because he understands us and exactly what we're trying to do. He doesn't touch us. He just lets us do what we want to do. He takes what we've done and tries to present it to the world in a way that he believes we would want it presented.[12]

Lee's statement was made just a year after Rush's *2112* album had sold 260,000 records and rescued the band's financial fortunes after three commercially unsuccessful albums. The band members still recount the period surrounding this album's release as tense and difficult, with Mercury Records putting pressure on them to move away from long, conceptual tracks and return to shorter, simpler rock fare. The band's decision to record *2112*, with a twenty-five-minute rock opera as its centerpiece, was a risky move and its success was anything but assured. Because the gamble succeeded, the band won deference from Mercury, which no longer had reason to doubt Rush's judgment. Thus, although commercial success permitted Rush to continue to compose and record according to its own interests, the group maintained the view that it was the artist's prerogative to do so without regard to sales figures. Moreover, the band credited a rigorous, honest work ethic as an important factor in its success. In 1986, Peart made this case to journalist Nick Krewen:

> As a writer, Hemingway thought that the most important thing was to sustain a reputation of integrity. Hopefully, all of the other fruits would follow from that. And for us as a band, myself as a musician, that was the idealistic goal with which we started out. I thought that all you had to do was your best and, sooner or later, all your rewards would come to roost. Again, that isn't always the case, but for us it was. We have squeezed through difficult periods. We have squeaked along without the benefit of radio and without the benefit of a hit single and without the benefit of media support. We started out at the beginning working non-stop and we figured we'll go out and play and we'll be good at that. And that will be the most important thing. If we get well known as a good live performing band then hopefully the rest will follow. And for once in modern life, cause and effect did tie together. . . . We were also under a tremendous amount of pressure to compromise, to make our music more commercial; to write nice little short songs, and to make them as repetitive and as commercial as possible. Against all that pressure we have prevailed—adopting the influences we wanted to adopt, and taking the course in songwriting that we wanted to take—and working with the people we wanted to work with, on our terms. It may sound a little egocentric, but it's not. It's just dedication to the values that drew us to music when we were teenagers, we thought that music was such an honest form of self-expression. And

then we went through the disillusionment of growing up and finding out that it wasn't that way at all—but that it was big business and that these musicians were just playing the music they thought would make them the most money and they were writing songs that would appeal to the lowest common denominator.[13]

Peart portrays Rush's career as built on integrity, hard work, heightened competence, and autonomy in its profession. From this, Peart claims, the band members attained artistic privilege, the freedom to make whatever music they chose. But there are, of course, several mitigating factors that permitted Rush to experiment musically before its commercial breakthrough. Peart himself acknowledged in an interview included in the *R30* DVD set (2004) that Mercury Records was in disarray at the time of *2112* and may not have been managing its affairs with the group as strictly as it might have under better circumstances. As such, Rush's artistic freedom at this time may have been due partly to the record company's distraction and internal structural problems, not simply to Rush's dogged tenacity.

In a broader historical context, it is fair to say that Rush's prerogative to experiment with rock's formal characteristics, to flout commercial restrictions and to please themselves creatively, was a byproduct of rock's shift toward "artistic" status. This privilege was won by mostly white, male rock musicians following the British Invasion of the 1960s. The Beatles, Cream, Pink Floyd, and progressive rock more generally had established the eclectic, experimental male rock band as a category to which the music industry had to adjust, especially as experimental albums like Pink Floyd's *Dark Side of the Moon* demonstrated its massive commercial potential. The rise of rock criticism also did much to argue for rock's special status as a more artistically pure, authentic form in contrast to commercial pop.[14] Much has been discussed about the social privilege made apparent by white male rock musicians assuming the mantle of artists and proudly flaunting a kind of artistic freedom that is seldom extended, except in rare cases, to female and black performers working in the domains of dance, pop, and soul. This imbalance of creative privilege was actively promoted in the way record companies themselves dealt with rock artists, especially in comparison to artists from other genres. Keith Negus, in his study of business practices in the music industry, states,

> The struggle is not *between* commerce and creativity, but what it means *to be* commercial and creative. . . . I found this to be apparent in the way in which white, male, guitar-dominated rock bands were being prioritized [by record companies] and accorded considerable investment. In contrast, soul and dance music was being treated in a less strategic and more ad hoc manner. As these priorities were established, a naturalistic 'organic' set of creative practices were accorded a privileged position over more 'synthetic' combinatorial approaches to popular music. These *creative* practices were then inscribed into the *commercial* priorities of the record companies, so that rock was prioritized over soul, albums over singles, and the self-contained 'live' guitar bands over the loosely structured 'studio' keyboard groups.[15]

Negus's analysis reveals that the industry's approach to rock bands' careers did, in many cases, offer rock bands a very privileged work environment which artists in other genres seldom received. From the late 1960s through the early 1990s, rock bands were given time to develop followings, to experiment musically, to expand their studio and performing resources, and most important to create "organically," writing and recording on their own schedule, according to their own preferred processes.[16] Of rock's privileged status, Lisa Lewis reminds us that "rock was made to stand as a higher form of popular music, as *the* representative of art and artfulness. . . . Rock discourse became useful to the goal of elevating white male musicianship and creating an ideal of white, male spectatorship. Its allegiance to art and folk values and its denouncement of commerciality and popular pleasure were made to conform to gender ideologies."[17] And Glenn Pillsbury discusses how the apparent detachment of thrash metal artists like Metallica from the commercial pressures of the music industry derives from broader values undergirding white, male identity, such as stoic independence and the imperative of self-control and self-determination.[18] Any discussion of

Rush's attainment of creative autonomy must be understood against this historical background.

While scholars justifiably made discussions of status and prestige in music center on social factors like race and gender, there is a class dimension that demands further explanation. Rush's concern with creative freedom exemplifies one of the most cherished possessions of the middle-class professional: occupational autonomy. In most of the "honorable professions" (e.g., law, medicine, or academia), the reward for long years of education, apprenticeships, and paying one's dues is the freedom to run one's own practice, to gain tenure or enter into partnership, or to have to answer to no one but oneself. To some degree, middle management also receives a measure of autonomy within some corporate departments, with the freedom to develop a leadership style, make some decisions, and guide a departmental culture. As Barbara Ehrenreich observes, autonomy in the workplace is one aspect that separates professional labor from lower-status types of work. The less subject the professional is to the priorities of others, the higher the prestige: therefore, "the pure researcher looks down on the industrial scientist, journalists look down on ad copyists. . . . This is snobbery, but it stems from an allegiance to that elusive middle-class value, occupational autonomy—the freedom to direct one's own work according to inner principles rather than externally imposed priorities, such as profit."[19] Ehrenreich further observes that the professional career is different from the stereotypical working-class job in that professionals expect to derive "secret pleasure" from their work, while having a working-class job means getting paid for doing something you would rather not do.[20] These points are paralleled in comments Alex Lifeson made in 1983: "We've considered ourselves successful for a long time. It depends on how you measure success. We felt we were successful for a long time before we had any kind of financial satisfaction. We were hundreds of thousands of dollars in debt . . . but we had control over what we were doing at least. We had control over the way we wanted to project ourselves and in that we found a lot of satisfaction."[21]

From this standpoint, the artistic autonomy claimed by rock musicians like Rush not only reflects a neo-romantic tension between art and entertainment, but also a struggle over the definition of the musician's occupation and the terms under which work and business are conducted. Many forms of the musician's occupation lack the degree of workplace autonomy that Rush carefully guards. Musicians for hire—in the form of session musicians or cover bands—fulfill roles that approximate lower-prestige forms of labor, not entirely lacking opportunities for creative work and input but also requiring significant capitulation to the employers' desires.[22] The devaluation of mainstream pop singers who work under the old Tin Pan Alley model (with singers, instrumentalists, songwriters, and arrangers usually fulfilling separate functions) arises out of a perception that their role in the creative process is too dependent on other specialists; the factory-like Tin Pan Alley model makes the performer's job resemble a cog in a machine.[23] The rhetoric in the Rush quotes above—about not allowing others in the studio, not wanting to answer to anyone, working "on our terms"—aims to present the band as self-directed professionals; Rush appears to be an organization that others work for, not the reverse.

Peart also highlights the issue of integrity, a concern that surfaces in a number of Rush songs (e.g., "A Farewell to Kings," "The Spirit of Radio," "Natural Science," "Grand Designs"). "Sustaining a reputation of integrity" is an important pillar supporting the ideology of middle-class professionalism. Michael Eraut explains that the professional, as an expert possessing specialized knowledge, is expected to protect the public from being duped: "Hence, the emphasis put by the professions on moral probity, service orientation and codes of conduct. . . . [Their] relative freedom from interference is based on unique expertise and moral integrity."[24] Under this ideology of professionalism, Rush's occupational autonomy is certainly a privilege, but it is leveraged against the band's pledge to use that autonomy to deliver the highest level of musical expertise it can. Professionalism is, by its very nature, elitist, and attaining a peak level of skill and competence is a very high priority. The professional's skill, Bledstein tells us, is built up as more than just a service for sale; it is seen as a calling and a human capacity of virtually unlimited potential.[25] Rush's much-vaunted obsession with instrumental and compositional virtuosity ties in with this aspect of professionalism in several ways. The band equates its early work (1975–1980) with developing technical skill and proving itself worthy of the mantle of musicians. Neil Peart recalls, "In the early years, it's true that we were learning to play, and the focus for probably our first six albums was 'let's get better as musicians.' A lot of [songs] were just exercises stuck together, but they had a purpose. It was our postgraduate study."[26] In another interview, Greg Armbruster of *Keyboard* magazine asked Geddy Lee, "In order to improve your technique, do you make it a point to write beyond your ability to play?" Lee replied, "I think you have to—that's how you get better. In the earlier days, around *Hemispheres* time, we always did that. I'd write a part and go, 'Wow! This is tough to play.' We would have to play it a lot in order to play it well. During this period, that was all we had to do: figure out something that was hard to play and in an odd time signature. We would write fourteen different pieces, or bits, that were in different time signatures and stick them all together to create a concept. . . . Now, our technical ability has gotten to a point where we can pretty well play anything we can think of."[27] The very idea of "postgraduate study" and the need to compose above one's current technical ability make it clear that the band members saw themselves as something less than credible musicians until they had achieved an elite level of musicianship.

These quotes also suggest that, from the band's point of view, songwriting was sometimes a medium for training themselves in musical technique as much as it was about crafting songs. This approach (and the band's discussion of it in interviews) seemed to be aimed at legitimizing themselves as self-taught musicians, bringing some order and rigor to a process that is often imagined as mysterious, ad hoc, and contingent. The band members' training, from the available evidence, is a fairly typical mix for rock musicians, including the aural imitation of recordings, private lessons, and learning from each other as they collaborated and performed. Each member also had some "extra" training and experience from outside the Rush context during the early years of adulthood. Alex Lifeson took a year's worth of classical guitar lessons in 1971, which did much to open up this avenue of musicianship for the guitarist. Peart, who went to England in the early 1970s, hoping to find his way into an English progressive rock band, spent the most time performing and interacting with other musicians. Geddy Lee also spent time in a rhythm and blues group in Toronto during the early 1970s. Nevertheless, they all actively cultivated a publicly visible regimen of technical improvement across their first seven albums, and the group put a great deal of effort into attaining virtuosity in a number of musical and compositional domains.

"La Villa Strangiato," an all-instrumental track from *Hemispheres* (1978), provides an excellent illustration of what Lee and Peart discuss and a rich example of the musical tactics Rush used to authenticate itself as a group of competent, professional musicians. Over nine minutes long, the piece is subtitled "An Exercise in Self-Indulgence," intended humorously, although it also acknowledges Rush's ever-present concern with creative autonomy. "La Villa Strangiato" contains ten different musical themes, each named after one of Lifeson's vivid nightmares, with three of the themes reprised near the end to give the piece a sense of coherence and closure. The introduction features Lifeson alone on classical guitar, playing a sparse, angular theme outlining a diminished chord, executed three times with increasing intensity. His fourth gesture is a virtuosic, rapidly accelerating flurry of notes in a descending pattern, reminiscent of Spanish flamenco music, ending in a chord strum and a shift to a quiet, gently arpeggiating electric guitar. This gesture is reminiscent of a cadenza, a sometimes-improvised passage in classical concertos meant as a climactic display of the featured musician's dexterity. The introduction serves two purposes. First, the invocation of classical music signifies seriousness, providing an indication that Lifeson's musical knowledge and experience extend beyond rock and into a domain that has traditionally carried a mantle of prestige. Second, by use of an acoustic guitar, Lifeson authenticates his virtuosity by playing a difficult, dazzling passage without the "crutch" of electronic amplification, special effects, or the easier action provided by an electric guitar's neck.[28]

The second theme acts as a bridge between sections, featuring Lifeson arpeggiating a C chord with an added ninth, gradually building from the quiet volume level of the classical guitar to the full dynamic loudness of

Rush's electric rock. Over this static background, Lee and Peart play figures on synthesizers and orchestra bells, demonstrating that their range of instrumental abilities extends beyond rock's standard rhythm section of bass and drum kit. This is followed by the "Strangiato Theme," which features two contrasting ideas. The first is a main riff in A major, which acts as the stable home from which the other themes take off. The second is a decidedly quirky episode, with the guitar playing a single-note lead line against the implied chords C major and F-sharp major (a progression that foreshadows the seventh theme). Peart drives the groove hard with busy, syncopated ride cymbal work, played in rapid sixteenth-note subdivisions. The guitar, bass, and drums play a kind of counterpoint here, in contrast to the more rhythmically unified A major riff. In the "Strangiato Theme," then, Rush uses two contrasting compositional techniques, one based on riff repetition, the other on linear, melodic invention, showing adeptness at rhythm section cohesion in one part and contrapuntal playing in the other.

The fourth section returns to a quiet, pensive dynamic and acts as the piece's main guitar solo. Recalling the introduction, Lifeson begins at a soft dynamic level with short, angular motifs, using a volume pedal to turn his notes into "swells," notes that fade in and out without an attack. Lifeson explores the lonely, doleful mood of the theme and then builds with the rhythm section to passages of greater intensity and activity, ending with several virtuosic, cadenza-like runs. The solo is played throughout over a groove in $\frac{7}{4}$ time, one of several deviations Rush makes from the standard $\frac{4}{4}$ orientation of most rock songs. Rush drew this interest in asymmetrical meters from progressive rock, a rhythmic device that has profound consequences for the feel and meaning of a rock groove, and signifies musical complexity and intellectuality. Rush helped to popularize the use of these meters in hard rock, leading to the emergence of "math rock," a category of rock where complex changes of time signature are a primary feature. Theo Cateforis explains the significance of asymmetrical meters in rock: "The *math rock* label has gravitated towards these bands because their nonrock influences make the music somehow more 'difficult to understand.' In this formulation, math rock is equated not with a particular style, but with the idea of complexity itself. Much as mathematics is often seen as a generic symbol of complexity, so math rock has become a free-floating 'complex' signifier."[29] Cateforis further surmises,

> Math rock seems notable for the degree to which it makes difficult the act of ritualized dance, negating one of popular music's most enduring social forces. . . . Listeners, it would seem, are offered few points of bodily identification. In the absence of a steady, divisible pulse, math rock has instead been depicted as "sharp," "jagged," and "angular" music. These descriptions can, of course, be applied to conceptions of the body [such as] the distorted bodies of a cubist Pablo Picasso painting.[30]

Cateforis's point is well taken: Rush's use of asymmetrical meters renders its music undanceable, although rather than bodily distortion, another interpretation is that math rock's unpredictable rhythmic character implies wakeful discipline, a body carefully choreographed to work through a constantly varying rhythmic terrain. As such, the use of asymmetrical meters signifies musical complexity and discipline, and adds a cerebral dimension to Rush's composition and claim of virtuosity.

The fifth section, entitled "Monsters!" contains musical quotes from Raymond Scott's composition "Powerhouse" (1936), a theme used famously in over forty episodes of Warner Brothers' "Looney Toons" cartoons.[31] The humorous use of quotation or allusion serves a number of purposes. With respect to the song's structure, following nearly six minutes of instrumental play, the theme provides something both amusing and familiar—a lighter moment—as a contrast with the lengthy, difficult guitar solo which preceded it. But more important, it is another gesture implying virtuosity. When done with a sense of caprice and wit, musical quotation signifies a musician's ease and familiarity with bodies of repertoire. Moreover, the achievement of a humorous effect with quotation—making a joke with music itself, not words or physical gestures—suggests a sort of mastery of music's expressive effects and signifying power. Although the simple act of quoting another composition is not, by itself, an act of virtuosity, the successful and imaginative contextualization of the quotation can be. In "La Villa Strangiato," Rush precedes the "Powerhouse" quotation with a 24-measure sequence of riffs in $\frac{7}{8}$, emphasizing the notes A and E. These are the same notes "Powerhouse" starts with, making it seem as though the quotation is a logical continuation of the previous pattern. Moreover, the first four bars of the quotation maintain the $\frac{7}{8}$ feel of the previous section, only then resolving to the expected $\frac{4}{4}$ of "Powerhouse." Rush's manipulation of the quote may be seen as a demonstration of mastery, the ability to take a familiar theme and recontextualize and alter it at will. For the sake of comparison, Charlie Parker and Dizzy Gillespie, two of jazz's most noted virtuosos, pursued similar kinds of humorous quotations and effects. For example, in their 1953 live recording of "Perdida," Gillespie elicits laughter from the audience during his solo by quoting a phrase from the 1943 Tin Pan Alley hit "Laura" (and fitting it perfectly to "Perdida's" chord structure), demonstrating a capricious and precocious mastery of the catalogue of jazz standards. Although Rush did not improvise its "Powerhouse" quote into the song in the same manner, a similar kind of virtuosic caprice seems to be at work.

The sixth theme places the focus on Lee and Peart, beginning with a tortuously fast and melodically twisted bass line, followed by a rapid series of ensemble shots in a chromatic descent. The arrangement alternates between ensemble shots and solo bass and drum fills, similar in structure to a big band jazz arrangement. This stylistic allusion is amplified by Peart's use of a swung, "closed-closed-open" pattern on the hi-hat cymbals, a jazz drummer's cliché. Again, as another indication of virtuosity, the band shows its flexibility and eclecticism here, the ability to draw from a number of musical styles and resources, using its musical diversity as a measure of professional accomplishment. In the seventh section ("Danforth and Pape"), Lifeson has another guitar solo, but the section is meant as an exercise in musical disjuncture. The rhythm section's groove seems set up to throw as many challenges at the soloist as possible. A pair of tritone-related chords (C major and F-sharp major) is used as the harmonic basis of the section, a distantly related pair of chords that would not likely intimidate many jazz soloists, but one that is quite rare as an underpinning for lead guitar playing in rock. The section is in $\frac{4}{4}$, but the timing sounds quite odd because Peart extends every fill past the downbeat and lands consistently on beat three. As such, the chord changes which are implied in the bassist's pattern are out of phase with the drummer's accents, creating a sense of rupture and unpredictability. Peart further amplifies this by forgoing the usual snare drum emphasis on the backbeat, never playing on beat two but accenting beats three and four in some bars, and the afterbeat of two in other bars. Meanwhile, Lifeson's solo is full of squawks, string bending, and dissonances against the chord changes implied by Lee's bass, resolving occasionally to almost singable melodic motifs. Rush achieves virtuosity in this section by setting up a very risky and difficult set of parameters in which to groove and improvise. This serves to reinforce the image of Rush as musicians willing to take up difficult musical challenges and push its ability to cohere as an ensemble to the limit.

The eighth section—the last with any new material—is entitled "Waltz of the Shreves," alluding to its setting in $\frac{9}{8}$ (compound triple time). This compound time is maintained during the beginning of the "Monsters!" theme's reprise, now in $\frac{12}{8}$, and the band metrically modulates into $\frac{4}{4}$ time (the eighth-note pulse remains the same, simply shifting from triple to duple accents) for the full restatement of the theme. The restatement of the "Strangiato Theme" is fairly similar to its earlier iteration, but contains two key shifts (C major to A major, A major to F-sharp minor), partly to facilitate sectional transitions, and also serving to demonstrate compositional merit through the band's ability to shift its themes to any key it chooses.

Overall, "La Villa Strangiato" demonstrates Rush's careful cultivation of musical complexity and virtuosity in five key areas: (1) speed and technical dexterity, (2) stylistic flexibility and eclecticism, (3) metric complexity, (4) compositional craft, and (5) ensemble tightness and cohesion. These areas of emphasis lead to some questions. First, what kind of musicians were the members of Rush striving to be? Second, why did they measure their competence and professionalism as musicians, especially during the first decade of their recording career, specifically in terms of technique, difficulty, and, as Lee emphasized, the ability to master odd time signatures? Why was the emphasis not placed in other domains, such as melodic imagination or the ability to play symmetrical rhythmic grooves more fluidly? For reasons similar to Rush's concern with creative autonomy, the band's idea of a "musician" seems tied to a very particular kind of elite professional status. Rush was clearly not interested in any kind of folk-music rhetoric, such as the idea of a rock musician drawing energy and immediacy out of naive simplicity, studied amateurism, or primitivism. Instead, the band constructed its style around features that signified prestige, intellectuality, and the attainment of mastery. In many ways, the model of the 1970s guitar hero, described by Steve Waksman as "offering the appearance of individual achievement and mastery in the face of the growing crowds that occupied the spaces of rock performance,"[32] was applied by Rush more generally to the whole band. Heroic displays of virtuosity became obligatory on Rush's albums through the late 1970s and 1980s, with fast guitar solos, nimble drum fills, and linear, melodic bass predominating. Peart and Lee became especially recognized by the early 1980s as among rock's most technically adept drummers and bassists. According to Peart, the members of Rush grew up admiring rock artists such as the Who, Cream, and Jimi Hendrix who could be considered "musicians' musicians," players whose spectacular technical acumen wins the admiration of their colleagues.[33] Rush attained this kind of appeal by the early 1980s.

In its approach to the band's own music and in the musicians' view of themselves, Rush participated in a larger set of trends in rock music in the late 1970s and early 1980s. At that time, musicians in hard rock—guitarists especially, though not exclusively—were increasingly expected to accomplish a certain level of technical mastery, playing scale-like passages with speed and precision and drawing inspiration from Baroque and Romantic musical resources. Robert Walser discusses the turn that heavy metal guitarists made, especially in the wake of Van Halen's success, toward a conservatory model of musical practice. The rehearsal of scales, arpeggios, and sequential patterns drawn from classical theory and repertoire became as important as developing a vocabulary of bent-note blues licks and folk-based modal chord progressions, which had hitherto been the basis of rock guitar playing. Heavy metal had always drawn inspiration from the blues and from classical music, and this new regimen of practice and emphasis on high-precision technique was an outcome, particularly, of the admiration these guitarists had for classical musicians and composers.[34] Elsewhere, Walser describes how some heavy metal guitarists linked their rigorous practice and attainment of virtuosity to the values of commitment, authenticity, and a willingness to make personal sacrifices for their music.[35] Their imitation of the rigors of classical concert performers was intended to draw favorable comparisons between the rock and classical player, co-opting for the former both the prestige and professional legitimacy of the latter.

Even if Rush did not carry these practices to the extreme that guitarists like Steve Vai or Yngwie Malmsteen did, the band's earnest cultivation of virtuosity was an attempt to attain prestige as professional musicians in much the same way. Professional labor gains both value and prestige by being rare, the domain of specialists whose knowledge or technique is difficult to attain and not widely shared. Bledstein explains that professionals do not necessarily hide their esoteric knowledge from the rest of society, but others in society do not usually learn professionals' knowledge to any degree and are not expected to understand it in detail.[36] "The more elaborate the rituals of a profession," he notes, "the more esoteric its theoretical knowledge, the more imposing its symbols of authority . . . the more prestige and status the public was willing to bestow on its representatives."[37] To some degree, Rush's use of asymmetrical time signatures, tightly rehearsed polyrhythmic shots, chord tensions, rarely used modes or scales, and advanced instrumental techniques were aimed at demonstrating the band's mastery of esoteric musical devices. Moreover, the carefully crafted, serious, and disciplined presentation of its musicianship in live performance (discussed in the next chapter) ritualized the band's musical professionalism in many ways.

The pursuit of musical sophistication and technical complexity, however, could have worked against Rush's efforts to amass a substantial fan base, since the intricacies of musicianship tend to be of consummate interest to a specialist minority only. As demonstrated in chapters 1 and 2, Rush's appeal was not limited to displays of technical musical prowess, but elite musicianship was nevertheless a key element in the band's style, and a crucially important feature to fans who identify themselves musicians, amateur or professional. For these fans, Rush functions as "musician's musicians," models of professionalism and skill which serve as instructive examples to those interested in developing similarly as players. Some fans were readers of musician's magazines, and I highlight these periodicals as an important part of Rush's mediation as elite musicians. Magazines such as *Bass Player, Modern Drummer, Guitar Player,* and *Guitar for the Practicing Musician* helped to forge a taste public or community of interest among suburban "bedroom" drummers, guitarists, bassists, and other would-be musicians by profiling influential and proficient musicians, transcribing their music and sometimes describing in detail important musical-theoretical aspects of the transcribed repertoire. Some of the magazines took on a pedagogical tone; *Guitar School* provided lessons using the songs transcribed in any given issue.

In contrast to the allegedly poor reception Rush received from mainstream rock critics, the attention Rush received in musician's magazines was flattering and often reverent. Rush was frequently included in "best of" lists and ad hoc canons. Neil Peart was voted favorite rock drummer in *Modern Drummer* magazine every year from 1980 to 1985; Alex Lifeson was inducted into *Guitar for the Practicing Musician*'s Hall of Fame in 1991.[38] In the same magazine in 1995, Rush's "Temples of Syrinx" was voted one of the "Heaviest Riffs of All Time";[39] in 1996, *Moving Pictures* was included in *Guitar for the Practicing Musician*'s "50 Albums That Shaped Rock Guitar," on the rationale that it "flawlessly merged heavy metal and progressive rock with the liberal use of suspended chords, arpeggiation, the acoustic guitar and monster tone."[40] The content of these magazines did much to affirm for its readership that, from the standpoint of the professional musicians who wrote for these magazines, Rush's music was indeed sophisticated and virtuosic. Transcriptions of Rush's music appeared frequently in these magazines, especially in the 1980s and early 1990s, with commentary illustrating Rush's musical sophistication. For example, *Guitar School* provided a lesson on the use of quartal harmony[41] in rock, using Rush's "Show Don't Tell" (1989) as its analytical example. Rush was positioned as an innovator in the use of quartal harmony alongside modernist composer Arnold Schoenberg and jazz pianist McCoy Tyner.[42] The article waxes eccentric by trying to link Rush's musical practices to Schoenberg's and Tyner's, but the comparison says much about the kind of legitimacy and prestige the author sought to project onto Rush by placing them in the company of a highly cerebral art composer and bebop musician known for his stunning dexterity.

In *Guitar for the Practicing Musician,* Andy Aledort's commentary on "Tom Sawyer" (1981) exemplifies how Rush's musical style is delineated in these magazines:

> Alex Lifeson uses chords with great sustaining qualities for this tune, and in conjunction with the synth chords, the sound is very full. Most of the syncopations are played by guitar, bass and drums, and along with the odd time sections (featuring the use of $\frac{7}{8}$, $\frac{7}{16}$, and $\frac{3}{8}$), the song has a fusiony feel to it, which is a staple of the Rush sound. Lifeson uses a powerful, distorted tone with ambient echo and chorus, using a guitar with single-coil pickups. Riff A is a good example of Lifeson's rhythm work, as he creates a part that combines a moving bass line with sustained unisons. Reading in $\frac{7}{8}$ can be confusing, so read carefully, counting eighth notes in your head; count sixteenths for the $\frac{7}{16}$ to avoid confusion. Lifeson's solo is based primarily on E Mixolydian (E,F♯,G♯,A,B,C♯,D) and features some of his characteristically unusual phrasing, squeezing and stretching notes alternately. I suggest tackling a few bars at a time and piecing them together, as opposed to the "sight-reading-burn-right-through-it" approach.... Geddy Lee's bass-line is highly energetic (as usual).... This is a great workout for all bassists, with Geddy Lee using E Mixolydian to great effect.[43]

Aledort's commentary assumes a degree of music literacy and theoretical knowledge on the part of the reader. This underscores how the readership for these magazines form, ideally, a cognoscenti with esoteric knowledge about music (though perhaps these magazines are more accurately regarded as a means for transmitting and acquiring this knowledge). In many ways, the elite musicianship of bands like Rush do not simply confer prestige on the performers, but flatters the tastes of fans who learn to appreciate it and furthermore to talk about that appreciation using the jargon of music theory and musicians' shop talk. The fans share in the prestige, enacting a connoisseurship of musicianly expertise.

Nevertheless, the elitism associated with Rush's musicianship was always fragile. The band clearly linked its cultivation of musicianly expertise with credibility, but in rock music, musical credibility can take many forms. In punk rock, for example, virtuosic display was associated with glibness and unnecessary excess, and a back-to-basics approach to instrumental arrangement was understood as a gesture of populism and honesty. There was never any guarantee that Rush's quality of musicianship would lead to critical approval or commercial success because standards in popular music are so highly contested. Indeed, at the same time that Rush and Van Halen were pushing the envelope for speed and virtuosity in hard rock in the late 1970s, punk was pushing rock musicianship in nearly the opposite direction. Many American and British rock critics endorsed the punk philosophy, seeing it as closer to the spirit of rock 'n' roll than progressive rock or metal. The punk rock explosion was a vexing development for the members of Rush, because the musical credibility which they had been building was suddenly threatened with irrelevance by punk's challenge. In 1994, Geddy Lee recalled, "We were real musos at that time.[44] We were real into the math of music, we were time signature freaks. . . . We put so much emphasis on the technical side of playing. . . . Back in the late 70s, when punk was going on, since we were heavy into this muso vibe, punk seemed very weird to us. We couldn't take it seriously, because we were players and these guys couldn't even play. It was comedy."[45] In the same interview, Peart noted, "I know a lot of musicians around that time felt threatened by [punk]," though the drummer confessed a surprising attraction to it: "At worst, it was amusing, and at best, an amazing spectacle. As the bands started to get better, when more thoughtful bands like Talking Heads came out and later the new romantics, I embraced it totally."[46] Though Rush initially felt alienated, perhaps even displaced, by punk and new wave, the band eventually found in this new kind of rock a potential source of influence and invigoration, and new wave sounds found their way into Rush's music from the early 1980s through the early 1990s.

Lee's and Peart's comments here raise two more issues regarding Rush's professionalism: status anxiety and eclecticism. Status anxiety plays a prominent role in the history and sociology of the Anglo-American middle class. C. Wright Mills observes that European and American experiences of status are very different: while many countries in Europe have a history of consistently honoring certain kinds of status claims, those same claims have a history of being treated very ambivalently and uncertainly in North America. The prestige associated with middle-class professions is subject to strain and disturbance. For this reason, says Mills, the middle class is often in a "status panic," striving to locate means for attaching prestige and importance to their work, and remaining very conscious of the ways in which authority and autonomy in their professions can be subjected to question and doubt.[47] Barbara Ehrenreich, who saw fit to name her book on the American middle class *Fear of Falling*, notes that losses of vitality, occupational status, and authority were among the greatest anxieties harbored by professionals. A significant literature has built up around this issue, with the middle class after the early 1970s seemingly always on the defensive.[48] It would be unfair to say that Rush came across as defensive about its career with any regularity, but defensiveness does creep into discussions about Rush's position in rock history, especially with respect to rock's emerging canon. In 1992, questioned about the band's lack of support from rock critics, Peart told *Spin*'s Bob Mack, "We're accused of being too busy, too convoluted, too far-reaching—but no one can question the sincerity of the attempt."[49] Peart seemed concerned that the band members' virtuosity, which had been so important in validating themselves as musicians, would be dismissed as charlatanism. Rush's cultivation of musical complexity and high-concept lyrics, he feared, might be open to charges of posturing and dishonesty. The following year, Perry Stern of *Network* wrote that Rush "suffered from an image problem," "hobbled by the perception that it exclusively wrote dungeons-and-dragons style epics or cyberpunk fantasies for nerdy 17-year-old boys. Rush found itself at odds with the way the music world classified it." Peart told Stern, "We were just as outside and experimental as Japan, Peter Gabriel or Brian Eno, but we certainly never won that respect and were never perceived as having those intentions."[50] Peart recognized that there was no certainty about how Rush's artistic aims would be perceived by music critics. What Rush regarded as experimentation or artistic insight was just as likely to be inscribed in rock's official journalistic discourses as the equivalent of an esoteric board game or pulp fantasy novel. Rush fans have similarly experienced "status anxiety" on the part of their favorite band, mounting internet campaigns to get Rush inducted into the Rock and Roll Hall of Fame in Cleveland, and complaining bitterly about the perennial failure of the induction board (made up partly by rock critics) to acknowledge Rush's prestige and authority as musicians.[51]

If affirmation of Rush's professionalism was scarce in mainstream rock journalism, the band found other ways to claim exclusive status in its vocation. Rush tends to emphasize an entrepreneurial aspect to its identity as a rock band. The band as a "small business" is a good metaphor for characterizing how the group views its career. The tropes of privacy and occupational autonomy that I discussed at the beginning of this chapter amplify the image that Rush cultivates as a small, private enterprise. The early history of the group—starting its own independent record label (Moon Records) in 1973 after its first album was rejected by all the major record labels—places this theme in Rush's story right from the beginning; the formation of its own vanity label in 1977 (Anthem Records) for all its Canadian releases similarly reflects the band's interest in fostering an entrepreneurial image. In 1978, Roy MacGregor of *MacLean's* magazine reported that Rush had "perhaps the best recording contract in the business (a $250,000 advance on each new album and a remarkably high 16% royalty rate)," and highlighted Rush as a new kind of rock band, one that openly celebrated entrepreneurial capitalism instead of criticizing it.[52] The rock band as a small business is not a concept at all unique to Rush—the Beatles pioneered this with Apple Corp., and 1970s hard rock acts like Deep Purple, Kiss, and Aerosmith all followed a similar model, right down to the pseudo-corporate logos that branded their names—but it clearly demonstrates how the musician's occupation can take the form of a lower-middle-class (petit-bourgeois) enterprise, with all its advantages and ambivalence. Rush, at the height of its career, occupied an ideal but threatened place in the music industry, with a remarkable amount of creative and contractual independence. But the petit-bourgeois small business is also uniquely vulnerable in the way it occupies a middling status: it is threatened from above by powerful corporate interests, competition, and lobbying power; it is threatened from below by powerful labor organizations. Similarly, Rush's success hung precariously between the power of the major record companies, who could withhold distribution and promotional services if Rush became burdensome or unprofitable, and the support of fans, who could become alienated if the band used its creative privilege to swerve too far from the interests of its taste public. Indeed, the band left Mercury Records for Atlantic in 1989 as its standing with its old label became uncertain; and since the mid-1980s, the band members have commented periodically on the pressure they receive from some fans who wish the band would return to its "classic" 1970s and early 1980s style.[53] Though Rush's career was never seriously impeded by these issues, at least not up to the time of writing, these issues hint at the contingency and fragility under which Rush's privileged career unfolded.

Stylistic change is another feature of Rush's career which derives from its investment in artistic autonomy, the development of virtuosity, and the demonstration of musical skill. As Negus notes, rock bands since the 1960s used stylistic change and eclecticism as symbols of growth, and such change gave shape to careers which more closely match the verticality expected of a professional career.[54] I have already discussed how Rush's cultivation of virtuosity and adoption of progressive rock symbolized stylistic expansion and an improvement in musicianship, so that the band "progressed" from a fairly typical, unremarkable 1970s hard rock sound and emerged as elite musicians by 1980's *Permanent Waves* album. From 1980, Rush's musical style was marked by a gradual and strategic backing away from its 1970s progressive rock style, which meant eschewing long tracks in favor of shorter, more conventional song forms, using influences from new wave, techno-pop, and reggae (a style then fashionable among rock bands), and eventually a simplifying of the band's musicianship. Of Rush's eclecticism, Alex Lifeson commented, "I don't think there's anything wrong with getting really good at different styles, so long as you have a style and it's not mimicking someone else's. I like to be proficient with a variety of techniques, but in my own way. And for me, I'm always evolving; I'm always learning something new. I hear something, or I play something I haven't done before, or I apply myself to a certain passage in a different way by adding textures I haven't added before."[55] The members of Rush prided themselves during the 1980s on their stylistic openness, and the band did indeed conjure a musical style that was as cosmopolitan as any in rock.

"Distant Early Warning," from *Grace Under Pressure* (1984), exemplifies Rush's marriage of disparate musical elements from across the popular music field of the early 1980s. The track begins with a sharp, ringing suspended chord, utilizing a thin guitar sound with its treble range emphasized. As the chord rings, Peart and Lee play in a half-time, reggae-like groove, with an emphasis on beat three. Lee's bass line is reminiscent of Jamaican dub music, though in straight, not swung, eighth notes. The pace of harmonic change is quite slow, with Lifeson unleashing a new suspended chord once every two to three measures. This is the texture underlying the song's verses, and is a stylistic gesture toward the new wave sound of bands such as the Police, Talking Heads, and U2. The chiming guitar timbre, the reggae-inspired groove, and relatively sparse texture were evidence of Rush's incorporation of post-punk styles into its stylistic ambit. The second texture is an instrumental theme, usually coming before the chorus, featuring Lee playing a figure on synthesizer (doubled by Lifeson's guitar) in $\frac{7}{8}$ time, with a shift into $\frac{5}{8}$ near the end. This theme gestures in two directions: it affirms Rush's continued link to progressive rock through the use of asymmetrical meters, and it demonstrates the rising importance of synthesizer technology to Rush's sound. Rush enthusiastically availed itself of electronic technology during the 1980s, and *Grace Under Pressure* in particular introduced sequenced synthesizer patterns and the electronic drum kit into Rush's sound. The chorus provides the third main theme of the song, an upbeat rock groove in $\frac{4}{4}$, with dense power chords. The chorus—closest in sound to Rush's hard rock roots—anchors the song stylistically, acting as the center with which the other styles contrast. In the context of rock in the 1980s, Rush's stylistic contrasts were somewhat eccentric, since post-punk rock styles (new wave, rock-reggae, electro-pop) were generically and discursively constructed in opposition to heavy metal and progressive rock, Rush's past stylistic touchstones. Rock critics' responses to Rush's mid-1980s albums provide evidence of this breached divide: Kurt Loder of *Rolling Stone,* no fan of Rush, dismissed *Grace Under Pressure* as the work of a "lumbering metal anachronism," a response difficult to reconcile with the album's lack of heavy metal stylistic traits, but a judgment that ghettoizes Rush on the "old school" side of 1980s rock.[56] David Fricke, who was Rush's champion at *Rolling Stone* and reviewed the *Power Windows* album (1985), praised the band's inventive linking of older progressive rock traits with new post-punk innovations, and declared Rush "the missing link between Yes and the Sex Pistols."[57] Rush's eclecticism acted as a gesture of detachment from rock's generic politics, and the band used its stylistic broadening as a way both to update its sound and to continue demonstrating its mastery of musicianship, since the band seemingly could play in any popular style. By incorporating the latest developments in rock, and the latest in pop music's technology, the band could present itself as "up on the latest research," competent with the state of the art, as well as in command of its artistic direction. Neil Peart equated eclecticism with artistic freedom, telling *Spin*'s Bob Mack, "'The Spirit of Radio' [an eclectic Rush track from 1980] is a valid musical gumbo, even now. The concept was to combine styles in a radical way to represent what radio should be. I think we really nailed that on 'Roll the Bones' as well. And it's happening on the fringes of pop music—like Faith No More [a metal/rap/progressive rock hybrid group]."[58] Peart also told *Canadian Musician*'s Frank Schulte, "I always think of Rush as widely spread on musical influences—from African to hard rock to Toronto R&B. There are no areas of frustration."[59]

Rush's eclecticism reached something of a peak with the song "Roll the Bones" (1991), which incorporated a funk groove as the main riff, an acoustic strum-along folk-rock chorus and a bridge featuring the band's one and only attempt at incorporating rap music. The band had turned away from sheer virtuosity and use of classical influences as ways of demonstrating elite musicianship. Stylistic diversity could now represent complexity, and the band also explored areas of musicianship with which it had not previously concerned itself. The band's interest, for example, in fluidity of groove or rhythmic feel increased during the 1980s. For example, Lee told Karl Coryat of *Bass Player,*

> I tried to use a much more rhythmic approach this time. I've enjoyed listening to Primus, the Red Hot Chili Peppers, and Soundgarden—bands that have a more active rhythmic role coming from the bass. That's a direction we started going on *Roll the Bones:* trying to use a bit funkier approach to rock and trying to make it more groove-oriented. As a bass player, I wanted to push myself in that direction, also. When I try to lock into a more repetitive, groove-like thing, I've found it's not about playing fewer notes—there are still the same number of notes per bar—but there is less of a variety of notes per bar. I had great fun doing the *Counterparts* [1993] bass tracks because of it; I felt like I was learning something all over again, and I was able to use things I already knew but applied in a different way. And I got a lot of support from Neil in that direction; he got right into it as well.[60]

But what does it mean that Rush—once so concerned with elite notions of musicianship, progressive rock, and classical-like virtuosity—was now drawing influence from styles unconcerned with such displays, like punk, funk, and reggae? Was middle-class professionalism and an elite form of musicianship still at stake?

Eclecticism opens up a complex area in the study of cultural preference and social class. Sociological inquiry into cultural consumption over
the past thirty years has documented an interesting shift in how cultural
taste—especially musical taste—is deployed by different status groups. In
North America, especially, highbrow status, which was once associated
with the exclusive consumption of European-derived high culture (opera,
classical concert music, theater, high literature), has shifted toward cosmo-
politanism and eclecticism. The "cultural omnivore thesis," explored by
sociologists such as Paul DiMaggio, Richard A. Peterson, Koen Van Eijck,
and Michael Emmison, is based on social surveys revealing that people
in higher echelons of occupational status, educational level, and income
usually report the widest range of cultural interests and consumption of
the greatest number of musical genres. In the lower range of these social
factors, respondents reported a less wide and diffuse pattern of cultural
consumption. Cultural omnivore respondents typically reported consuming cultural material ranging from traditional highbrow forms, like classical music, to middle- and lowbrow forms, such as jazz, Broadway, and
country music. DiMaggio and Van Eijck provide an intriguing twist on
this thesis, showing that the most omnivorous social group seems not to
be the upper class, but rather a young, mobile component of the middle
stratum.[61] DiMaggio observes, "Being a successful member of the middle
class requires some mastery of prestigious status cultures, but it is abetted
by an easy familiarity with cultures of occupation, region and of ethnicity
as well. . . . Middle-class adults learn how to 'culture-switch' as they move
from milieu to milieu. Such individuals command a variety of tastes, but
(and here's the key to the puzzle) they employ them selectively in different
contexts."[62] Emmison notes, further, that professionals tended to have the
most "diversified cultural portfolios" since their occupations require the
deployment of "a range of cognitive skills and personality attributes."[63]

Peterson and Kern, addressing the question of why there has been a
shift in America from highbrow exclusiveness to omnivorous cultural consumption, suggests five factors: (1) a shift in the social structure, in which
increased immigration and social mobility forced all cultural participants

to adapt to diversity; (2) a shift in intellectual paradigms from Eurocentrism and universalism toward relativism and tolerance of difference; (3) a change in the highbrow artistic field, where the appropriation and aestheticization of mass culture (in postmodern ways) has become normalized; (4) a change in intergenerational politics since the Second World War, with younger people of all classes and ethnicities similarly consuming television and other mass cultural fare; and (5) a shift in status group politics.[64] Of this last point, Peterson states, "Dominant status groups have regularly defined popular culture in ways that fit their own interest, and have worked to render harmless subordinate status-group cultures. One recurrent strategy is to define popular culture as brutish and something to be suppressed or avoided; another is to gentrify elements of popular culture and incorporate them into the dominant status-group culture."[65] The shift toward eclectic taste discussed by these sociologists has probably been accelerated by the internet, and the web may have flattened its class significance to some degree, but during the period of Rush's highest degree of eclecticism (1982–1991), the band used stylistic breadth as a way of signifying continued artistic and professional growth. The band showed itself to be culturally—hence, socially—mobile through its style, a demonstration of broad and diverse musical interests. Eclecticism also allowed Rush to resist being pigeon-holed musically and kept its musical identity open-ended. It was a strategy used to prevent the band from being typecast as "classic rock" in a narrow sense, and allowed it to make claims on being a relevant, dynamic part of rock into the 1990s. This is not to suggest that Rush had no established, recognizable musical style; rather, the band aimed to keep the parameters of that style open to revision and reinterpretation.

Rush's visual image should not be overlooked as part of its cultivation of an open-ended musical identity, and a part of how it positions itself as a group of professionals. Lee, Lifeson, and Peart have generally shunned the idea that they have an image, and the effacement of image plays an important role in both the band's and its fans' perceptions of the group. The band members claim a kind of ordinariness of appearance that allows them to make statements about "selling the music, not ourselves," or about being "musicians, not celebrities." In one of the *R30* DVD interviews, Geddy Lee makes this plain: "The fact that we've been such an anti-image band, but not really militantly . . . kept us away from a lot of the lifestyle press. It's put us off in a more quiet place, which I think has been very healthy for us and probably another ingredient in why we've been around so long." In the same interview, Lifeson continues, "We're not personalities like some other artists might be. You're not going to see us in *People* magazine. . . . We've never been the kind of group that is a personality-type group. We're probably not the best looking guys at the best of times, there's not something you can latch onto with us physically that's attractive, maybe. [laughter] And it's never been important to us to be regarded that way."

Rush fans generally concur. According to nearly every questionnaire respondent and consultant I queried, Rush has no image, or at least none that could be regarded as important to either the band or its fans. One consultant, Allen Kwan, noted,

> The only thing I notice is Rush trying not to have an image. Everyone else tries to pigeon-hole them. They've created an identity for themselves, but that's different from having an image. Having an image implies a flash-in-the-pan, moving-target sort of thing. Building an identity, though, is a concrete thing, a foundation on which to grow.[66]

I confess that I, too, as a Rush fan in my teens and early twenties, did not see, refused to see, Rush as having an image. During one of my graduate classes, I once asserted that Rush is a band that avoided having an image; I described them as possessing a "non-image" (whatever that is!). A fellow graduate student, himself a Rush fan, questioned me on this, pointing out that the band had at least three distinct looks throughout its career, each of which was quite relevant to Rush's musical phases. Certainly, up to the end of the 1970s, Rush had an image that was quite congruent with its progressive rock/heavy metal leanings, with long, flowing hair, robe-like garments, and bell-bottom trousers, all in keeping with the mythical and sometimes mystical aspects of its fantasy epics. During the 1980s, Peart achieved the most average appearance in the group, keeping his hair short and his shirts and pants quite plain. Lee and Lifeson, however, began dressing in a more upscale manner, with sports blazers and skinny ties common stage attire. Their decidedly business-casual look reminded me of the confident, well-dressed New York jazz-fusion musician, the stereotypical model of the slick, 1980s professional musician. By the mid-1990s, Rush began dressing in a manner congruent with the rock culture of the time, typically in T-shirts, plaid overshirts, and dark jeans. In each of these eras, Rush leaned to the conservative side of rock fashion, more or less blending in with the sartorial practices of the time, which may explain the perceived invisibility of Rush's image. Insofar as a musician's image is tied closely to musical genre, Rush's images from the early 1980s onward gestured toward generic ambiguity.[67]

Rush's effacement of image returns us to the theme of privacy, specifically the band's oft-voiced desire to be respected as musicians but not viewed as celebrities. Here, the band's concept of professionalism rubs up against the realities of the entertainment industry in some uncomfortable ways. In interviews, Lee, Lifeson, and Peart have stated that they would be happy to have a straightforward professional-client relationship with their audience, sharing the fruits of their expertise as musicians, perhaps taking some time to meet with small numbers of fans in controlled, low-key exchanges, but wanting solitude and anonymity during their downtime. As Peart told *Metal Hammer*'s Malcolm Dome,

> My first glimmers of fame really just left me feeling that it was a weird scene. It always makes me very uncomfortable. . . . You then begin to feel imprisoned against your will and feel as if you're in a fish bowl. It all begins to get a little predatory and you are the prey! Yet trying to explain all these things rationally to people is impossible, because it's so far outside their experience. I don't feel I deserve all this adulation, I just do a job of work, and if you enjoy it then that's great. It's an exchange; if I enjoy doing it and you enjoy the results then that should be the end of it. You don't owe me a living, I'm not owed a loyal audience.[68]

But the very nature of fandom—and the meaning of popular culture for fans—leads to very different perceptions of the band/fan relationship.

For some fans, the music and concerts rank among their deepest, most transcendent experiences, and as many studies of popular music have shown, personal identity gets strongly invested in expressive culture. "An exchange" is simply too mundane, too business-like, to describe the meaning the music brings to their lives. Many Rush fans respect the band's desire for privacy and accept Rush's expectations of how the band and fans should interact, but the cultural and psychological effects generated by mass culture and mass popularity cannot easily be squared with the more conventional paradigms of middle-class professionalism. Ultimately, for fans, the identity journeys provided by Rush's music, the ritual moments supplied by its concerts, and the lifestyle example set by the musicians' public careers take on the mythic quality that gives popular music its power and impact.

4

"Experience to Extremes"

Discipline, Detachment, and Excess in Rush

There is a striking moment near the end of Rush's "Freewill," a propulsive rocker from the *Permanent Waves* album (1980). Following one of Alex Lifeson's most searing, rapid-fire guitar solos, the band prepares the final chorus with one last verse where Geddy Lee sings in the strained, upper register of his tenor voice. This moment stands out for a couple of reasons. First, it marked the last time Lee sang like this on Rush's studio albums. *Permanent Waves* inaugurated a new phase in Lee's vocal style, where his lower and mid-ranges would be used almost exclusively. Because Lee's shrieking high range had been a trademark of the band's style in the 1970s—an acquired taste that offended the ears of the uninitiated as often as it delighted fans—this was a significant change

in Rush's sound. As Lee lowered his voice to a more moderate, widely appealing range, Rush's album sales rose; in some sense the piercing last verse
of "Freewill" could be heard as a farewell to Rush's early style. But even
more significant, this verse emphatically brings to the fore two diverging
tendencies in Rush's music which seem contradictory on the surface but, as
this chapter reveals, reflect mutually dependent middle-class desires. Discipline, detachment, and seriousness compose the first tendency; excess,
spectacle, and extremity mark the other.

In "Freewill," Peart's lyrics broach philosophical questions that provide
a tone of seriousness and detachment. The lyrics explore metaphysical issues of volition and determinism. The song asks, what do you think guides
your life's course? A deity's predetermined plan? Preexisting circumstances beyond your control? The impersonal vagaries of luck? Your own
agency? Peart, ever the individualist, casts his vote for personal volition;
your life is whatever you choose to make of it. In the final verse, though,
Peart acknowledges life's random elements: all of us are separate "cells
of awareness," with our own flaws and limitations. We search for who
we are and what our best destiny is, with no guarantee that the answers
will ever be found. We are all random "genetic blends," Peart concludes,
with unknown capacities and potentials awaiting discovery. These are
the kinds of lyrics that garnered Rush its reputation as "the thinking-
person's heavy metal band," tackling heady issues in a linguistic register
that features pseudo-scientific terms ("cells," "genetic blends"), nebulous
metaphors ("a planet of playthings," "celestial voice," "heaven's unearthly
estate"), and a rhetorical positioning that implies analytical distance and
objectivity. Peart achieves such rhetoric by assuming the viewpoint of a
detached observer. Each verse begins with the phrase "There are those
who . . . ," as if issuing abstract generalizations drawn from dispassionate
observation. The song's rhetoric also derives from the use of universal-
izing language. The use of "we" and "each of us" imply that the song's
observations and philosophical discussion transcend social and cultural
context. The word "I" appears only at the end of the chorus ("I will choose
freewill"), a conclusion to the song's argument. The "I" of the song appears

objective as well, because the perspective is left invisible; no context is given, and the observations simply stand as ahistorical, almost proverbial statements of truth. While the language and metaphors used are colorful and illustrative, the tone of the lyrics is mostly dispassionate and logical, with little overt affect. The lyrics a few lines before the second chorus contain the most affect-laden words, describing those misguided ones who resign themselves to providence as "prisoners in chains" and "victims of venomous fate" who have been "kicked in the face." The lyrics make the alternatives to Peart's secular and rationalistic notion of freewill (in this case, religion and superstition) seem ominous and threatening. This is a strategic part of the song's rhetoric, but this ominous affective component is not overwhelming.

Lee's vocals in the final verse provide a marked contrast with the tone of the lyrics, delivering Peart's words with cutting, visceral intensity. The singing here recalls various moments of extreme affect in Rush's 1970s repertoire where such high vocals were used, like the righteous anger of "Bastille Day," the suicidal pathos near the conclusion of "2112," the panic at the end of "Cygnus X-1," or the rising, claustrophobic madness in the last vocal phrases of "Xanadu." All these past songs, however, were narratives featuring violent events that called out for highly emotional delivery. Why was a similar vocal performance used in "Freewill"? What does it mean to deliver lyrics like these with such seething intensity? What relationship exists between the lyrics' dispassionate detachment and the vocals' affective excess? It is possible that, after the song's vigorous instrumental section, it simply made musical sense for the vocals to maintain the level of energy built up during the guitar solo before the song wound down. But acknowledging the logic in this part of the song's arrangement still leaves questions open about why Rush unites such divergent sensibilities. This apparent contradiction is a Rush stylistic feature found throughout its repertoire, particularly as live performers. Even if Lee's vocals moved toward a lower, more reserved style during the 1980s and 1990s—matching Peart's detached, sometimes abstract lyrics—the music remains highly intense, loud, and vigorous.

This chapter explores Rush's uses of affect and rhetoric to create an identity that mediates between the detached, disciplined, and controlled on the one hand, and the excessive, spectacular, and extreme on the other. The ways in which these tendencies are deployed reflect much about middle-class attitudes toward the mind, body, and emotions, and provide an excellent opportunity to think about the ways in which rock music's affective characteristics have been appropriated in middle-class, and predominantly masculine, contexts. This chapter looks at how a disciplined and detached character is constructed in Rush's lyrics and music, using "Freewill" and "The Camera Eye" as paradigmatic examples; I then explore this same character in Rush's performance practices, looking at how the musicians' presentation of discipline and detachment is set against spectacular stage and lighting effects. Observations of Rush's stage show are taken in part from my own field notes of concerts attended in 1996 and 2002, as well as from the various live video and DVD releases Rush has made, including *Exit . . . Stage Left* (1981), *Grace Under Pressure* (1984), *A Show of Hands* (1989), *Rush in Rio* (2003), and *R30* (2004), all of which were commercially available at the time of writing. For the interested reader, the three concert films from the 1980s are available under a single cover, *Rush: Replay X3* (2004), providing a convenient and suitable companion to this chapter. The chapter's conclusion reconciles Rush's presentations of discipline, detachment, and excess by showing how they interrelate in constructions of white ethnicity, masculinity, and middle-class identity.

The theme of detachment, which is well illustrated in "Freewill," is traceable throughout Rush's lyrical repertoire. The sense of social distance which I discussed in Rush's 1970s escapist narratives placed great emphasis on transcendence, an attempt to get outside society or the self in order to gain knowledge. This emphasis carried forward into the mostly non-narrative songs of the 1980s and 1990s, but with topical and descriptive strategies replacing storytelling. "The Camera Eye" (1981) provides an excellent example of a song that uses detached description as its main conceit, and helps to further establish this chapter's themes. An eleven-minute track from the *Moving Pictures* album, "The Camera Eye" describes New York and London, contemplating the urban character of each city. The song imitates photojournalism, providing glimpses of people, buildings, streets, and the ambience created by the weather. Symbolically, the camera's eye represents the photographer's detached observation, seeing the city from above, from street level, capturing revealing moments in a lens that the lyrics describe as sometimes in "sharp focus," other times in "wide angle." Documenting the two cities from different angles, the photographer's voice in the song analyzes what emerges from these composite pictures of London and New York. Manhattan's denizens are an "angular mass" swarming through the city; as "head-first humanity" they move inexorably forward, barely pausing for stop lights. The city's skyline is equally angular and headlong, as the buildings disappear in their "limitless rise." A spring rain drizzles down on the city, but the people themselves seem detached, barely noticing it as they storm through the sidewalks. The photographer is taken in by the heartbeat of this city, the "purposeful stride" of its citizens, the possibilities and "hard realities" that commingle within it.

The description of London captures a different sensibility. Though it, like New York, is awash in a spring rain, London's scenes and vistas look backward toward history and tradition as much as Manhattan looks forward. Ancient, weathered, and wistful, London evokes pride in its modern citizens through the city's deep past, its growth and survival through the centuries, and the stories its streets and buildings tell. New York is aestheticized in terms of modernity, forward movement, and progress; London is described in terms of history, tradition, and rootedness. Though these are clearly subjective aestheticizations, a sense of detachment is maintained because the photographer is subtly positioned as an outsider, exploring and taking in the city through the camera's scenic gaze. The song's cinematic conceit ensures that the experience of New York and London is limited to visual representations; we meet no individuals in this song, and we sample none of the cities' tastes or scents. Like pictures or paintings on the wall, we can respond aesthetically to the song's vignettes without actually being in any of the scenes; a sort of distance is maintained. Jacqueline Warwick has observed that popular music that assumes this kind of distanced posture has appealed for some time to middle-class audiences. Discussing male singer-songwriters and their lyric writing, Warwick suggests that they take on the role of

> a dispassionate, self-aware observer of events happening at some distance, like Baudelaire's *flâneurs*. Baudelaire identified a specific kind of bourgeois Parisian in the mid 19th century who strolled the city streets observing and analyzing the complexities of modern life, but shying away from the dangers of involvement. The *flâneur* exists in an interior/exterior space simultaneously, occupying the landscape of his mind and the physical landscape of the city as he wanders.[1]

The voice speaking in "The Camera Eye" is remarkably similar to the *flâneur* concept Warwick invokes, exploring New York's and London's urban landscapes while remaining aloof from them.

The music of "The Camera Eye" plays a number of interesting roles in counterpoint with the words. For example, Peart's lyrics are not particularly lengthy, but Lee and Lifeson chose to set them quite expansively, with considerable time allotted to instrumental passages. Like the cities, the music sprawls. The band sets up a series of musical episodes that match affect to the themes of the lyrics. The song's opening synthesizer passage, for example, sets up New York's modernity with a rising sequence of fourths (a very "modern" sound in comparison to the more traditional diatonic and triad-based music that follows it). Lifeson's most characteristic guitar riff in the piece, an unharmonized major-key line with wide, angular leaps, provides an optimistic and buoyant "main theme" for the portrayal of the cities. The riff, however, has the oddity of having a call phrase in D-flat major and a response phrase in C major, giving the riff a chromatic, modulating twist. Perhaps musically dramatizing the city's skyline above (D-flat) and the people below (C), both parts are united in the uplifting affect provided by the riff. As Lee delivers the verses that describe New York or London, the music remains energetic and optimistic, as Lifeson strums a distorted electric guitar and moves between low-tension tonic and subdominant harmonies. As the lyrics change from description into more subjective reflection ("Are they oblivious to this quality?"), the band shifts into half-time, with clean, gently rolling arpeggios accompanying Lee's vocals; as the lyrics back away from direct observation of the cityscape, the music's intensity eases off as well. Energy builds back up toward the end of each city's description, where Lee muses about urban possibilities and hardships, and the final refrain ("the focus is sharp in the city") is hammered out by the band in rhythmic unison, harmonized by a sharply dissonant suspended chord.

In contrast to the climactic moment in "Freewill," "The Camera Eye" is conceived as a tightly integrated composition, faithfully matching lyric theme to musical affect. "The Camera Eye" is also a good example of Rush's propensity for presenting a highly disciplined musical sense. Rush achieves this partly through its song forms, which tend to be very modular.[2] Boundaries between the various sections of Rush songs are often very abrupt, with sharp changes of tempo, timbre, key, rhythmic feel, and dynamics being common. The introduction, for example, establishes a mid-tempo, synthesizer-dominated texture based on a chordal riff in C. After a long buildup using this riff, the section's ending is interrupted by an alarming new synthesizer pattern in D-flat, over which electric guitar shots are anticipated with highly syncopated and unpredictable drum fills. This new section acts as a transition into the main guitar riff (described above), which has a much more up-tempo feel than the song's introduction. The vocal sections could be divided into three distinct verse themes, but no conventional verse-chorus or AABA structure is apparent; the final theme ("I feel the sense of possibilities . . .") is the closest to a refrain, as it closes the first main vocal section and reappears after the guitar solo late in the song. Although Rush creates feelings of reprise and closure through the song's form (it is not just a collection of randomly juxtaposed sections), the song's length and large number of themes make the section changes difficult to predict. The need for precision in the song's execution is increased by the band's characteristic use of changing and asymmetrical meters, particularly noticeable in the first verse, where the groove alternates between $\frac{5}{4}$ and $\frac{6}{4}$.

The way the song is constructed contrasts with an approach that melodically sets up verse-chorus forms over an unchanging riff or chord progression, or that strives for smooth transitions between sections. Rush's tendency to fuse musically disparate sections together creates particular challenges for the musicians; the band members must know when a section change is scheduled to happen, must be prepared, if necessary, to alter their equipment settings quickly as the change happens, and must lock into the new feel or tempo quickly and in sync with the other musicians. Rush's compositional approach offers the musicians little leeway for improvising or "faking" their way out of a mistake. Almost orchestral in approach, Rush's way of arranging songs requires tightly rehearsing or choreographing pre-composed changes, rather than taking the more processual approach of jazz combos or jam-rock groups like the Grateful Dead or Phish. While jazz musicians use formal conventions (like a song's form or set of chord changes) as a template, their melodic phrasing, accompaniment figures, and order of soloists in a given song are open-ended and can change from performance to performance. Rush took the opposite approach, treating nearly all details of a song's arrangement as integral structural units not to be changed or omitted. This was a considerable deviation from Rush's seminal influences, such as the Who, Led Zeppelin, and Cream, all of whom made use of improvisation and open-ended jamming. As Peart explained in a 1988 *Modern Drummer* article,

> I have told the story before about how I was a big Keith Moon fan as a beginning drummer. All I wanted to do was get in a band that would play some Who songs so I could wail like he did. But when I finally found a band that actually wanted to play these songs, I discovered to my chagrin that I didn't like playing like Keith Moon. It was too chaotic, and things just weren't placed rationally. I wanted to play in a more careful, deliberate way—to think about what I played where, and not just "let it happen." I am driven by a strong organizational, perfectionist demon. Of the two extremes, I must confess I probably prefer the dull and "correct" to the adventurous foray that doesn't quite come off.[3]

This is a candid description of Peart's musical aesthetic in which discipline, control, and structure are favored over intuition and improvisation. The value judgment that Peart makes in the final sentence is also particularly interesting: he criticizes himself for his preference for preplanned, overly organized playing. Being "correct" and "dull" implies a self-consciousness about taking an approach that is too WASPish, too whitebread, too middle class for a style of music that is supposed to rebel against these things.

Peart takes a similar approach to lyric writing; he told Frank Schulte of *Canadian Composer* that

> lyric writing is as technical as drumming is, and should be approached with purpose and discipline. I have long discussions with Geddy about which type of lyrics work and which don't. I realize that sometimes the lyrics are secondary. Lyrics used to be so good and so finely crafted in the '30s and '40s—no one would put out second-rate lyrics. Then the '50s came out with things like "Be-Bop a Lula." A sense of care and craft is not definable. . . . I please myself with structure but realize that it doesn't matter.[4]

Peart's appraisal of the lyricist's work elevates technique and craft above inspiration and immediacy, and his invocation of the lyrics of the 1930s and 1940s, the age of Ira Gershwin, Cole Porter, and other Tin Pan Alley songwriters, recalls a time when lyricists could be dedicated, specialized professionals. Song texts during Tin Pan Alley's heyday were carefully honed in certain ways, matching linguistic rhythm and accent to musical phrasing, working out extended internal rhymes, and composing clever metaphors and poetic structures. Peart contrasts this ideal with 1950s rock, when lyrics could be ad hoc and priorities were oriented more to the processual or performative than the textual. Peart, though he makes no indication of liking Tin Pan Alley music itself, clearly identifies with its professionalized, disciplined (and middle-class) model. Thus, "pleasing" oneself with structured work, even while acknowledging that such a self-imposed restriction is arbitrary or unnecessary, is clearly aligned with the middle-class value of disciplined, structured self-direction.

As live performers, Rush offers further evidence of its commitment to this exacting, disciplined aesthetic. Rush concerts typically involve very precise reproductions of its studio recordings, in keeping with the band's compositional approach. Even details that sound improvised, such as fast drum fills and guitar solos, are carefully rehearsed and perfected to match the studio versions. Rush has given considerable forethought to how studio versions could be reproduced live, partly because the band believed that the ability to match live performance to recorded sound was a mark of competence and authenticity. Recalling his own experience as a concertgoing fan, Lifeson notes,

> I always went to a concert expecting the band to sound like it did on record. If I liked the record, I felt cheated if it wasn't played exactly like that. I remember thinking at times, you can't play it the way you did on the record? I don't think everyone was like that. But it was important to me that we play live as we recorded. We never put a rhythm guitar in where it wasn't going to be live. We stuck to that rule. . . . I don't think anyone expects us to do long, drawn out jams in the middle of "Manhattan Project." We're not that kind of band.[5]

Lifeson's reading of fans' expectations has a great deal of merit. Given how much stock fans place in Rush's virtuosity, the live performance provides visible, tangible evidence that the dazzling playing on the record was not studio trickery or a collection of lucky takes.

Some rock critics saw Rush's approach to live performance as very much at odds with rock's aesthetics of immediacy and spontaneity, and puzzled over enthusiastic fan responses to a band whose concerts seemed so studied and predictable.[6] They missed the point: the Rush concert is, to some degree, a ritualization of musical structure, in which even the audience may take part. For example, the fixedness of Rush's musical arrangements allows fans to air-drum in perfect synchrony with Peart's elaborate drum fills, miming each rhythmic gesture, an act which celebrates not only the band's discipline but the fan's finely tuned grasp of the structure and details of the musical arrangements. Similarly, some fans mimic the guitar parts, sing along with the bass lines, or pump fists in the air in time with polyrhythmic ensemble shots, providing visible evidence of their approval of Rush's composerly approach to rock, and a desire to physically embody or inhabit those musical structures.

In Rush's live performances, discipline and detachment are closely intertwined, and this becomes especially apparent in the band members' minimal presentation of themselves as stage performers. The band's movements are generally limited to the scope needed to play the instruments, Lee's banter with the audience is brief and sparse, addressing the crowd only after every three or four songs, and the band generally maintains an air of concentration and aloofness when performing. As William Johnston remarked, "The interaction with their audience is limited almost exclusively to their music. . . . It's not like going to a Stones concert, [where] there's lots of interaction between the audience and the band on stage. There's some exchange back and forth, even if it's just glances or waves, or someone tosses a beach ball on stage and a band member kicks it back. Whereas, when you're watching a Rush concert, they are sort of self-contained on stage, and that's as far as it goes." While Rush does not ignore its audience per se, the group does strategically underperform in a certain way, ensuring that what it offers as entertainment—the songs, the musicianship—is never upstaged or overshadowed by anything the musicians do other than play.

To underperform, however, is not simply self-effacement, but a powerfully rhetorical stance, especially in the context of a large arena-rock concert. It represents attitudes of seriousness toward the music being performed, professionalism, and a desire to direct attention toward musicianship rather than showmanship.[7] Symbolic of discipline and detachment, the understated manner in which Rush performs actually works hand in hand with the spectacle of virtuosic musicianship and epic song structures on which the group's career significantly depends. Each of the three members of the band actualizes a detached, disciplined sensibility in a different way, and in each case, it contributes to the experience of musical extremity that Rush's fans celebrate. For example, Neil Peart's onstage persona is probably the most emotionally detached of the three, maintaining an almost dour look of concentration as he plays. Peart moves quite fluidly and economically as he plays, executing what appear to be very calculated, pre-choreographed movements with the confidence, focus, and emotional neutrality that characterizes masters of the martial arts. Peart adds fun frills like twirling or throwing his drum sticks on occasion, but it is mostly all business as the drummer negotiates his way around his drum kit. One of the nicknames Lee and Lifeson gave to Peart, "the Professor," stereotypically captures the demeanor he achieves as he plays: his air of remoteness and seriousness underwrites his reputed mastery of the drums. In one sense, his remoteness and reservedness seem to contradict the spectacle he unleashes as he sits amidst one of the biggest drum kits in rock, playing frequent roller-coaster drum fills and spry rhythmic patterns. In fact, the musical excess Peart performs is amplified by the very expert remoteness with which he delivers it.

As a performer, Lifeson provides a distinct contrast, seeming far less remote and even-tempered. Whenever he appears on the stage's video screen, Lifeson's face is quite animated, always responding to the musical gestures he executes on guitar. Squawking high notes are accompanied by clenched teeth and wincing eyes; slashing power chords are unleashed with pursed lips and a furrowed brow. Lifeson's bodily gestures are open and sweeping, adding weight to ringing suspended chords by strumming with an exaggerated follow-through. For Lifeson, the dramatization of intensity and effort is a characteristic of his style, and the disciplined control he demonstrates over his instrument is manifested in visible signs of effort and strain. This is a common rhetorical strategy of guitarists playing hard rock, where the metaphor of weight in heavy rock music is visually manifested in the apparent effort exerted by the players. The purely rhetorical aspect of this cannot be overstated: the electric guitar requires the lightest touch of any type of guitar, and electronic amplification makes it possible to unleash deafening walls of sound with almost no effort. But the electric guitar's sound in hard rock is richly and powerfully iconic, as Susan Fast observes, acting upon the body as a symbolic gesture of strength and force.[8] Thus, for most guitarists, it is difficult to make these sounds without miming bodily intensity and effort. Detachment is a less significant quality in Lifeson's musicianship than in that of his bandmates, but discipline dramatized through effort is a key part of the show Lifeson puts on: excess effort is displayed as a sign of rigorous control over his instrument and his committed mastery of Rush's repertoire.

As a performer, Lee's role in Rush has been quite complex. As vocalist, bassist, keyboard player, and front man, his performing style is defined by his ability to successfully multitask. This requires an obvious show of discipline: especially after 1982's *Signals* album, Lee was often confined to one region of the stage, in close proximity to his microphone and banks of keyboards. During tours for *Power Windows* and *Hold Your Fire* (1985–1988), Lee imposed significant demands on himself due to the nature of the material the group was recording. These albums contained Rush's most frequent use of overdubbed synthesizer parts, sometimes simultaneous with Lee singing and playing bass. The band considered hiring a fourth member to cover the keyboard parts, but Lee decided to keep the technology under his own control. No matter how much this reduced Lee's ability to move on stage, this decision meant a lot to the band. Instead of always playing the keyboards, Lee sometimes triggered sequencers that play synthesizer lines automatically, which became necessary when Lee was playing bass at the same time, and Lifeson and Peart were sometimes called upon to trigger sequencing gear from their positions on the stage as well. This approach potentially opened up troubling questions for fans about how authentically "live" Rush concerts really were, especially when machines were playing some of the music automatically. But by using foot pedal triggers, a musician on stage maintained at least some level of control over the technology. As Lee explained in 1991,

> There's nothing that we use onstage that's triggered by anyone else, because there's this kind of unwritten code that if we're going to use a sampled piece or a sequenced piece it has to be triggered by us, which is why we have this elaborate foot pedal setup. Nothing happens without

some connection to performance for us. . . . You've got to be there at the right time, you've got to trigger it in time, you've got to add that element of performance, and if you screw up, you can't use the part. . . . We make sure that there has to be that element of human error that makes the difference.[9]

Keeping the potential for human error as part of Rush's use of sequencers was clearly a way of authenticating the use of automated music technology, a gesture aimed at placating rock fans suspicious of this technology and its capacity to subvert traditional expectations of live musicianship.

Moreover, this approach kept Rush's traditional trio format intact without adding backup musicians, something Lee assumed was important to its audience: "We came to the conclusion that our fans would rather see us use technology to try to pull it off than have somebody else on the stage. And I really think that was the main reason why we opted to do it ourselves. . . . We figured that technology was a more acceptable answer than not being a three-piece."[10] Fans, Lee surmised, wanted to see Rush struggle successfully with the challenge of realizing song arrangements on stage that seemed too complex for a trio. It actualized what Rush fans believed about the band, namely that it was more virtuosic, well-rehearsed, and disciplined than the average rock band. While Lee's multi-instrumentalist role minimized his ability to move about the stage, it actually enlarged Lee's reputation as a musician, and the musical excess of having one musician provide the vocals, bass lines, and synthesizer parts turned Lee's in-concert musicianship itself into a spectacle of power and control.

My discussion thus far of Rush's live performance practices suggests that, in spite of playing rote renditions of its album tracks and hewing to an aesthetic of understated physical and emotional performance, the Rush concert remains an arena-rock spectacle. It is an exhibitionist display abetted by the musician's apparent detachment from it. The sheer size and adornment of a Rush stage set underscores this point. Drawing on its progressive rock and heavy metal influences, Rush adorned the stage as if it were a theater, using gigantic props taken from album cover art

to fill out the stage set (three enormous spheres for *Hold Your Fire*'s tour
[1987–88], giant magic hats for *Presto* [1989–90], massive nuts and bolts for
Counterparts [1993–94], and so on). Special effects were added annually,
tour after tour, with flash-pot explosions, laser light displays, and a giant
projection screen displaying music video footage or thematically relevant
film montages, all becoming standard in Rush concerts by the mid-1980s.
Visual and aural spectacle surrounds and envelops the musicians, almost
like an aura, while the musicians themselves perform in physically modest
ways. Of course, Rush is hardly unique in this sort of concert presentation,
comparing favorably to other progressive rock performers, such as Pink
Floyd, Yes, or Genesis, whose relatively subdued physical presence was set
against grandiose stage sets and special effects.[11] As Edward Macan notes,
"Compared to performers of other rock genres, progressive rock performers have tended to be relatively static and motionless on stage. . . . Audiences
often spent far more time concentrating on the laser lights, the dry ice fog
and other elaborate visual effects than on the performers themselves."[12]
Progressive rock certainly seemed to discipline, repress, or minimize the
performer's body even as it provided large and elaborate visual displays
that filled arenas.

But what connects these aesthetics of discipline and excess, detachment
and spectacle, control and extremity? What reconciles them? Scholars
studying hard rock have generally theorized these as important underpinnings in the performance of gender and the accomplishment of racial identities, but discussions of how this involves social class are rare. Though my
conclusions focus on discipline and excess as important parts of middle-
class identity, I review recent literature that links these values to identity
in rock music, and consider how they impact my analysis.

The issues of detachment, control, and extremity in hard rock are most
directly addressed by Glenn Pillsbury in *Damage Incorporated: Metallica
and the Production of Musical Identity*, and his discussion is quite relevant
for Rush in part because the two bands share a number of musical and
ideological features (modular compositions, odd meters, individualistic
lyrics), and Metallica even acknowledges Rush as an important precur-

sor. For Pillsbury, Metallica's musical identity is built on the interrelated pillars of detachment, control, and complexity, all of which support particular constructions of whiteness and masculinity. Like those of Rush, Metallica's lyrics often sidestep overt political stances (even while raising significant ideological and social issues) as a way of projecting a detached, neutral point of view. This strategy, Pillsbury notes, was part of Metallica's desire to control its public image and avoid being pinned down to a discrete identity, political orientation, or subjective position.[13] Complexity was an important complement to Metallica's detached stance, he notes:

> Metallica's desire for detached political statements, their arguments for 'opinions' and 'explorations,' and their assertions of independence provided a context for the level of musical complexity.... Musical complexity was seen as a practical expression of the band's intelligence, as 'studied.' Along with the lyrics which were elevated to the status of the sublime by the description 'poetry,' the critics generally celebrated Metallica's 1980s material specifically for its complexity, almost thankful that *finally* there was a heavy metal band that could write real music.[14]

The discipline and complexity that marked Metallica's music was, for rock critics, related to the band's abandonment of any tangible influence from the blues, making Metallica's style a significant revision to the generic code of heavy metal. Metallica's modular songs, with riffs based on precisely articulated rhythmic figures resembling fast drum rudiments, all but denuded heavy metal of its blues influence. The positive critical reaction to Metallica's blues-less style activates, for Pillsbury, a binary of virtuous "white discipline" set against black, blues-based "ineptitude."[15] Metallica's commitments to control, complexity, detachment, and neutrality must be understood, Pillsbury says, as part of the racial politics that help to shape and mold popular American genres. Pillsbury shows how Metallica's music, interview rhetoric, and critical reception are suited to the production of a nameless, invisible, neutral whiteness.

Similar ideas can be found in the discourse around Rush. For example, John Stix's 1988 article on Rush for *Guitar for the Practicing Musician* was

entitled "Alex Lifeson: Classical Precision, Blues Touch," immediately establishing an image of European classical music as studied, exacting, and
disciplined, while blues is associated with an emotive and instinctual way
of making music. Stix does not see Rush as having abandoned the blues
ethos, but as having merged it with classical notions of composition, structure, and performance. Stix develops this idea as he describes Lifeson's
playing: "As the chief colourist and harmonic base for Rush, guitarist Alex
Lifeson is the musical glue that holds the elements of improvisation and
exacting form together . . . both as the blues component who rocks in solos,
and as a strong believer in the classical virtue of repeating performances
exactly as recorded. It is this basic dichotomy that somehow explains both
the passion of Rush's fans and the ferocity of their critics."[16] To be fair, Stix
does not divide the blues and classical traditions into an inept/competent
dichotomy per se; he seems to view the blues as a subtler language than the
European classical tradition, which he equates with an almost deadening
technical emphasis: "Each member of Rush is a virtuoso on his instrument, who prefers the finesse of nuance (which is the essence of blues) to
the bludgeon of velocity."[17] Stix's characterization of Rush acknowledges
a disciplined, exacting character in the band's music (classical, therefore
symbolically white), but also recognizes how Rush balances that character
with certain kinds of affect and intensity (associated with the blues, thus
putatively black).

Geddy Lee has acknowledged in a number of interviews a strong association between Rush's music and a distinctly white generic construction
of rock. Comments about this arose in the early 1980s, when Rush began
incorporating reggae-style rhythmic passages into its music, and again
in the early 1990s, when funk rhythms appeared on *Presto* and *Roll the
Bones*. Invariably, Lee expressed a feeling of distance from "black" styles,
explaining that as "white guys" or as "white Canadians," Rush produced a
rhythmic feel that was inevitably mathematical or marked by dry, technical
precision. Asked about the band's then-recent interest in reggae beats, Lee
told Pete Makowski of *Sounds* in a 1982 interview that "I think our whole
direction has moved towards feel, I notice that was something that was

missing on our earlier records. A lot of our earlier records sounded forced. We put all our energies into developing feel and I guess reggae is one way that it's coming out." But Lee also stated that "Reggae is pure feel, it's nothing real technical. You don't have to play well to be able to play it."[18] In the early 1990s, Lee regularly joked about Rush as "white Canadians" trying to play funky beats and barely pulling it off. For example, commenting on the layered riffing in the song "Roll the Bones," Lee told John Stix, "Alex and I lock[ed] into this funk, and I use the word very tentatively. We're talking about three white guys from Canada, you know. So we have this section that was relatively funky for a *rock* context."[19] Although such jokes were intended to be self-deprecating, they reveal a consciousness of how Rush's approach to music-making was coded as white, intellectualized, and disciplined. On the flip-side, Lee's comments also expose a problematic assumption that black styles like reggae eschewed precise musical technique in favor of rhythmic feel (an assumption made all the more questionable by Lee's quips about Rush's inability to perform reggae or funk grooves smoothly). If anything, these self-deprecating jokes about being "too white to groove" were defensive gestures of detachment from the racial politics of popular music, and inferred that Rush's appropriations of funk and reggae were harmless and inconsequential since they were neither serious nor successful. Lee's invocation of Rush's Canadian identity in this context is particularly interesting, since its intent is to further distance the band from racialized musical dialogues. Speaking to American journalists, Lee used his Canadian background to deflect any uncomfortable questions about what it meant that Rush played around with African American styles. Not being American, Rush's "Canadian" music could more easily be positioned as politically neutral (even naive) about supposedly American debates over music and race.

The relationship between discipline and detachment has also been explored with respect to masculinity. Michael Bannister discusses different constructs of male identity in *White Boys, White Noise: Masculinities and 1980s Indie Guitar Rock,* providing an insightful historical account of how masculine strategies of nonperformance or underperformance developed in rock music. There is no question that bodily spectacle has held an important place in rock's history, but Bannister feels that the emphasis on this has oversimplified the analysis of rock's myriad masculinities, and that gender constructs in genres like psychedelia, indie rock, punk, art rock, and progressive rock will be better understood if we include those kinds of masculinity based on things other than physical force, machismo, or theatricalized androgyny. Bannister explores how masculine control can be manifested in music through intellectualization and distance. Bannister points to the studio-bound artistry of bands like the Beatles, Pink Floyd, and the Beach Boys, the rise of record producers like Phil Spector, and the merging of art and pop culture by Andy Warhol as ways "for white masculinities to assert their cultural authority over popular culture by aestheticization—the cultivation of distance, refinement and a disengagement from the body, and the gradual replacement of bodily performance with an ideal of mental control, the artist not as performer but as critical observer."[20] Particularly in the cases of Spector and Wilson, Bannister notes that these men "habitually absented themselves from their own work—disavowing their own physical presence" while compensating for this in the very "grandiosity" of their work.[21] This accomplishes a remarkably narcissistic form of masculine power, where control is exercised and maintained through a withdrawn, indirect gaze.[22]

Bannister's ideas intersect tellingly with the performance aesthetics of progressive rock groups like Rush, Pink Floyd, Yes, or Genesis. Their live shows were generally visual spectacles that dazzled the eye apart from the musicians themselves. The band members' minimal physical presence was placed amid musical and visual grandiosity, with technology providing lighting, pyrotechnics, and projected imagery. This juxtaposition allowed the musicians to exhibit control and power without applying much physical effort or taking any obvious, direct control over the stage environment. Although not absent from their work the way Spector or Warhol were, Rush and their prog-rock kin presented stage spectacles that were orchestrated by teams of roadies, technical personnel, and film crews whose work was dependent on the musicians' directives without the musicians carrying out any of the labor. The musicians' underperformance amid visual grandeur was a display of power, reveling in an ability to fill large spaces, to entertain and awe while doing little else other than playing their instruments. Performing apparently obliviously while magnificent lighting and technical displays unfolded around them, the musicians seemed all the more detached, stoic, unflappable, and in control: the marriage of spectacle to detachment made these male virtues even more conspicuous.

Of course, displays of excess, discipline, and detachment play a role in class as much as gender identity. For example, the excess and spectacle provided by Rush's live performances are consonant with middle-class visions of upward mobility. The ostentatious onstage display of musical technique and technological toys is that of the *arriviste*, the individual or family which has upped its material and cultural cachet. "Showing off" is always a sign of upward mobility, or at least the desire to appear mobile. As Peter Bailey explains, this sort of "peacock" display of achievement is something embedded in lower-middle-class conceptions of masculinity, in which efforts to "make the scene" in higher social circles or "keep up appearances" are a deeply felt need.[23] Although Rush's commercial success is undeniable, its ongoing practice of flaunting it through the development of a live, touring, big-event spectacle provides abundant visual evidence of its social mobility as successful musicians, and a desire to keep up with the band members' closest peers on the arena-rock circuit.

Middle-class identity is also palpably present in the detached quality that surfaced in both "Freewill" and "The Camera Eye," in which the subject speaking through the lyrics takes on the position of a neutral, objective, invisible observer. Such a subject has been well critiqued in the American context as representing a privileged whiteness and masculinity, so that the unmarked and unhyphenated "American" (or "Canadian") is presumed to be white and male. Pillsbury discusses this as an important factor in Metallica's cultivation of detachment: "Carving such a [deracialized] space for Metallica but never acknowledging the existence or characteristics of that space results in the kind of cultural void so distinctive to whiteness."[24] Assuming the position of an invisible, universal, unnamed subject is an important strategy of whiteness, as many studies of this ethnicity bear out,[25] but it is also a crucial part of North American middle-class identity. In fact, the kind of ethnically empty whiteness that has recently been critiqued depends a great deal on an interrelationship with class. Historians have shown that entry into the middle class often accompanies a loss of ethnicity and absorption into whiteness; for example, historian Loren Baritz documents in detail how Italian, Jewish, and Irish ethnicities began to dissolve into a more generic American whiteness at exactly the moment, after World War II, when these one-time ethnic minorities began taking white-collar jobs in larger numbers and moved into the suburbs.[26] For some, Baritz points out, this process involved a quite painful loss of culture, especially as parents watched their suburbanized children grow up as "unhyphenated" Americans.[27]

The rhetorical ethnic emptiness of American whiteness, it seems, is abetted by assuming a middle-class identity and lifestyle. Anthropologist Sherry Ortner explains, "Class is central to American social life, but it is rarely spoken in its own right. Rather, it is represented through other categories of social difference: gender, ethnicity, race and so forth."[28] The evasiveness maintained by white, middle-class Americans about class and racial identity is further discussed by Lorraine Kenny, who observes "in functioning as a privileged norm . . . everyone else has a race except whites and class is reserved for those with and without money, either the very rich or very poor. In striving to name the un-nameable and see the invisible, the ethnographer of middle-class whiteness works against the very foundations of the culture she embodies and has come to study."[29] Thus the kind of neutral, detached subject position, found in some of Rush's lyrics, can be read as white, but at the same time as middle class, and detachment and distance, as discussed earlier in the book, are aesthetic dispositions closely tied to the material conditions of class.

The interrelationship between discipline, control, spectacle, and excess within middle-class identity can be further illuminated by looking at how attitudes toward emotion and behavior have been shaped historically in North America. These attitudes have been rigorously traced in the work of historian Peter Stearns. In both *American Cool: Constructing a Twentieth-Century Emotional Style* and *Battleground of Desire: The Struggle for Self-Control in Modern America,* Stearns focuses particularly on the evolution of middle-class mores and behavioral norms in the United States, and observes that even as attitudes toward the body have become more casual since Victorian times, the strictures placed on emotional behavior have actually tightened.[30] For middle-class Americans, Stearns blames this on the conditions of professional and white-collar work. Such work was best accomplished if relations between white-collar professionals and clients were friendly, casual, impersonal, and devoid of overt emotional intensity.[31] White-collar employees, often mediating between "angry bosses" and "demanding subordinates," were put in a position where disinterest and emotional detachment were useful strategies in coping with conflicting interests.[32] Much stock was therefore placed in middle-class child-rearing on teaching kids restraint, self-control, and the suppressing of overt (especially negative) emotions. This intermingled with middle-class ideas about discipline and deferred gratification, insofar as upward mobility and professional advancement typically required middle-class people to put their work and training ahead of their feelings and immediate desires.

Inevitably, the middle class's emphasis on restraint, detachment, and self-control impacted the popular culture it consumed. Leisure, notes Stearns, became an outlet; as the emotional character of middle-class Americans became "cool," their preferred popular culture became "hot."[33] But of particular interest is how this popular culture became hot: for Stearns, it was not simply that the films, fiction, popular music, and TV shows became more emotional, but that they became more intense. In many cases, the drive to produce intensity and excitement superseded any actual emotional content. Popular culture, Stearns notes, became louder, more brash, and more extreme during the twentieth century, but its function was sometimes more about producing a sensation, a surge or a thrill, than providing surrogate emotional expression. This was particularly true of horror films, where fear was generated as a way of impersonally experiencing intense excitement, but the danger and loss of life depicted was never meant to arouse complex, personal emotions (such as regret, mourning, or guilt). Stearns feels that some of the popular music that emerged after World War II "celebrated intensity with no explicit emotional strings, and the addictive popularity of the new styles suggested a search for leisure styles which could overwhelm, that were exciting but did not require elaborate emotional expression."[34]

This provides considerable insight into the apparent contradiction which began this chapter. Rush's "Freewill" expressed a basically impersonal, detached, philosophical musing through the lyrics, but Lee's vocals at the end wrapped them in piercing intensity. Indeed, the entire song, with its thundering drums, rich guitar distortion, and jarring rhythmic contrasts, is representative of Rush's musical style, which is typically energetic and extreme in certain ways. The lyrics express ideas in a detached way, while the music, vocals, and performing practices provide exactly what Stearns describes: stirring, sometimes overwhelming intensity without deeply personal emotional content. In this context, detachment and intensity are not in opposition but are complementary. The powerful and authoritative character that Rush takes on when performing live is facilitated by this mix of intensity and detachment, and while not all of Rush's music is necessarily intense or detached, it remains a significant aspect of its style and an important part of its appeal.

5

"Reflected in Another Pair of Eyes"

Representations of Rush Fandom

R ush has been the only band that matter[s] to lone-wolf suburban kids,"
critic Bob Mack wrote in his 1990 review of Rush's *Presto* album. Although clearly typecasting, there is here, as with most stereotypes, a
kernel of truth in Mack's characterization of Rush fandom. Suburbia,
isolation, and individualism merge in Mack's appraisal, and some who attended suburban Canadian or American high schools in the 1980s probably
recall the stereotype of the reclusive but obsessive drummer or the bookish
loner wearing a Rush tour shirt as one of several music-related identities
that circulated during that decade. This lonely, suburban character surfaces in several Rush songs, including "Circumstances" (1978), "The Analog
Kid" (1982), "Middletown Dreams" (1985), and "The Big Wheel" (1991), so

there is no doubt that Rush addressed such an audience directly. At the same time, such typecasting only provides one view of Rush fandom. At various times, and from various points of view, Rush's audience has been characterized as zealously loyal cult fandom,[1] a subset of the homogenous white-male consumer base for corporate rock,[2] a diverse, multi-generation, and multi-ethnic taste group,[3] a musician-based fan community,[4] a rowdy, drunken, hard-rocking crowd,[5] and—conversely—an unusually mature, sober, and contemplative arena-rock audience.[6] As Matt Hills observes in *Fan Cultures*, fandom can never be explained by a single motivation, and for an observer reading social aspects of class, gender, or ethnicity from fan discourse, the terrain is quite complicated.[7]

Moreover, mapping the terrain of any given fandom is not a straight-forward ethnographic task. Much data offers itself up for analysis: the internet today provides plenty of forums, message boards, and blogs where fans voice opinions, leave testimonials, share news, debate points, and reflect on their fan experiences. Surveys and questionnaires can be circulated among fans; consultants can be located and interviewed at length; participant-observation can be done wherever fans publicly congregate. Gathered through these means, the data reveal important patterns, and a picture of a particular fan group may emerge. But the picture will still be incomplete, representing only the fandom visible in certain contexts. Fans who don't post on the internet, who are not frequent concertgoers, or who don't attend fan conventions may nevertheless have deep connections to Rush, but will be, to an ethnographic gaze, practically invisible.[8] Publicly available fan discourse, too, may be incomplete or opaque in a number of ways. As Hills observes, academics must be cautious about taking fans' voiced justifications for their attachments at face value, and he notes that fans sometimes fall back on well-worn "discursive mantras" (well known, socially acceptable, and oft-repeated tropes) when explaining their fandom.[9] As a Rush fan reflecting on my own past fandom, I understand why Hills voices this concern. In casual discussions with fans and nonfans, I remember trading all sorts of clichés about why I liked Rush, which I probably learned from fellow enthusiasts, rock publications, and the residual romanticism that circulates all over popular culture. And some of these discursive mantras were taken directly from Rush itself, including tropes about the band's integrity, its willingness to change and evolve, the musicians' down-to-earth attitudes, and so on, all of which could be readily found in newspaper and magazine interviews with the band members. Fans may choose not to articulate the underlying sociocultural reasons for their fandom, they may not be conscious of them, and they may have no interest in becoming conscious of them. For these reasons, the character of any fan base should be assessed through a combination of resources, archival as well as ethnographic, insider as well as outsider.

Acknowledging these concerns, I investigate *representations* of Rush fandom in this chapter, including those from fans, journalists, and the band members themselves. I am particularly interested in how Rush fans characterize themselves and their fandom, what kinds of divisions they make among themselves, what issues most urgently divide or unite fan opinion, and what kinds of discourses about Rush they both privilege and disparage. Observations of Rush fandom made by outsiders are also important in characterizing Rush's fan base. Journalists, for example, provide observations of the fan base across a number of years and a number of North American locales, allowing some aspects of change and continuity in the audience to be inferred. Rush musicians themselves, despite copious contact with their fan base over more than thirty years, nevertheless provide an outsider's view. In interviews throughout their career, they have made numerous observations about who they think composes their fan base, and, more significantly, what relationships they imagine Rush fans having with the band's music. At times, the band emphasizes certain kinds of band-fan relationships over others, which influences what is perceived in online Rush fan communities as normative fan behavior. Other characteristics of Rush's audience, including gender balance, ethnicity, its substantial musician following, and its overlap with other taste publics and subcultures add significant details to this book's class theme.

Some statistical information is discussed here, but much of the data is qualitative. Statistical information for this chapter was drawn from three rounds of Rush fan surveys conducted in 1996, 2000–2002, and 2008. These surveys queried fan opinion and obtained a rough sense of Rush fan demographics. I make no assertive claim for how accurately the statistics I gathered reflect the demographics of Rush's North American audience. A full-blown ethnography of the type produced by Daniel Cavicchi on Bruce Springsteen fans or Sara Cohen on the Liverpool rock scene of the 1980s would require a book-length focus.[10] My ethnographic inquiry into Rush fandom was kept to the scope required for this chapter. In keeping with comparable studies, like Fast's on Led Zeppelin and Echard's on Neil Young, my use of quotations from fan respondents and consultants, as well as internet discussion, serves to bring fan discourse into this musicological study and to bring my academic work into dialogue with fans' priorities.

The 1996 survey (107 responses) focused on the gender balance of Rush's audience and the perceptions of Rush's music in gendered terms. The 2000–2002 survey (64 responses) dealt more generally with the reception and interpretation of Rush's music in different stylistic periods. The 2008 survey (101 responses) was keyed more directly to the themes of the book (suburbia, escapism, individualism, professionalism, fandom, critical reception). All three surveys, however, gathered demographic information (age, gender, occupation, region), asked about fan "initiation narratives,"[11] and asked respondents to characterize Rush's fan base and opine about the band's appeal. The 1996 questionnaire was distributed through the internet to respondents whose email addresses were available from Rush fan sites. The 2000–2002 round of surveys was partly done through similar internet distribution methods, as well as from my own Rush fan web site.[12] I include in this second round of surveying my distribution of printed questionnaires, based on the same questions, at the first annual Rush Convention (RushCon) in Toronto in 2001. The most recent survey was posted on a popular fan blog, www.rushisaband.com.[13] Among the 272 respondents from all three surveys, the vast majority were American, most from the Northeast, the Midwest, and California. Smaller but significant numbers of fans responded from Ontario and the American South. An even smaller number of fans—about ten for each round of surveys—came from the

United Kingdom, and there were even single respondents from Japan, Italy, Sweden, Germany, Argentina, Mexico, Brazil, and Suriname.

A number of internet domains facilitated my observations of fan discourse, including the Usenet group alt.music.rush (the oldest forum), as well as fan message boards, such as The Rush Interactive Network (or TRI-Net, now defunct), the Counterparts Message Board (www.rushmessage board.com), The Rush Forum (www.therushforum.com), and GeddyLee .net (also defunct). Rush concert clips and videos are now available through sources such as YouTube, and fans can post comments and testimonials keyed to specific songs and performances, providing another source of information. I maintained a log of the topics, debates, and opinions discussed in these domains in an effort to get a sense of the issues to which fans are attentive, and to grasp what shapes discourse about Rush on the internet. Discussion online is plentiful, and I do not attempt to characterize it in all its breadth; my interest here remains an examination of public representations of Rush fandom.

Because social class is such a rarely discussed identity marker in North America, I tend to infer issues of class from fan discourse rather than draw them directly from statements. Some respondents did flag class directly in characterizing themselves or Rush's audience, but this occurred too infrequently to form clear patterns. Durrell Bowman provides some useful points on discussing fans and class; his dissertation addressed social class in characterizing Rush's audience. Bracketing gendered and ethnic aspects, Bowman highlighted class and occupation as the most significant commonality among Rush fans. The largest proportion of his fan sample[14] fell into the categories of non-manual service industry workers ("new collars") and professionals in the knowledge industry (lawyers, architects, teachers, software engineers, known as "bright collars").[15] The terms new collar and bright collar, from an article by Ralph Whitehead Jr. in *Psychology Today,* map onto non-manual working-class jobs and some middle-class professions, respectively, forming a middle ground between traditionally blue-collar labor and the highly privileged and restricted professional domains of the upper middle class.[16] These provide suggestive markers for locating Rush's core audience on the socioeconomic spectrum, although Whitehead's terms are less well used than more established sociological categories of lower middle class, new middle class, and "embourgeoised" working class.[17]

In my own surveys, 71 percent of Rush fans reported white-collar occupations, including attorneys, accountants, engineers, civil servants, professors, teachers, principals, corporate managers as high as vice-presidents, retail managers, librarians, entrepreneurs, and information technologists. Nineteen percent reported blue-collar occupations, including police officers, construction workers, couriers, caretakers, chefs, workers in manufacturing, utilities workers, sound and television technicians, and security guards. Ten percent of respondents fell into an undetermined category, with high school students, artists, musicians, and homemakers difficult to gauge in socioeconomic status or outlook. There are also ambiguities in some categories such as "entrepreneur," where the term may apply to someone actually running a company with a team of employees (clearly qualifying as petit-bourgeois), but the term was also used by respondents working on a freelance basis. Of these in the latter category, some respondents worked freelance in non-manual domains, such as advertising, while others worked on contract in manual occupations such as electronics repair. Among blue-collar respondents, ambiguities also emerged from those who hold postsecondary and even postgraduate degrees, but who found that some blue-collar occupations pay better than jobs related to their fields of study. In any case, based on the evidence here, a large chunk of Rush's audience is middle class or lower middle class, though a significant working-class following is evident as well.

Bowman and I also queried other social divisions. Though our statistics fluctuated slightly in different rounds of surveying, Rush's concertgoing audience, convention attendees, and online fan communities averaged a bit more than 75 percent male and just under 25 percent female. Bowman found that 90.5 percent of fans self-identified as white, the rest as non-white.[18] In all three rounds of surveying, I found the average year of birth (1970) for Rush fans remained consistent. The core seems to be fans in the younger segment of baby boomers (born in the early 1960s), as well as Generation X, fans born between 1965 and 1980. Both our survey outcomes were consistent with regard to Rush fans who self-identify as amateur or professional musicians with experience performing on an instrument; between two-thirds and three-quarters claim this status. This is clearly an important self-perception of Rush's fan base, and calls for some analysis.

These statistics suggest that Rush's audience is weighted heavily toward a white, male, middle- or lower-middle-class demographic, though with some crossover into other demographics. Critics represent the relative homogeneity or diversity of Rush's audience in a fairly consistent way. During the 1980s and 1990s, journalists typically reported a narrow demographic appeal. Reviewing a 1980 concert in Los Angeles, Steve Pond wrote, "In one way, Rush is a lot like Shaun Cassidy, Teddy Pendergrass and *Super Vixens:* its audience is made up almost entirely of one sex. In Rush's case, it's nearly all males—or more precisely, judging from this crowd, nearly all sixteen-year-old males with long hair, faint mustaches and adrenaline to burn."[19] Sixteen years later, Keith Spera acknowledged that Rush's audience remained pretty much as it had always been—"mostly white, mostly male"—even if the age spread had enlarged somewhat.[20] Of course, these observations are made mostly by writers only casually observing concert audiences, but as reviewers, they witness crowds at performances of many different artists. Rush band members have also noted at various times that their appeal is highly slanted toward a white, male demographic.[21] In my 2001 interview with Alex Lifeson, the guitarist noted that a small but conspicuous female fan base became evident by the early 1990s, but he was particularly struck by the growing age range in Rush fandom, with an obvious passing of musical taste from parent to child. Geddy Lee, in a 2002 interview with Vit Wagner, also noted a broadening in age and gender of the visible fan base, but he described the teenage fans he met as a younger version of the older hardcore: male musicians.[22]

How homogenous or diverse do fans themselves perceive Rush's audience to be? In my fan surveys, I asked the respondents to comment on who they thought Rush's audience was. The answers were spread widely, with many fans (58 percent in all) quite candid about what they saw as the white, male homogeneity of Rush's audience. Others made cases for diversity in the fan base, with diversity taking many forms, including age, gender, class, and race. Among these, some fans argued that Rush's music transcends social boundaries, so diversity in the audience is to be expected. For some, diversity meant that hardcore or cult fans shared the band with more casual rock fans. Some felt that Rush's audience had once been quite homogenous, but that its appeal broadened during the 1990s and 2000s, especially with respect to gender. But others wondered if this had really occurred, since it had become increasingly common, especially since the mid-1990s, for older hardcore male fans to bring their spouses and kids to Rush concerts. Had mixed-gender family units simply replaced or supplemented male-bonding groups in the concertgoing audience? There was no significant split in audience perception between male and female fans; both saw Rush's audience as either diverse or homogenous in roughly the same proportion. Assumptions that Rush fandom must be diverse because the music transcends social boundaries turned mostly on the notion that music, being a form of art, is always universal—a decidedly Western, bourgeois idea, ironically. Many characterizations of Rush's audience sidestep social divisions altogether, opting instead for other kinds of descriptors. Some described the audience's apparent range of demeanor (thoughtful, mature, intellectual), personality types (inquisitive, obsessive, intense, aloof), and taste orientation (eclectic, interested in science fiction, classic rock, and progressive music). Many respondents also emphasized the high prevalence of musicians in the audience, a fact which remains important for fans and the band members alike.

This contradiction—the disagreement between fans that see diversity in Rush's audience and those that see homogeneity—underscores the difficulty in faithfully representing audiences ethnographically. Both views have their merits. On the one hand, there are good reasons why Rush's audience would be weighted heavily to a white, male demographic. The point in rock's history when Rush rose to fame was marked by a shift from "broadcasting" (music projected to the widest possible markets or taste groups) to "narrowcasting" (the courting of loyal, predictable niche markets).[23] The strategies of the music industry played an important role in this, but identity-seeking audiences were equally implicated in the formation of narrower, specialist taste publics at the end of the 1960s. Thus, whereas 1960s artists like the Beatles initially appealed across gender, class, and, to a lesser degree, race boundaries, 1970s hard rock acts like Rush, AC/DC, Styx, and Aerosmith emerged to serve a narrower rock audience whose taste gelled along particular racial (white) and gender (male) lines. The niche radio format developed to cater to such tastes, known as album-oriented rock (AOR), was the format that embraced Rush.

On the other hand, this narrowcasting process, no matter how successful it was in drawing audiences from expected demographic ranges, always leaked. For example, Susan Fast points out that hard rock, so often presumed to be music made by and for males, was as open to female appropriation and interpretation as any other part of popular culture. It is the unimaginative, restricted ways in which audiences are written and talked about that seem to simplify and essentialize our view of audiences.[24] In researching an audience, an awareness of how the pleasures and practices of fandom diverge depending on one's social perspective requires a flexible approach. As Thomas Lindloff and his colleagues note, "A typical media audience is not a cohesive membership that behaves according to a shared code. Instead, actors in mass-mediated events use and interpret the 'same' text in divergent ways . . . subject to the demands and constraints of their social order."[25] This does not mean that commonalities or patterns cannot be observed in audiences, but that the analyst must acknowledge significant play and slippage in the cultural practices of fans. The various representations of Rush fandom that follow below need not be understood as prescriptive "types" of fans, but rather as orientations that help characterize different fan practices and affinities. In many cases, the various representations of Rush fandom—such as a musicianly fandom, a literary (or "readerly") fandom, or fans of "old Rush"—are points of endless discussion and redefinition within fan communities. These representations, and the debates over them, reveal much about the social ground over which Rush fandom takes place, and I show how various aspects of class, gender, and ethnicity are implicated in the following representations.

The image of Rush's audience as a musicians' community is quite salient in both fans' self-representations and in Rush's own perception of its fan base. Rush's reputation as virtuosi inevitably drew the attention of some listeners who played bass, drums, or guitar as a hobby or with professional aspirations. This aspect of Rush fandom is consistent with the group's close relationship to genres like heavy metal and progressive rock. As noted by Robert Walser, a large proportion of the audience for heavy metal during the 1970s and 1980s took up the guitar, bass, or drums and fostered an interest in the details of instrumental technique, music theory, and audio gear.[26] The growth of a taste group centering on the appreciation of rock musicianship paralleled the development of the power trio and the "supergroups" of the late 1960s. Cream and the Jimi Hendrix Experience are good examples of bands that influenced Rush in its earliest phase, and both groups elevated the charismatic and accomplished instrumentalist to the same level as the lead singer. In the case of Hendrix, the guitar playing arguably outshone the quality of the lead vocals, placing high emphasis on the expressive and virtuosic nature of the instrumental performer, attracting (and holding) fans and enthusiasts who identified directly with the guitar playing. This inspired considerable hobbyist imitation and spawned the rise of rigorous rock pedagogies (private lessons on rock instruments and a sector of the music publication industry dedicated to transcriptions of "great" rock songs, complete with detailed reproductions of instrumental solos). Bands like Cream and the Who are notable for extending the role of heroic instrumentalist to the bassist and drummer. Jack Bruce of Cream and John Entwistle of the Who developed melodically and rhythmically busy styles of bass playing that would influence later bassists like Geddy Lee; the aggressive, "around-the-kit" drumming of Cream's Ginger Baker, the Who's Keith Moon, and Led Zeppelin's John Bonham set a standard for heroic percussion styles in hard rock, developed further by Neil Peart. Both 1970s progressive rock and heavy metal carried these stylistic trajectories further as the fan base for this kind of musicianly rock galvanized and developed its own aesthetic discourse.

The members of Rush recall their own pasts as fans of rock while it made this musicianly turn. Peart told *Metal Hammer's* Malcolm Dome, "We started out as fans of the late sixties style of music, which was dominated by the likes of Jimi Hendrix and Cream—musicians. I was personally inspired by the Who, they were the first band to make me want to play drums and write songs. . . . That's where our values were forged."[27] Speaking with *Bass Player's* Robin Tolleson the same year, Lee echoed Peart's sentiment: "Cream was one of the groups that I loved when I was growing up and first got into music in a more serious way. We used to play Cream songs way back when. What I liked about Jack [Bruce] was that his sound was distinctive—it wasn't boring, and it wasn't typical. And he was very busy. He wouldn't keep his place, which I really liked a lot. He wouldn't keep quiet as a bass player. He was obtrusive, which I like in a bass player."[28] Similar sentiments emerged from my questionnaire respondents when discussing Rush's appeal; one respondent said, "I would say about 90% of the avid Rush fans I know play a musical instrument. Personally, I never played an instrument until I was so darn inspired by their musicianship that I felt I just had to pick up an instrument. So, I would say that I would not play an instrument had it not been for their music." Another respondent emphasized an exclusive, esoteric aspect to the musicianly appreciation of Rush: "Instrumental music is an abstract language, and Rush are very interesting and articulate speakers in that language. I can listen to long instrumentals and instrumental passages and get as much or more from them as music with lyrics." One respondent connected his fandom with learning his craft as a drummer, and also revealed an important link between Rush fandom and the readership for musicians' magazines:

> I'm a semi-pro musician and have been playing in bands for 25 odd years. Neil was the primary inspiration for me to start taking drum lessons as a 12 year old—I got into school band, etc. and had my own rock band. In the early days of my music education, *Modern Drummer* magazine was a huge source of inspiration—the technical information it provided was

invaluable and Neil seemed to be closely associated with this magazine. Neil's interviews and ask-a-pro responses taught me a lesson about his "prime motivations" when it came to music—just wanting to play better, experiment, develop new skills, being open to different approaches, etc. I adopted his basic attitude towards music and it influenced my music career immensely.

In a broader context, this kind of Rush fandom fits into a history of fan fixations on the musicianly qualities of recorded popular music extending back at least to the 1920s. Burton Peretti, writing on the popularization of jazz during that decade, recounts that "jazz inspired adolescent white males to create cliques of appreciation and instrument playing, which led many into musical careers. Phonograph records and instrument instruction inspired high school boys . . . to form bands."[29] This pattern, noted in jazz's social history, continued in rock, with similar stories being recalled by fans of psychedelic, metal, and progressive bands like Cream, Yes, Rush, Van Halen, Metallica, and Dream Theater, revealing it as a long-lived leisure practice associated with teenage male music fandom. It is a kind of fandom that clearly serves to construct a particular kind of cultural prestige, combined with significant gendered meaning.

The issue of musicianly prestige in Rush's career was addressed substantially in chapter 3, but the role of fandom in cementing this perception of Rush as master musicians is critical here. A number of interviews with Lee, Lifeson, and Peart broach the subject of the band as mentors for aspiring young musicians, highlighting their pride in passing on musical knowledge, influence as well as values (usually couched in terms of perseverence, maintaining high standards of craftsmanship, or remaining open to new music).[30] As Peart has noted in interviews, the perception of Rush fans as informed and competent musicians makes him somewhat self-conscious when performing, aware of drummer-fans watching his every move, analytically dissecting the performance as it unfolds.[31] Peart clearly cherishes and fosters this mentor-apprentice relationship that Rush has with some fans, having written articles for *Modern Drummer* and releasing an instructional video in 1996, *A Work in Progress,* in which he shared his techniques, philosophy, and the process he underwent in constructing the drum parts for Rush's *Test for Echo* CD. Through such efforts, a symbiotic relationship between Rush and its musicianly following is strongly inferred. The quality of the band's musicianship is affirmed by the fans' attention and ability to discourse about each band member's playing; the fans' connoisseurship is actualized by their own sophisticated grasp of Rush's putatively complex body of work. The band and musicianly fans affirm each other as specialists, exchanging cultural capital based on knowledge of musical theory, technique, and gear.

It is worth noting what fans mean by the term "musicianship." The word could denote just about any act of making musical sound, but for Rush fans, as well as most heavy metal and progressive rock fans, it is used in a fairly specific and conservative way. The practices established in the late 1960s for playing guitars, basses, drums, and keyboards are at the core of what is considered authentic musicianship, and the self-conscious pursuit of technical proficiency and a personal, original style are touted as important aesthetic considerations. I call this a conservative definition of musicianship because of what it excludes. Synthesizers, though not automatically excluded, are viewed with suspicion because of their association with artificiality and their capacity to play automatically, seen by fans of bands like Rush as fakery. Such fans expect synthesizers to be deployed in very particular ways to qualify as acceptable musicianship. From 1977 to 1984, when Geddy Lee was actually playing chords and melodic figures on synthesizers with his own fingers, fans generally accepted the instrument's role in Rush's music. From 1985 to 1991, when Lee began using presequenced patterns, the use of synthesizers became a more contentious matter among fans. This explains the performing practices discussed in chapter 4, in which the musicians insisted on triggering any automatically sequenced synthesizer parts themselves on stage, so that they were still, in some sense, playing it. DJing or creating collages of samples, so important to rap and electronic dance music, is not generally considered valid musicianship to much of this audience. Instrumental musicianship is generally valued more than vocal capability, and groups that perform in playing/

singing/dancing combinations are not generally favored or desired, as this detracts from the instrumental musicianship itself. Among this audience, Rush is seen as the exemplars and the defenders of a particular ideal of musicianship, which seems precious and prestigious to them in part because the onward march of technology and new musical practices threaten to displace it.

In spite of its patina of musical prestige, musicianly Rush fandom does not clearly or simply inflect an identity based on social class. The performance and consumption of virtuosic display in popular music has a very ambiguous history with respect to class. Guitar virtuosity in heavy metal—even when it drew on European classical influences—had a wide appeal across the spectrum of social class, acting as a widely recognizable embodiment of individuality, power, and male potency, the appeal of which is not limited to the working or middle classes. Instrumental prowess and musical complexity in the domain of 1970s progressive rock seems to derive consistently from middle-class origins in Britain, but its reception along class lines in North America is not well documented. Macan claims that American progressive rock audiences contained a much larger blue-collar portion than was evident in the United Kingdom, which may indicate that enthusiasm for classically influenced rock musicianship crosses class lines in the United States, but Macan provides little evidence to back up this claim.[32]

To some degree, virtuosic musicianship is ambivalent as a marker of class identity, especially as it relates to the occupation of a musician. Though I made the argument that Rush constructed its career as musicians along middle-class professional and entrepreneurial lines, there are many ways that Rush's musicianship may be seen by fans. On the one hand, dextrous drumming, nimble bass playing, and fast guitar work are a sort of manual labor, no matter how much lofty rhetoric is used to glorify it. And it suits working-class values to derive power from the work of one's hands, power that is manifested in visible displays of skill and earning power. The virtuosic rock star, then, can take the form of a working-class hero whose skill models individual empowerment and upward mobility. Musicianly fandom, too, celebrates the musicians' mastery of technology and machines, and, as I found when interviewing some musicianly Rush fans, sharing one's knowledge of guitars, basses, amplifiers, and other equipment used by Rush was important. These fans would vividly discuss the combinations of equipment, the techniques Rush used with them, and the acoustical results, with the conversations homologically resembling similar working-class male shop talk about cars, power tools, and other machines, where comparing knowledge of mechanical attributes provides a way of bonding. Virtuosic musicianship, on the other hand, may be seen as more refined by some fans. Associated with the fine arts, the careful cultivation of musical complexity, especially in the compositional domain, can be perceived as evidence of cerebral, non-manual expertise. Rush's musical structures, modalities, suspended chords, and asymmetrical meters, as discussed in musician's magazines, provide opportunities for discussions of music theory, and these discussions foreground a conceptual complexity in Rush's music that goes beyond manual dexterity. The appreciation of Rush's musicianship in almost formalist and music-theoretical terms aligns more closely with the distanced middle-class aesthetic disposition discussed in chapter 1.

If Rush's musicianly fandom appears class-ambiguous, the same cannot be said of its gendered dimension. Popular music's history bears out an enduring split in gender roles between the instrumentalist, who is almost always male, and the singer, whose gender identity is wide open. Challenges to this status quo have occurred variously since rock 'n' roll's inception, but in nearly all popular genres, female instrumental musicians remain a conspicuous minority.[33] Cults of musicianship, which have formed around highly dextrous jazz musicians, blues guitarists, metal guitarists, and progressive rock musicians, have held ground as sites of male bonding and masculine self-actualization. But this phenomenon calls out for nuanced explanation, since these reputedly masculinist cults of musicianship do not appeal to all (or even most) men. As Matthew Bannister observes, masculinity in popular music should not be explained through simple top-down models of gender hierarchies, as this overlooks the ways in which masculinity is marked by internal divisions, rankings, and multiplicity.[34] We need to ask what kind of masculinity this segment of Rush fandom, which centers on dextrous musicianship and an obsession with instruments and music theory, performs. One important quality of musicianly Rush fandom, and other similar cults of musicianship, is the way they provide access to highly technical and formalistic musical domains. The development of a style of hard rock that provides not just loudness, harsh timbres, and a rebellious stance, but also entry into a series of abstract musical "systems" (scales and modes, odd time signatures, additive or sectional forms), creates a technocratic musical world, fusing rock's power with the abstraction of music theory. All this can be usefully contrasted with the aesthetics of hardcore punk and indie rock, again predominantly male rock subcultures, which retain the rebellious and homosocial aspects of rock musicianship but reject fetishizing the technical or theoretical materials of music.[35] Hardcore punk creates a space for the effusive display of righteous and politicized anger, a register of emotion that is compatible with fairly normative masculine characteristics. After all, in many forms of popular culture, the sight of men becoming angry, even violently angry, for "justifiable" reasons (having been victimized, protecting the weak, seeking revenge under certain circumstances) is quite common, and is an important part of action-based heroic narratives.

But rock's technocratic side, represented by Rush, neo-progressive groups like Dream Theater, or neo-classical metal artists like Yngwie Malmsteen, Randy Rhoads, or the group Cacophony, portrays a different masculinist sensibility, where intensity and vigor is merged with a conspicuous command of music's abstract technical and theoretical qualities. In fact, valid comparisons could be made between the virtuosity- and time signature–obsessed fandom of technocratic musicianship and the culture created around computer programming. Sherry Turkle's sociological study of computer science students found that programming—requiring the mastery of a machine as well as an esoteric, rarefied language for discussing it—attracted a demographic weighted heavily toward males. The reasons for this, Turkle surmised, had much to do with a greater tendency among males to embrace long hours of asocial engagement with machines and their specialist programming language. She found that for female computer science students, this social isolation was one of the least attractive and most uncomfortable aspects of the profession. But a number of male students reported feeling more comfortable working in a solitary programming project than in more socially collaborative spaces. Male students often became obsessed with computing as teenagers (just as some of their counterparts became obsessed with playing musical instruments). "Computers," Turkle observes, "become particularly seductive at a certain moment in psychological development: the moment of adolescence. There are new sexual pressures and social demands. The safe microworlds . . . of sports, chess, cars, literature, music, dance and mathematical expertise—can become places of escape." Moreover, "in our society, men are much more likely than women to master anxieties about people by turning to the world of things and formal systems."[36] Musicianly Rush fandom, with its shop talk about meters, modes, brands of guitar, and drum kit setups, is highly suggestive of the kind of "microworld" Turkle discusses.

In fan internet forums, the importance of Rush's musicianship—the perception of them as elite musicians—is generally consensual; few fans publicly question that Rush's virtuosity is a widely cherished aspect among the audience. However, overtly technical forms of musicianly fandom are open to criticism from other Rush enthusiasts. For example, one female fan on the *Counterparts* message board aired frustration with musicianly male fans for "over-analyzing" every detail of every song, and for somberly watching Rush perform live, as if studying the band.[37] She positioned herself playfully and ambiguously in her post, acting as both a marginalized victim and a sardonic critic of musicianly fandom. On one hand, she pointed out how elitist and exclusive she found these musicianly "guys" and their shop-talk to be. On the other hand, she seemed to dismiss their practices as pathetic attempts to compensate for insecurity by posing and preening with their "superior" knowledge of music. She recognized that musicianly fandom reflects a desire for cultural status and prestige, but also that social anxiety (like the kind Turkle discussed) is a subtext of this fandom. Her way of representing musicianly fandom cleverly brings to bear two perceptions of that fandom: an insider's view of fan-musicians as knowledgeable, discriminating aesthetes, and an outsider's view of them as obsessive nitpickers with too much time on their hands. I highlight this post not only because it lays bare the gendered aspect of musicianly fandom, but because it also underscores its class-ambiguous character: fan-musicians create and trade a sort of cultural capital using musicianly knowledge of Rush's music, and this parallels the refined, educated appreciation of high culture in a much broader cultural field. But this musicianly capital seems to have limited exchange value or prestige outside this fan subcommunity. Metaphorically, it is a small cultural economy that is fairly insular.

Another important representation of Rush fandom is that of the literary or readerly fan, where Neil Peart's lyrics are the focus. As composer of nearly all of Rush's song texts since 1975, Peart worked hard to establish himself as a reputable writer, and part of Rush's fan base responded strongly to his style. Writer Perry Stern argues that Peart's early fantasy-based lyrics galvanized a taste public focused on his words: "Originally immersed in 'Sword and Sorcery' imagery with elaborate lyrical fantasies and complicated musical compositions, the band developed the kind of loyal following politicians would kill for. The people who read only science-fiction would elevate Rush as the one band that could articulate their baroque cosmologies with a rock sensibility."[38] Journalist Nick Carter sized up Rush's audience as a contemplative—if also opiated—interpretive community, on the outskirts of hip popular music trends: "Adolescents in the late '70's and early '80's fell into one of two camps: those who would rip a band like Rush to pieces while combing back their hair, adjusting their skinny ties, and listening to Elvis Costello in the school lunch room, [and] those who could be spotted at the basement weekend beer bash, splayed out in a bean bag chair and musing over the band's pseudo-spiritual lyrics while passing around a bong and gazing at black light posters (of bands such as Rush)."[39] Philip Bashe, writing in *Circus* magazine, found a correlation between Rush's pseudo-literary lyrics and the kind of audience it draws: "If there's one thing rock journalists dread more than watery drinks at press functions, it's facing the wrath of Rush fans disgruntled over a less than favorable review. Not only are they a vocal lot who will gladly spring for the postage in order to castigate the offending scribe, but they're unusually articulate. Basically intelligent fans for a basically intelligent band; it's a unique relationship."[40]

Readerly Rush fandom falls into its own tradition of popular music reception. The idea of popular song as a modern form of poetry or literature has flourished since the mid-1960s, and fandom based on an intellectualized, pseudo-literary appreciation of song texts emerged during that period.[41] Bob Dylan stands out as an artist whose audience celebrates his talent as a wordsmith, so much so that some fans publish monographs of interpretive ruminations on his work.[42] The development of readerly fan bases like this one was partly the outcome of middle-class, often college-educated, popular music fans learning to evaluate and aestheticize the object of their fandom in the same manner as the literature they studied in school.[43] In many cases, this kind of fandom is based on relatively private contemplations or discussions of the semantic and symbolic meanings of songs, but for some fans, this becomes a public project with a scholarly veneer. Among writings on Dylan, Michael Gray's *The Song and Dance Man* stands as an excellent example of a book that brings terms and methods from academic folklore studies and English literature to bear on Dylan's songs, self-consciously locating Dylan's poetic lyrics in deep traditions both literary and vernacular.

This manner of bringing academic analysis into fan discourse is emblematic of what Hills calls the "fan-scholar," a fan whose work has the rigor of scholarship, even though the work is made outside the academic's professional field.[44] In Hills's view, fan-scholars differ from scholar-fans insofar as the latter make scholarship their profession, and their work is sanctioned by academic institutions. In contrast, fan-scholars' work, even if published, is considered an epiphenomenon of popular culture that may be worth studying as a text, but is not typically taken seriously outside its fan context. At its best and most erudite, academics are most likely to view the work of fan-scholars as an example of vernacular theory to be "examined as sources of 'critical' fan knowledge, but not as a site where academic knowledge may circulate outside the academy."[45] Among Rush's North American audience, fan-scholars have surfaced from time to time. Bill Banasiewicz, for example, published the first Rush biography not written by a journalist (*Visions*, 1988), mixing some archival research with his own interviews and contacts with the group. Though far from a definitive and polished work, it remained the latest book-length biography of the group for more than ten years, providing an example of a fan trying to provide reference material for other fans. Robert Telleria's *Rush Tribute: Merely Players* is an excellent example of what Hills describes as a "fan dissertation," a work of archival compilation that, in Telleria's case, resembles a reference encyclopedia, indexing set lists, tour dates and locations, musical gear used by Rush over time, record sales, thematic material, bibliographic and discographic catalogs, and memorabilia.[46]

Carol Price's *Mystic Rhythms: The Philosophical Vision of Rush* is the most extensive readerly fan publication dealing with Rush's lyrics. *Mystic Rhythms* discusses at length a significant swath of Rush's repertoire, paraphrasing, interpreting, and comparing ideas gleaned from Peart's lyrics to those of philosophers from Socrates to Heidegger. Price shows parallels between some Rush songs and works of high literature and popular culture. Price's stated intention in writing the book was to provide a resource and reading guide for teenagers, using rock music to interest young people in philosophy.[47] As a fan-scholar, Price takes on a leadership role, providing critical interpretation of lyrics and aiming to educate younger fans coming into the fold. The book clearly assumes a readerly fan orientation and constructs an image of Rush fandom that is distinctly middle class. For Price, Rush fandom is cerebral, using rock music as a pretext for discovering and debating ideas. She positions Rush amid the great philosophers and writers of the Western tradition, although she does not leave American popular culture out of the discussion. Price implicitly represents Rush fandom as educated, versed somewhat in Western high culture as well as popular culture. This may be a middlebrow vision of Rush fandom, but because she sees such a wide-ranging set of cultural references (from highbrow to lowbrow) as important to the appreciation of Rush, her ideal fan appears very much as a middle-class cultural omnivore.

Readerly fandom appears as the inverse of musicianly fandom: the reader is positioned more squarely as middle class, but the gendered associations are more ambiguous. As established in the previous chapter, Peart's lyric writing style, especially after 1980, was marked by a prevailing tone of detachment, abstraction, and objectivity, producing a rhetorical point of view that has a long history in the West of being coded (tacitly) masculine. The lyrics strongly infer a masculine point of view, but their reception is less straightforward. In the first place, the absence of a clear gender address in the lyrics may in some ways open up interpretive possibilities for female fans. Also, reading literature itself has a gender-inclusive history within the middle class. From Victorian times, reading and writing with some level of erudition has been desirable among middle-class women, and the appreciation of novels, poetry, and art songs acted as a marker of gentility for men and women alike. While my survey and interview sample contained musicianly fans who were almost exclusively male, those whose fandom was marked by readerly fan discussion and activity included both women and men. This included one woman, Cat Ashton, who wrote short stories based on Rush's fantasy epics. Her writing included a continuation of Rush's "Cygnus X-1" narrative, which followed the astronaut's exploits beyond the world described in the band's "Cygnus X-1 Book II: Hemispheres." Both this and Price's fan-scholar writing are visible examples of readerly engagement with Rush lyrics, providing a way of engaging deeply with Rush's repertoire entirely outside the musicianly realm. It is also telling that, although none of Rush's publicly acknowledged musical influences were female, Peart's literary interests have included women such as Camille Paglia and Ayn Rand.

In spite of its connotations of intelligent, active engagement, readerly fandom is represented in an ambivalent way in internet fan communities, and the band members themselves discuss it surprisingly infrequently. Readerly publications, like Price's book or Leonard Roberto's *A Simple*

Kind of Mirror: The Lyrical Vision of Rush, are monologues, interpretations of Rush songs that arise from private, individual reflection.[48] In public internet forums, readerly interpretation appears restricted; lively dialogues about meanings, symbolism, the political significance of songs, and flights of subjective interpretation, which one might expect in such an interpretive community, seem rather muted. There are several reasons for this. First, there is a strong allegiance among fans to the romantic idea of auteurship, meaning that Peart's status as author invests his interpretations with an authority that outweighs those of any fan, however well expressed. Subjective readings of songs are considered subordinate to Peart's public statements about his lyrics. As Hills notes, this is a common feature of cult fandom, where a recuperated, auteur-centered romanticism is far more prevalent than any kind of freely subjective, postmodern interpretive stance.[49]

Peart's own rhetoric in interviews serves to protect this sort of auteurship. Discussions of his role as lyricist emphasize his literary influences,[50] his inspirations for specific songs, and his attitudes toward his craft.[51] When he addresses fan interpretation, it is often to discredit what he sees as excessive. Peart once quipped that Rush could start a "flake of the week club" based on some of the lyric interpretations fans write down and mail to the group, some of which had pseudo-religious connotations.[52] No doubt some of Peart's discomfort stems from fans finding meanings he could never have foreseen in his songs and which substantially contradict his views. Peart told the *Chicago Tribune*'s Lynn Van Matre, "People extract amazing interpretations out of things. Someone told me one of my songs was about me going to search for God and finding Him. Yeah, right. Sure." He elaborated: "There's a good portion of our audience, just like any other group of people, that we simply have no point of relationship with, and you just have to accept that. But then there's the ideal fan, the person who appreciates every move we make and knows if we make a mistake and acts as kind of a built-in judge factor. Those are the people we write our songs for."[53] Even for Peart the lyricist, then, it seemed that he found more connection with musicianly fans than with those paying close attention to his words. This is consistent with most Rush interviews where fandom is broached; the band members welcome feedback regarding their musicianship, but lyric reception is seldom discussed the same way. Although literary meaning is neither fixed nor limited to the author's intention, Peart is careful not to license what he sees as errant interpretations of his lyrics. His comments here also reveal an interesting split in his perception of Rush fandom in the early 1980s. The musicianly audience member represents the ideal fan, an educated, discerning observer. The reader/interpreter, even if not entirely dismissed, is simply tolerated as a secondary fan whose literary analysis is open to suspicion.

Although not all Rush fans on internet forums acknowledge or accept Peart's claims to ultimate interpretive authority, there are numerous fans who do and who quickly counter the personal takes that overly creative listeners post there. Some fan sites, like *The Rush FAQ,* where song themes are catalogued, warn potential fan contributors that the webmaster is "not interested in your pet theories" about song topics, messages, or symbolism.[54] All contributions to this site are required to be supported by references to Peart's own statements, thus maintaining a patina of objectivity while reinforcing Peart's attempt to control his work. This reflects patterns observed by Derek Johnson in his study of fandom, where he notes that producers or auteurs of popular culture find ways of limiting or preventing fans from publicly contesting authorial control over their material's meanings.[55] But the fact that some fans are also complicit in this suggests a desire to protect the semantic meanings of the songs from something—perhaps overinterpretation, misreading, or even criticism.

Peart's unease about overtly readerly fans may also reflect an ambivalence about the band's status as an object of cult fandom. This is not simply a matter of fans reading too much into the songs, but of fans investing too much of themselves in their fandom. More than admirers or enthusiasts, fan cults are marked by high degrees of personal involvement and depths of identification with a text or celebrity that are intensely felt and long-lived. The band members' own stated opinions diverge with regard to their perception of Rush's cult audience. In a number of interviews, Geddy Lee has credited the band's ultra-loyal cult following with facilitating Rush's creative freedom and career longevity.[56] He has generally seemed at ease with, even approving of, Rush's audience being characterized as a cult following. Peart's ambivalence here is somewhat ironic, given the role he has played in helping to create this type of fandom. His vigorous cultivation of virtuosity—evidenced in his becoming a contender for the title of "best rock drummer" by the early 1980s—inevitably drew drummer-fans seeing him as a larger-than-life hero. His lyrics and song concepts—the grand ideological statements, the epic narratives, the metaphysical topics, uses of science fiction and fantasy—were perfect ingredients for the creation of "cult texts." Few casual fans are drawn to such things. Moreover, Rush could attract fans from existing sci-fi cults by writing pieces such as "2112," "The Twilight Zone," and "Cygnus X-1," and its Rand-influenced songs and libertarian-inflected lyrics also drew on existing cult texts. Indeed, Rand's Objectivist movement has been analyzed as a secular cult, drawing a following almost religiously devoted to her highly ideological literature.[57] As Hills theorizes, cult followings do not develop randomly; there are specific kinds of texts that tend to draw such audiences, texts typically associated with charismatic or visionary auteurs, sometimes involving the creation of alternative worlds and/or open-ended narratives.[58] It is not simply that Rush (especially in the years leading up to its commercial peak) provided such texts, but that it also referenced musical, literary, cinematic, and televisual genres that include well-known cult texts, from heavy metal and prog-rock to Tolkien and Rand to Rod Serling's *Twilight Zone*. Rush was nothing if not poised to accrue a cult fan base, both musicianly and readerly.

In fan discussion forums, the cultish dimension of Rush fandom is represented in a variety of ways, both critical and affirmative. One representation is the "fanboy" or "fanboi," an unflattering stereotype of the male adolescent who is naively enthusiastic, extreme in his views, and intolerant of criticism. Some internet forum members use the term to upbraid those who flame any statement even mildly critical of Rush. The fanboy is considered to possess an undesirable aesthetic disposition because he seems to lack the detached, critical distance so broadly important to a mature masculine and middle-class identity. It may even be seen as an emasculating term, denoting a fandom perilously close to stereotypical images of preteen girls screaming for Elvis, the Beatles, George Michael, or the Backstreet Boys, a perfect opposite to male rock fan self-perceptions. In this sense, the fanboy is an insult particular to male fans, and is also unseemly for middle-class fans, who presumably should have a more disinterested, critical, and sober appreciation of their choice of popular culture. At the same time, some fans will characterize themselves as fanboys, partly to poke fun at themselves. Such self-ridicule serves a defensive purpose: the cult fanatic is already laughing at himself, taking Rush very seriously, but not taking his own fandom seriously, thereby disarming any mockery from others. As is common in many fan communities, an ironic posture provides a suitable disguise for an otherwise serious (and perhaps embarrassing) level of cult fandom.

But cult fandom is also represented in a more positive way as a community of shared interests and knowledge. In this sense, the cult is a privileged group of initiates or insiders whose fandom coalesces around something putatively esoteric or hidden from the mainstream. This seems to resurrect the issue described in chapter 3, where Rush tries to mark itself as separate from popular music's commercial mainstream, even as the band sells millions of albums and performs in massive arenas. But cult fandom, as a representation of fandom, goes a step further by creating a category of fan that is in some sense more knowledgeable, devoted, and authentic than others. For the cult fan, it does not really matter that Rush has a mass audience so long as there is a relatively small hardcore of aficionados who understand Rush in a way that the masses don't. Again, this is an ideological effect of rock extending far beyond Rush, but Hills notes further that fandom across the media spectrum (music, TV, literature, film) is both implicated in the commercial entertainment industry and acts outside of it. That is, fans are part of the commodity-exchange economy of the culture industry, but there is also a "use value" associated with what fans consume that is mostly out of the industry's provenance and control.[59] In cult fandom, such usage assumes an intensity and specificity that may cast it as deviant consumer behavior, but this is easily turned to the fans' own purposes in making their fandom feel exclusive. The cult fan community becomes an "us" who share knowledge which "they" (softshell fans, non-fans, critics, the industry) do not understand.[60] But even then, cult fandoms are not necessarily unified, and they may split into factions. Moreover, there are disagreements and debates over what exactly is the object of cult fandom. For example, among Rush's fandom, there are long-lived struggles over the issue of repertoire or canon: hardcore fans are split about the status of "old Rush" versus "new Rush," with some insisting that the group lost its creative spark at some point in its career. When that moment of lost vitality occurred is itself up for debate, but the *Signals* album (1982) is an important fault line, since Rush's emphasis on its original heavy metal and progressive influences began declining at that point. Other fans insist that the entire canon (all eighteen studio albums) has roughly equal aesthetic merit, notwithstanding a few unimportant lapses and failed experiments.

Another common representation that connotes cult fandom is the Rush fan as geek or nerd. In questionnaires, several fans openly admit that Rush produces "geek rock" with a significant constituency who might be de-scribed in such terms. One male respondent described Rush's audience as comprising "a million geeks, and that includes me," while a teenage female respondent described Rush's audience as mostly males "who are a slight bit geeky but also very worldly and smart." While this descriptor seems whimsical, it is also one of the most revealing representations of Rush fandom because it spotlights the social terrain on which a certain kind of Rush fandom is situated. In white suburbia, the nerd or geek pro-vides a good example of an insider-Other,[61] someone whose social litany (white and/or male, probably middle-class) is entirely hegemonic, but who nevertheless feels relegated to the margins of their peer group as a misfit. Through connotations of intelligence, the geek is favorably positioned for acquiring educational capital, and the assumed career prospects for geeks include non-manual, mind-oriented occupations that are highly skilled and white-collar. Professions such as information technology, science, mathematics, architecture, and engineering (and in some cases music) that require highly technical skill sets are most frequently associated with geek culture. Despite this, the jobs, academic interests, and leisure pursuits affiliated with the geek are considered strange, dull, or unseemly to the wider suburban peer group. Obsessive or excessive engagement with leisure pursuits is often portrayed as geek behavior, making extreme musicianly or readerly Rush fandom appear similar to the zealous *Star Trek* fan, the hardcore Dungeons and Dragons player, or the obsessive *Rocky Horror Picture Show* enthusiast.

The geek or nerd is typically a kind of white male identity, but it is a socially stigmatized one. In her study of nerd culture, Mary Bucholtz observes that nerds occupy a social category of marked rather than unmarked whiteness. She notes that normative, unmarked whiteness in American youth culture is constructed around a paradigm of "cool," where types of slang, music, comportment, and fashion which have African American origins are foundational, even if those cultural features have been so fully appropriated by whites that they are no longer recognized as black.[62] Bucholtz also finds that nerds typically disrupt this kind of normative whiteness by refusing to take part in most of these youth culture trends. Furthermore, nerds tend to speak in "Superstandard English," a dialect comprising "lexical formality, carefully articulated phonological forms, and prescriptively standard grammar," which normally exists more as a written dialect than a spoken one. This, together with a tendency to dress in conservative or unfashionable clothes and maintain a stiff, low-affect demeanor, leads geeks or nerds to be seen by their peers as "too white" or "hyperwhite."[63] In this respect, their ethnicity is marked and seen as excessive or abnormal. It is not surprising, then, that some Rush fans who acknowledge a geek component to the band's audience also flag its predominating whiteness. One respondent, paralleling Bucholtz, wrote, "Actually, we geeks were too cool for cool. And we're so, so very white, but not without soul."

The Rush fan as geek, then, is a representation implicated in many of this book's themes. As an insider-Other, this kind of fan embodies individualism. The misunderstood outcast-as-hero, reappearing frequently in Rush's repertoire, is easily read as an individualistic revenge fantasy, where the nerd is validated and glorified despite past social castigation.[64] The potential for the geek to withdraw into technical, virtual, or imaginary worlds (whether of fantasy, musicianship, ideology, or technology) is a form of escapism from the social world. The technical yet creative vocations associated with the geek are pursued in terms that favorably compare with the sorts of professionalism and occupational autonomy valued in Rush's musical career. Finally, there is a remarkable congruence between the geek and middle-class identity at large. Both identities are bound up in a kind of shame derived from being socially unremarkable, but both identities connote similar virtues associated with hard work, upward mobility, and intellectual vigor.

There are other representations of the audience that the band members and their fans discuss relatively infrequently. Casual fans, who may have been interested in the band for only an album or two, were important audience members in terms of beefing up Rush's album sales and raising its profile during the height of its commercial success in the early 1980s. Rush's recent North American concert tours (2002–2008), with attendance figures holding steady while album sales dwindled, suggest that casual fans, in some cases classic rock fans who gravitate toward bands of Rush's generation, are important substratum audience members who help keep the entire Rush enterprise operating in the new millennium as a large-venue, arena-touring group.

6

"Scoffing at the Wise?"

Rush, Rock Criticism, and the Middlebrow

ccording to conventional wisdom, Rush was never a critic's band. The group's biographers have frequently used the putative indifference and hostility of rock critics as a dramatic contrast with Rush's commercial success and longevity.[1] Rock journalists themselves have also associated Rush with an abiding lack of critical acclaim. As far back as 1977, Max Thaler in *Circus* magazine framed Rush's then-recent breakthrough as "not bad for a band that had no critical respect for about four long years, despite ever-enlarging audiences and record-buying support. . . . Simply, Rush has never been appreciated by the critics, and none of their albums qualify as 'critics' choices.' Their concerts are likewise either misconstrued or misjudged by most critics despite public reactions to the contrary."[2] In

1980, *Rolling Stone*'s David Fricke began his review of Rush's *Permanent Waves* by stating, "It's easy to criticize what you don't understand, which at least partly explains why Canadian power trio Rush have suffered so much at the hands of rock journalists since the band's debut album in 1974."[3] And again in the mid-1990s, Bob Mack set up his double review of Rush's *Test for Echo* and Porno for Pyro's *Good God's Urge* by observing how the critics beat up on Rush for its intellectually pretentious lyrics and Geddy Lee's abrasive vocals while at the same time praising alternative rock groups like the Pyros for possessing exactly the same traits.[4]

Neil Peart once puzzled over the group's reputation as "the band that's always being dumped on," noting that Rush managed to receive its share of positive press,[5] and during my 2001 interview with Alex Lifeson, the guitarist noted, "I always thought we had a good relationship with the press."[6] In my research into Rush's critical reception, I have found that, indeed, Rush's reputation as "the band critics love to hate" is inflated and oversold. Across the group's thirty-year career, Rush's reception from *Rolling Stone*–type critics such as Michael Bloom, John Rockwell, Jon Pareles, and Michael Azzerad might be described as lukewarm, respectful of Rush's technical virtues as musicians but critical of its songwriting and lyrics. Crushingly bad reviews were not unheard of, but reviews for other progressive rock bands like Genesis, Queen, or Emerson, Lake, and Palmer were frequently more scathing. Critics only occasionally used the stereotypical dismissal of heavy metal and progressive rock as "pretentious, yet stupid" to describe Rush, and a large number of reviewers regarded the band as one that aimed high even if it sometimes came up short. What is interesting is that in nearly every case, regardless of how good or bad the review was, critics writing for *Rolling Stone* and similar periodicals established a marked aesthetic distance from Rush and the rock genres they invoked. Even when reviews of Rush were good, such as those by David Fricke or Bob Mack, they tended to place Rush outside the critics' sphere of "valid rock"; for better or worse, Rush's image in the press was indelibly marked as noncanonical.

Perceived critical dismissal has stoked outrage among Rush fans for some years. *Rolling Stone*, the highest-profile rock publication in North

America, is the focus of a lot of Rush fan discontent, since its critics are key figures in nominating and inducting artists into the Rock and Roll Hall of Fame in Cleveland. Rush has never received a nomination, and in 2000, critic David Wild confirmed that Rush lacked the acclaim necessary to make such an honor imminent. Moreover, Rush has never been featured on the cover of *Rolling Stone,* which traditionally ensures canonical status in the rock 'n' roll firmament.[7] One of the most popular Rush fan sites, *The National Midnight Star,* circulated a fan petition to get Rush inducted into the Rock and Roll Hall of Fame during the late 1990s; an angry thread emerged on *The Rush Interactive Network* in August 2000 calling for a boycott of *Rolling Stone* when that year's nominees were announced. Fans bitter about *Rolling Stone* ignoring Rush are at least tacitly acknowledging the symbolic value of being the lead feature in this magazine. As discussed in chapter 3, fans considered Rush's musical style to represent elite artistry and their appreciation of the band to reflect their own connoisseurship; the reviews in *Rolling Stone* and similar publications, even at their best, usually issued praise too thin to satisfy the fans.

This chapter explores Rush's apparent failure to merit canonicity in the eyes of American rock critics. The topic fruitfully contrasts with my discussion of Rush fandom because rock criticism generally comes from outsiders (i.e., non-fans) who are nevertheless dedicated, middle-class rock enthusiasts. Moreover, critics both explicitly and tacitly reveal conflicted aspects of class identity when they write about topics like Rush or progressive rock.

Rush's critical reception, summarized in brief, is middle-class rock dismissed by middle-class critics for being too middling. As always, the middle position is something to be escaped, negated, or transcended. *Rolling Stone*–style rock criticism is a genre of writing that models itself on a kind of hip intellectuality: it rhetorically embraces grass-roots, black, and working-class popular culture, but it self-consciously cultivates the educated, critical register of twentieth-century American high-culture *literati*. In doing so, I argue, it reproduces the tripartite cultural model commonly associated with modernism, with its highbrow, middlebrow, and lowbrow levels. On the one hand, rock criticism tends to assign value to artists who present a lowbrow, lo-fi, or working-class sensibility (the Ramones, Nirvana, Iggy Pop), and on the other hand, to artists who present a particular kind of clever and ironic intellectuality (Morrissey, David Bowie, Roxy Music, Bob Dylan). Though Rush, drawing on tendencies from progressive rock, gestures toward high culture in a number of ways, the group does not epitomize the kind of intellectuality that rock critics typically value. The same is true of Rush's approach to "lowbrow" hard rock: it is too complex and tightly rehearsed to provide the kind of thrill critics admire in the reckless abandon of Iggy Pop, in the artfully frenetic blur of early Hüsker Dü, or in the barroom swagger of AC/DC. As always, Rush is somewhere in the middle, and we can learn something about middle-class cultural tensions by looking at the characteristics of Rush's critical reception.

The doubt about Rush's canonicity says much about the power and authority of the *Rolling Stone* school of American rock criticism. After all, why should recognition from these critics matter? By other measures, Rush has enough acclaim to make a case for its canonicity. The various musician's magazines—their writers as well as their readership—have provided plenty of accolades, and Rush's perennially strong showings in reader's polls show a continuing popularity among amateur and professional musicians. With respect to the music business, Rush's coverage in *Billboard*, the industry's American trade publication, was almost always favorable. All the *Billboard* album reviews and most concert reviews were positive, and Rush was flagged as a "good risk" early in its career; the band was regarded as a stalwart, blue-chip rock band that rarely disappointed commercially in its later years.[8] The Recording Industry Association of America (RIAA) issued nineteen consecutive gold or platinum album awards to Rush, among the longest series of such awards in rock history, just behind the Beatles, Elvis Presley, the Rolling Stones, and Kiss.[9] In 1997, the Canadian government acknowledged Rush's contribution to culture by making them the first rock band to receive the Order of Canada, a prestigious award more commonly given to groundbreaking scientists, authors, and noted politicians.

Despite all this, bands and artists that lack acclaim in certain critical circles are not typically considered canonical. American rock critics who write for *Rolling Stone, Musician, Creem, Spin,* the now-defunct *Crawdaddy,* and the music columns in the *Village Voice* have attained a certain authority as tastemakers, mythologizers, and essayists that is difficult to dismiss. Though some of us who don't share their taste may rue this fact, there is no denying that these critics have become rock's intelligentsia, and their writings have been important in enhancing the cultural prestige of rock. As Bernard Gendron observes, "Critical approval, respect, canonization—all these are desirable goods even for those primarily occupied with commercial success. Early careers are kept alive by critical acclaim before the economic returns can set in, and the prospects for career longevity are certainly enhanced by canonization."[10] Moreover, as writers of popular music's postwar history, they are in a position to influence what will be remembered about rock in the coming years and what will be excluded.[11]

In order to understand critics' responses to Rush, I should first give some background on the cultural ideas and aesthetics mobilized by rock critics. American rock journalism emerged in the 1960s as a literary genre whose principal role was not simply to report to its readership what was good and bad in contemporary popular music, but to articulate what the music meant culturally. Value and meaning are, of course, culturally relative, and rock criticism developed particular points of reference in explaining rock's significance. Critics were especially concerned with arguing for rock's cultural importance and aesthetic legitimacy. Since many rock critics were university educated, many ideas from literary criticism filtered into rock critics' writing, giving it a modernist bent early on (and a postmodernist one later). Glenn Pillsbury explains clearly rock criticism's modernist presumptions, citing Ralph Gleason's equation of rock with social and aesthetic revolution, *Oracle* magazine (a San Francisco countercultural publication) on rock's political and intellectual seriousness, Robert Christgau on placing rock in the "high" position on the high/low culture divide, and Lester Bangs on newness, originality, authenticity, and transcendence as important aesthetic values in rock.[12] Keith Negus explains that aesthetics like these were applied to rock at exactly the moment when middle-class, educated young people appropriated rock music for their own purposes, and thus their means of legitimizing the music came through "an aesthetic vocabulary derived from an appreciation of 'high culture.'"[13] This process of legitimizing rock music not only involved making it look favorable according to modernist precepts, but also making its appeal seem exclusive in a number of ways. As Simon Frith describes it, rock criticism makes rock fandom seem like an exclusive club, with the journalism helping to create a hip community of listeners "in the know": "For most rock critics, then, the issue in the end isn't so much representing music to the public (the public to the musician) as creating a knowing community, orchestrating a collusion between selected musicians and an equally select part of the public—select in its superiority to the ordinary, undiscriminating pop consumer."[14] Rock criticism thus makes it feel as if the consumption and appreciation of select artists and albums provide access to an elite, alternative taste public, and the intelligent, evocative descriptions provided by rock journalism delineate and confirm this form of high taste. This mirrors what Bourdieu has shown in the wider arena of Western culture: that high culture's value is based, in part, on its rarity and the way in which access to that culture is restricted. But it does not matter if rock fandom is neither rare nor exclusive as long as it feels as if it is.

Yet rock critics could never simply make a case that rock was a manifestation of high modernism. Rock was, of course, a form of popular culture, based on working-class and black musical forms, and its aesthetics also embraced such things as immediacy, simplicity, folk populism, energy, and rhythmic (read: bodily) vitality. Rock criticism needed to embrace these things as well, and it drew on literary and critical precedents in order to do so. Jazz criticism, which worked to legitimize and intellectualize a once-popular, disreputable, and working-class dance-based music, provided one such model. The literature that grew up around the American subculture known as the Beats provided another resource of aesthetic ideas, in which an intellectualized, modernist posture was realized through a largely white, middle-class appropriation of features from black, bohemian, and underclass cultures. For example, the Beat poetry of writers like Allen Ginsberg captured at once the disjuncture and dissonance of modernism while plying it to the rhythms of jazz or African drumming. Norman Mailer's famous 1957 essay, "The White Negro," acted as a succinct summary of the views of the Beat generation (and later the counterculture), representing whites who rebelled against "straight" American society by imitating African American lifestyles. Mailer admonished young white Americans to "give up 'the sophisticated inhibitions of civilization,' to live in the moment, to follow the body and not the mind, 'to divorce oneself from society.'"[15] Though ostensibly taking an anti-intellectual stance, Mailer's essay was nothing if not a sophisticated theoretical exploration of the critical potential his representation of black masculinity could have for radical white aesthetes. A byproduct of the intellectualization of jazz and rock was a reinscription and valorization of the mythic otherness of the black underclass; appropriated blackness was at once a resource for "hip" whites to reconnect with the body and a way to take up a position critical of the Beats' and hippies' own white, middle-class roots by reimagining themselves as both working class and steeped in African American culture. Although this posture validated African American culture in one sense, it also essentialized it and reconfirmed some white American views of blacks as body-centered, unintellectual, and primitive.[16] Drawing from this Beat tradition, rock criticism came to use terms such as "instinctual," "primitive," "brutal," and sometimes even "stupid" as accolades praising the most stripped-down and raw examples of rock music.[17]

By merging modernism with vernacular culture, rock criticism cultivated an aesthetic that validated both the highbrow and the lowbrow. Critic Simon Reynolds, whose writings bristle with highbrow references from De Certeau, Kristeva, Foucault, and Barthes, comments on the highbrow-lowbrow alliance in rock criticism: "It stems from the schizoid position that rock critics occupy: as cultured, educated individuals who nonetheless love what the parent culture stigmatizes as juvenile, trivial and empty. Burning with an inferiority complex toward the 'high' culture in whose discourse they themselves are fluent, their overweening concern is to validate pop culture. This they have done by bringing to bear on it all the gamut of 'high' culture tools and terms."[18] The middle-class rock critic, then, is primarily interested in the "other"—the highbrow other and the lowbrow other. The obverse of this can be found in the objections made to rock which is most assertively "middle class," especially progressive rock. Prog-rock musicians are close to most rock critics in terms of social class and educational level, yet critical opinion of this genre has been ambivalent to say the least. Dave Marsh, in a 1977 *Rolling Stone* review of albums by Genesis, Queen, and Starcastle, overtly proclaims the impact of social class on critics' judgments of progressive rock. Marsh confirms that such groups are not normally critics' choices, and he states that he finds this music cold and empty in comparison to other forms of rock. In the review, titled "Rock's Icy Edge," Marsh observes that "what really leads to charges of iciness is . . . a kind of *class-based cult of musicianship, which is truly arrogant because it refuses to articulate just what moods its complex structures are meant to evoke. Eclecticism is determinedly middle-class*—thus, the general obsession with synthesizers and other gadgets, the devotion to science fiction and pop mysticism and, in the case of Genesis, a ruinous lyrical preoccupation with *half-digested English literature courses.*"[19] The review is not a total dismissal; Marsh goes on to temper his critique by admitting that progressive rock lyrics are really no more pretentious and obfuscatory than some of Joni Mitchell's or Elton John's. He even states that Genesis, "however haughty they may be about it, however short of the mark they may fall," is trying to accomplish something musically worthwhile; it's just that "the producers of successful product rather than failed art are the ones I am more comfortable listening to."[20] Marsh makes it clear that the unambiguously middle-class strains of progressive rock are outside the critic's aesthetic framework. The dichotomy he sets up is a revealing one: he prefers "successful product" (presumably, good works of mass culture that do not pretend to be anything else) to "failed art" (a typical epithet applied to middlebrow fare which attempts to elevate mass culture to artistic status).

In American rock criticism, reviews of Rush varied widely. This incon-sistency, in and of itself, is not of great import, but the roots of it reveal much about how bands like Rush represent a middlebrow cultural layer which does not converge neatly with critic's expectations of canonical rock. Consider, for example, how rock critics responded to Rush's lyrics. Neil Peart's writing was always marked by highbrow aspirations, making refer-ences to the likes of Shakespeare, Hemingway, and T. S. Eliot, exploring philosophical and metaphysical concepts and, especially after 1980, main-taining a tone of impersonal, analytical detachment in a number of songs. A very small minority of critics took this at face value and regarded Rush as one of the "smarter" bands on the rock scene. Bob Mack, for example, writing in the *Village Voice,* declared Rush's lyrics "unbeatable," with an intelligence unmatched by anything in the critics' rock canon.[21] For *Roll-ing Stone's* David Fricke, Rush's attempts to invoke the "highbrow" in its songs in the early 1980s were a positive feature, for "despite their occasional over-reach, [the lyrics] are still several refreshing steps above the moronic machismo and half-baked mysticism of many hard-rock airs."[22] Among positive reviews, Fricke's comments are representative; Rush's lyrics are positioned above the most crass of the lowbrow, but they are not usually compared with the poetic genius of Bob Dylan, Joni Mitchell, or Leonard Cohen. Jon Pareles's 1981 review of the live album *Exit . . . Stage Left* car-ries a similar tenor: "Rush have been unfairly maligned as just another barnstorming heavy metal act, fit only to vibrate arena walls. Actually, the group is a lot more interesting than cock-rockers like Van Halen or AC/DC, and is far less compromised than Journey or Styx."[23] Pareles notes that Rush fulfills a certain demand for powerful "virtuosic, storytelling, philos-ophizing" rock for the audience once served by Yes, Genesis, and Kansas, but his tone in describing Rush's lyrics is abrupt and dismissive enough to make it clear that he does not take them very seriously. For Pareles, Rush reaches for intellectual weightiness, but its songs can be briefly and glibly summarized as "pessimistic screeds suggest[ing] that in the upcoming apocalypse, every-man-for-himself will turn into stomp-the-other-guy," no analytical finesse required.

Other critics heard Rush's lyrics as false attempts to dress up rock in mock intellectual profundity. For Michael Eck of the *Albany Times,* Rush's "thinking person's rock band" aura was nothing more than a facade: "Rush has always flown a banner of intelligentsia amidst the rest of the rock 'n' roll blockheads; but the fact that drummer/wordsmith Neil Peart borrows every lyric he writes from someone else's book only proves that he's got a library card, not a high I.Q."[24] Mikel Toombs of the *San Diego Tribune* affirmed that Rush "has lofty aims—where most heavy metal bands don't appear to have cracked open a book (except perhaps a comic book) in years, Rush has apparently digested the collected work of Ayn Rand. Rush is not Rand, though, and its otherwise novel approach comes off as more pretentious than illuminating."[25] For these critics, Rush's intellectual stance is not the result of any significant insight or erudition on the band's part, just the mimicry of well-known literary works.

Evidently, critics found Peart's merits as an intellectual lyricist to be debatable, probably a result of the kind of intellectuality he projected during interviews. He made it clear that he had bookish obsessions, reading voraciously on tour, which underscored his reputation as one of rock's more learned stars and offset the well-known fact that he was a high school dropout who had given up formal education to pursue music well before the end of his teens. The rugged individualism that Peart espoused was actualized, in part, by his reputation as a self-made intellectual, a man whose knowledge and critical faculties were honed outside official educational institutions. Some journalists, finding him well read on a variety of topics, referred to him as a "Renaissance man" and "a rock 'n' roll Bodhisattva."[26] As a writer, Peart contributed to his worldly reputation by publishing book-length travelogues, documenting bicycle and motorcycle trips through West Africa and North America in *The Masked Rider* and *Roadshow: Landscape with Drums.*[27] But as I discuss below, this kind of self-made, individualistic intellectuality was not the kind of highbrow construct that critics typically valued; it was, if anything, seen as a quaint, outmoded gentility far out of step with popular music's more ironic, postmodern trends.

If Rush's sometimes highbrow lyrical allusions left some critics shaking their heads in skepticism, the band's songwriting style, which privileged elaborate forms and left plenty of space for showy musicianship, placed many critics in an equally ambivalent position. Early in Rush's career, critics acknowledged that the band was taking a genre typically associated with the lowbrow (heavy metal) and bringing a more refined sensibility to it. Reviewing *2112* for *Crawdaddy,* Bart Testa wrote, "Rush have at last graduated from mindless power-trio plodding to technoid forensics,"[28] implying that Rush's musicianship took on a precise, studied, almost scientific character, with asymmetrical meters and polyrhythms bringing a mathematical aspect to the music. Though this indicates that Rush was approaching its music with a new intellectuality, Testa dismisses *2112* for not really being rock 'n' roll, labeling its science-fiction theme "lousy reruns of third-rate David Bowie."[29] A year later, John Lamont, reviewing *A Farewell to Kings* in the same magazine, echoed Testa's appraisal: "In six albums, Rush has transformed itself from a rudimentary, noise-oriented power trio into an intricately disguised, ornately embellished, pretentious power trio."[30] Lamont saw Rush's attempts to intellectualize its music as clumsy, but in a quite entertaining way, and he felt that the band's "faults are actually the essence of Rush's charm."[31] These reviews place Rush's style in the mid-to-late 1970s in the middlebrow category, failing as art but succeeding in elevating or gentrifying traditionally lowbrow forms to some degree.

As Rush approached maturity at the end of the 1970s, the esteemed music critic John Rockwell wrote a review of Rush's "Tour of the Hemispheres" show for the *New York Times.* Rush biographer Brian Harrigan highlighted this review because Rockwell "showed respect and a deal of understanding about what Rush were attempting to do. . . . Although the review doesn't exactly rate alongside the conversion of Saul on the road to Tarsus it was the kind of press that Rush needed at the time. They were still being ignored by the radio station people in the States at the time so coverage by well-read and respected journalists was essential."[32] Written for one of the most prestigious newspapers in the United States, the review is an excellent example of a critic making positive statements about Rush while maintaining an aesthetic distance from the band and its milieu. Nevertheless, the review also contains a subtle tinge of condescension, beginning with Rockwell's observation that while post-punk new wave is the primary aesthetic domain of rock critics in the late 1970s, "an occasional dunking in the old wave probably wouldn't harm them any." Rockwell acknowledges that critics have been out of step with the band's fans: "Rush, a Canadian rock trio that was at the Palladium Saturday night (and again last night), no doubt thinks of itself as venturesome, and it can hardly be denied that a big, demonstrative crowd was on hand Saturday. Even if Rush feels a bit miffed about the way it's ignored by the supposed tastemakers of rock, it can take consolation in its audience's enthusiasm." Rockwell also sees Rush as a more intelligent alternative to other hard rock acts: "Basically this is a power trio, meaning lead guitar, bass guitar and drums. Except that 'power trio' implies gonzo assaults of the Ted Nugent variety. Rush is a lot cleverer than that, both in musical style and in the addition of periodic keyboard lines—from Geddy Lee, bassist—and in the complexity of the parts played by Alex Lifeson, guitarist, and Neil Peart, drummer." Nevertheless, Rockwell believes that Rush's emphasis on musicianship does not compensate for what he feels is lacking in its songwriting: "To this taste, the whole thing seems busy and empty in the manner of too many of these souped-up, neo–King Crimson outfits. But there can be no denying that Rush answers some sort of need, and answers it with crisp, professional dispatch."[33]

The review is honest and fair, but Rockwell's observation that Rush "no doubt thinks of itself as venturesome" implies that he does not necessarily agree. His positioning of Rush vis-à-vis the critics indicates that, already in 1979, barely five years into the band's recording career, Rush is not bound for canonicity: the group is part of the "old wave," already obsolete. In the absence of critical acclaim, Rush can only take "consolation" in the enthusiasm of its "big, demonstrative" audience. Mass popularity, however, has little bearing on critical acclaim or canonicity, and carries no special cultural prestige. In fact, because rock criticism absorbed so much from modernism, mass popularity was sometimes (but certainly not always) put forward as evidence of a *lack* of aesthetic merit. As Simon Frith explains,

"'The crowd liked them' remains a standard line in a scathing review. . . . The themes that haunted modernist writers and critics at the beginning of the century (their 'high' cultural concern to be true to their art, to disdain mere entertainment, to resist market forces; their longing for a 'sensitive minority' readership, for what Ezra Pound called 'a party of intelligence') still haunt popular music."[34] Through the late 1970s and 1980s, critics often saw Rush's swelling fan base as a large, faceless, arena-rock audience, not a "sensitive minority." Arena rock audiences seemed to reflect the worst image of suburban North America: there were so many fans of a similar socioeconomic class and ethnic background, it simply did not produce the small, hip, diverse and bohemian community that critics fantasized about. Rockwell did not disparage Rush's audience in this review, but the intention behind his comment on the group's mass popularity is, at best, ambiguous. Finally, Rockwell's observation that "Rush answers some sort of need" implies that the need is not his, and he does not know precisely what that need is. Though Rush is acknowledged as clever and professional, the critic subtly positions himself at a distance from the band and its audience.

The critical posture that I have outlined here is, perhaps, nothing new or surprising. Criticisms of Rush's virtuosity as dazzling yet empty, and its lyrics as overwrought or intellectually pretentious, are of a type that have always haunted progressive rock. Academics sympathetic to progressive rock have reflected, sometimes bitterly, on the genre's critical reception. Musicologists and music theorists—among the most vocal academic defenders of progressive rock—have had difficulty relating to the critics' objections because when they submit the music to conventional musicological and theoretical analysis, progressive rock seems to be among the most pleasingly complex and musically substantial genres of popular music. From the standpoint of theory and musicology, the charges of "musical emptiness" directed at rock musicians who cultivate virtuosity seem unfair or uncomprehending; some academics also argue that lyrics that attend to literary or philosophical matters—or that show "conceptual density," as progressive rock champion Bill Martin phrases it—are not necessarily empty pretension, but may have an honesty and critical potential behind them that the critics have cynically dismissed.[35] Thus, sympathetic academics have struggled to explain the aesthetic distance and displeasure that rock critics have voiced toward this kind of music. In *Rocking the Classics,* Edward Macan insists that the problem is most centrally political, and claims that rock critics have a neo-Marxist agenda; they only privilege music that speaks for an underclass, something progressive rock so clearly did not do.[36] In *Listening to the Future: The Time of Progressive Rock,* Bill Martin suggests, on the one hand, that the critics were seldom musicians themselves, and were therefore incompetent in making their judgments; the musical complexities of progressive rock were simply beyond them.[37] Above all else, Martin bases his reproach of rock criticism on the assumption that these critics were anti-intellectual and were devoted to an orthodox image of rock as an eternally, and in some way redeemingly, lowbrow cultural form. After surveying critics' comments on various progressive rock groups, Martin muses: "I have to wonder if the idea is that a musician who is in danger of developing too much of a musical vocabulary (which is really all that [progressive rock's] virtuosity is about) should take steps to ensure that this does not happen. Perhaps someone on the verge of 'conceptual density' should just stop thinking so much."[38] Martin believes that the critics "have embraced the absurd notion that rock music should only develop so far, and no further."[39] Sociologist Deena Weinstein goes further in chiding the critics for anti-intellectualism: "The rock critics, for the most part, do not attempt to educate the mass audience . . . but instead [pander] to its prejudices. For more elevated analyses of rock music, one needs to seek out subcultural groups that informally, and in 'zines' and online formats, educate one another."[40]

Martin also suggests that the critics upheld racist and classist assumptions about authenticity through their insistence on rock staying close to its black and working-class roots; critics therefore condemned progressive rock bands for failing to do so.[41] Other commentators have picked up on this idea that rock critics were being racist, or engaging in some kind of reverse racial chauvinism, by reacting with displeasure at progressive rock's "whitening" or "Anglicizing" of rock. Macan explains that "the basic premise behind [the critics'] line of thought is the belief that black music is 'authentic' and 'natural' in a way that white music is not. . . . The critics' equation of the blues tradition and 'authenticity' is inherently flawed by a series of simplistic assumptions [and] their criticism of styles such as progressive rock as 'unnatural' and 'inauthentic' cannot be taken at face value."[42] Musicologist John J. Sheinbaum and music theorist Kevin Holm-Hudson echo a similar sentiment, suggesting that rock critics were obsessed with musical purity and rejected progressive rock for its eclecticism and lack of commitment to working-class and black roots.[43] Although I agree that social class is relevant, the idea that the critics were racist is difficult to swallow. Those making such accusations need to explain why progressive rock's growing indifference to the black heritage of rock 'n' roll had less troubling racial implications in the 1970s than the critics' continuing fondness for it.

In any case, as a long-time fan of progressive rock, I am sympathetic with the frustration of these academics over the portrayal of this music as empty, pretentious, and tasteless. But since we are academics using journalism as primary and secondary data on musical reception, I am uneasy about the tenor some of this discussion has taken. There is a fine line between critically interrogating the socially relevant reasons for rock criticism's biases and using our institutional positions of authority to condemn critics for offending us as fans. In one sense, critics are more diverse in their points of view than some of the commentators above allow. Considerable differences, for example, emerge between Chuck Eddy's willful, brash anti-intellectualism, Simon Reynolds's flights of *haute*-postmodern analysis, Richard Meltzer's precocious, irreverent play with the philosophy and aesthetics of rock, and Greil Marcus's keen sense of cultural history so evident in his writings on Elvis, Sly Stone, and the Sex Pistols.[44]

These writers frame their criticisms of progressive rock with the issue of believability: much of the time, the critics seemed to regard progressive rock as pretentious, striving for a high register of intellectual and musical complexity, but failing to reach it convincingly. In their eyes, progressive rock claimed to be more than it really was in terms of its artistic merit, intellectuality, profundity, and complexity. But most important, there is a subtext of middle-class shame at work here: many critics recoiled at progressive rock's "gentrification" of popular music because, in their view, it looked like an embarrassing failure. It tamed and watered down the visceral vitality that critics cherished in earlier styles of rock; but worse, for all its pretensions to intellectuality or gentility, it looked like nothing that would ever be taken seriously by the highbrow establishment. Progressive rock was a middlebrow compromise between highbrow and lowbrow culture, and the middlebrow is notoriously difficult to celebrate: like the middle class itself, it has a history of being seen as safe, unsexy, and second-rate. If we look briefly at the history of middlebrow culture and its reception in America, we get a better sense of the wider cultural background in which rock critics wrote.

According to Joan Shelley Rubin's *The Making of Middlebrow Culture*, one of the few book-length histories of the topic, the middlebrow emerged in the early part of the twentieth century in North America as a response to the decline of genteel nineteenth-century culture and the growth of the mass media. As highbrow modernism became increasingly esoteric, beyond the comprehension of all but a tiny cultural elite, the desire for cultural forms that retained elevated (and elevating) elements of old high culture, purveyed in an accessible form, resulted in the products of an expanding middlebrow culture: digest reductions of canonical literary works, popular science books and magazines, light orchestral fare, and, as television gained prominence, quiz shows and popularized, made-for-TV mediations of high cultural works.[45] Consumption of this material allowed North Americans of middling education and some degree of social mobility to feel "cultured," conversant with the West's great works of art and thought. It provided an alternative to the "lowbrow" fare carried almost ubiquitously in the mass media, even though middlebrow culture was also carried through the same media.

North American intellectuals responded to the proliferation of middlebrow culture with indignation and derision. Digest introductions to works of Plato, Shakespeare, or Beethoven were considered watered-down versions of high culture, and the attempt to raise the respectability of low culture forms tasteless bowdlerization. In the diatribes of author Virginia Woolf or cultural critic Dwight Macdonald, the middlebrow appears as a singularly virulent threat to the health of America's cultural development. As Macdonald encapsulates the highbrow intellectual distrust of middlebrow culture: "The danger to High Culture is not so much from mass culture as from a peculiar hybrid bred from the latter's unnatural intercourse with the former. A whole middle culture has come into existence and threatens to absorb both its parents. This intermediate form—let us call it midcult . . . tries to have it both ways: it pretends to respect the standards of High Culture while in fact it waters them down and vulgarizes them."[46]

Some intellectuals were prepared to grant low culture a modicum of respect while naming the middlebrow as a genuine threat to all that is honest and decent. For example, Virginia Woolf, proudly describing herself as a "highbrow," wrote of her respect for lowbrows, praising their non-pretension and practicality, while she vented her disgust with proponents of the middlebrow and their misplaced missionary zeal in trying to raise the intellectual and cultural sophistication of lowbrow culture.[47] What ruffled the feathers of the emerging American intellectual elite about the middlebrow were the false promises it made about bringing its consumers a higher level of cultural competence. The literature, art, and music purveyed to middlebrow consumers was seen as a parochial, old-fashioned, and nonthreatening image of high culture, with all risky experimentalism carefully avoided. Middlebrow culture, in their estimation, was a safe middle ground. The outer fringes of culture—both the modernist avant-garde and the enlivening rhythms and practices of low culture—were where the real excitement was; what lay in between was, in Macdonald's famous phrase, a "tepid ooze."[48] Indeed, as historian James Gilbert observes, middlebrow culture in America "has not so much been ignored as dismissed as white noise that blurs the more exciting rhythms and melodies of mass and elite culture."[49] According to these accounts, the middlebrow is symbolically the suburbia of culture, the middling space that many may inhabit but which commands no attention.

These elitist attitudes toward the middlebrow echo in revealing ways in rock criticism, and are thus relevant for understanding the critical reception of Rush and much progressive rock. This is illustrated in a particularly pithy and scathing review of Rush's *A Farewell to Kings* by Robert Christgau in the *Village Voice*. He clearly regarded the band as an unwelcome example of middlebrow culture: "Rush," he wrote, is "the most obnoxious band currently making a killing on the zonked teen circuit. Not to be confused with [Montreal-based blues-rock group] Mahogany Rush, who at least spares us the reactionary gentility."[50] By "reactionary gentility" Christgau refers to Rush's many allusions to old high culture on the album, including a song based on Samuel Taylor Coleridge's "Kubla Khan" ("Xanadu"), the baroque-style guitar and keyboard interlude on the title track, a song named after a sixteenth-century vocal genre ("Madrigal"), as well as the orchestral percussion used liberally throughout the record (orchestra bells, tubular bells, tympani, and bell trees). Christgau levels at Rush the two biggest, paradoxical complaints typically made against middlebrow culture: it attracts a large mass audience as if it were tripe aimed at the lowest common denominator, yet tries to flatter that audience's "refined" taste and intelligence by deploying old-fashioned, high-culture influences. This paradox mirrors almost exactly what Gilbert notes about the reception of middlebrow culture at large:

> For a nation [the United States] that continuously refers to itself as middle class, meaning everyone except a fringe of wealthy and poor at either extreme, it is curious that middle-class culture—or better—middlebrow culture—rests so uneasily in a no-man's land between mass and elite culture, disparaged by the devotees of both. Curious too is its paradoxical reputation as pretentious as well as excessively democratic. In part, this is the result of semantics, aspirations and upward mobility. While few Americans admit to being working class, they still live in a world of homogenized consumer culture which retains a strong suspicion of genteel culture. Hence a "middle class" that still retains its mass culture prefer-

ences and a middlebrow culture that has few defenders. Perhaps this is why historians of literature and culture have avoided serious discussion of the middlebrow world while paying far more attention to mass culture, consumerism and Hollywood on the one hand, and the exploits of literary rebels and undaunted artists on the other.[51]

This brings us to the central issue of this chapter. American rock critics, in large proportion, were professional writers; most were white, educated, and middle class. Yet they found themselves uneasy about rock music that most closely resembled their own social and educational position. If it would be fair to call the music of Rush, Genesis, and other progressive rock bands "determinedly middle class," and "middlebrow" insofar as they mediated high literature and highbrow concert music for a mass audience, then perhaps the distance rock critics articulated from them reveal, in part, an anxiety about belonging to a middling educational, social, and occupational position. As the critics aligned themselves with the outer extremes—highbrow aesthetics and lowbrow culture—they quite pointedly distanced themselves from anything suggestive of a middlebrow position.

To maintain this distance, the critics developed very different "highbrow" reference points from progressive rock musicians, as well as different ideas about how rock should be intellectualized. With its extended forms, metrical experiments, virtuosity, and advanced harmonic and modal constructs, progressive musicians tried to intellectualize rock from the standpoint of production; rock critics, by adopting a highbrow posture in their appreciation of lowbrow music, tried to intellectualize rock's consumption. Thus, critics were not interested in complexity from a musician's standpoint; instead, they injected their own complexities into their writing on reputedly simple music. Rock criticism also praised particular kinds of highbrow interpolations into rock, but these were of a very different order than those used most often by progressive rock. Critics tended to praise rock that drew inspiration from avant-garde art and bohemian literary movements, with a special emphasis on deconstructionist, postmodern, and anti-art ideas. Thus, when Bob Dylan, the Doors, and some punk groups borrowed from

Bertolt Brecht and Arthur Rimbaud, the critical response was positive; similarly, Andy Warhol's toying with the concept of rock culture in his Pop Art spectacle, The Exploding Plastic Inevitable, made Warhol's house band, the Velvet Underground, legendary among critics. As Will Straw observes, critics in the 1970s and 1980s were drawn toward artists whose intellectuality was a function of their distant, ironic, and self-reflexive approach to rock, which "may be said to involve the eroticization and stylization of knowledge through its assimilation into an imagery of competence. There developed in the 1970s a recognizable genre of rock performance (Lou Reed, Patti Smith, Iggy Pop, even, to a lesser extent, Rod Stewart) based on the integration of street wisdom, a certain ironic distance from rock mythology, and in some cases, sexual ambiguity (whose dominant significance was an index of experience)"; such music as described here "involved a significant degree of intellectualization."[52] Straw also observes that critics highly regarded those artists who displayed a self-conscious sense of their place within rock's "archives," a kind of self-reflexivity with respect to rock's history, with artists such as David Bowie, Bruce Springsteen, and Roxy Music standing out in this regard.[53] Bernard Gendron, studying interactions between art and pop, suggests that the lowbrow allegiance rock critics had (which found its most perfect expression through punk rock) was merged with specific "highbrow" aesthetics; thus, "the punk pop aesthetic, which presents itself as being an anti-art aesthetic, functions also as a strongly pro-art aesthetic. Being against art simply meant being against the unmediated appropriation of mainstream art notions and their pretensions into popular music—the pieties of singer-songwriters, the virtuosic convulsions of some heavy metal, and the classical music quotationalism of British art rock."[54] To put it another way, the concept of highbrow rock that emerged in rock critic discourse "was driven by the binary of art/pop, in which each term is held in dynamic tension with the other rather than being absorbed by the other. The tendency [among critics] has been to opt for art that is also pop, to combine art with pop and to disdain any 'pretentious' rock music that borrows indiscriminately from art (e.g., classical music) while losing its pop edge."[55]

While the distinction Gendron describes here is somewhat artificial (after all, how is Yes's borrowing from classical music more "indiscriminate" or "pretentious" than Talking Heads' borrowing from New York's avant-garde art scene?), it does lay bare one key issue: both rock criticism and progressive rock are concerned with highbrow cultural status, but they choose different ways of claiming it. Broadly speaking, many rock critics align themselves with traditions of avant-garde anti-foundationalism, hence the interest in punk interpreted as a late manifestation of Dada,[56] in the Brechtian explorations of ironic artifice in glam rock, or Reynolds's eager comparisons of Baudrillard's and Jameson's postmodern aesthetics with the guitar textures of Sonic Youth and My Bloody Valentine.[57] Progressive rock aligns itself broadly with older traditions of high culture, influenced by Baroque and Romantic music, Shakespeare, William Blake, and Samuel Taylor Coleridge. According to Gendron, critics tended to see such influences as "mainstream art notions," which implies that progressive rock's artistic trajectory was not nearly hip or exclusive enough to count as genuinely highbrow. Progressive rock generally appropriated high culture that is widely recognized as such; the critics preferred music that intersected with high culture that is more exclusive and narrow in terms of public visibility.

Ultimately, however, these ways of claiming cultural prestige were tied to a particular historical moment, one that has largely passed, both for rock critics and musicians like Rush. For this reason, Rush's critical reception provides interesting commentary about how cultural prestige was negotiated during the era when the band was most active. Like the rest of progressive rock and neoclassical heavy metal, Rush came to fame in the final years when a large, middle-class audience sought a style of music that wedded a popular style to genteel aspirations. By the early 1990s, some commentators argue, the last embers of middlebrow culture in North America had dimmed considerably. The game of cultural prestige and hierarchy underwent a shift that led to the decline of the middlebrow, at least as a significant cultural market. In place of the highbrow-middlebrow-lowbrow categories, some cultural critics see the arrival of a "nobrow" culture in which no meaningful distinctions remain between art, commerce, the elite, or the vernacular.[58]

The decline and death of middlebrow culture in North America means that a career like Rush's is unlikely to be repeated. This does not mean that a middlebrow genre like progressive-hard rock has ceased to be an audience niche, but that niche has become much smaller in the past fifteen years. More recent bands that have tried to operate in a similar musical and cultural field—Dream Theater, Tiles, Ozric Tentacles—have not and will likely never attain the heights of commercial success and public visibility that Rush enjoyed during the most productive twenty years of the group's career.

NOTES

Introduction

1. See Theodor Adorno, *Introduction to the Sociology of Music* (1962; New York: Continuum, 1976); C. Wright Mills, *White Collar: The American Middle Classes* (New York: Oxford University Press, 1951).

2. Rita Felski, "Nothing to Declare: Identity, Shame, and the Lower Middle Class," *PMLA* 115 (2000): 41.

3. The members of Rush have been perennial winners in readers' polls in musicians' magazines such as *Guitar, Modern Drummer,* and *Bass Player.* According to Robert Telleria, Rush accrued the third-longest string of gold and platinum albums awarded by the RIAA, behind only the Beatles and the Rolling Stones, and tied with Kiss, as of 2001 (*Rush Tribute: Merely Players* [Kingston, Ont.: Quarry Music Publishers, 2001]: 137). Nevertheless, the Rock and Roll Hall of Fame in Cleveland, whose decision-making body includes a number of prominent American rock critics, has refused several requests to induct Rush on the grounds that the group has not been sufficiently influential.

4. Brian Harrigan, *Rush* (New York: Omnibus Press, 1981); Steve Gett, *Rush: Success under Pressure* (Port Chester: Cherry Lane Books, 1984); Bill Banasiewicz, *Visions: The Official Rush Biography* (New York: Omnibus Press, 1988); Robert Telleria, *Rush Tribute: Merely Players* (Kingston, Ont.: Quarry Music Publishers, 2001); Martin Popoff, *Contents under Pressure: 30 Years of Rush at Home and Away* (Toronto: ECW Press, 2004).

5. William Johnston, telephone interview with the author, November 14, 2001.

6. See Stephen Davis, *Hammer of the Gods* (New York: Ballantine Books, 1985), 142–143; Susan Fast, *In the Houses of the Holy: Led Zeppelin and the Power of Rock Music* (New York: Oxford University Press, 2001), 71–72.

7. Daniel Cavicchi, *Tramps Like Us: Music and Meaning among Springsteen Fans* (New York: Oxford University Press, 1998); Fast, *In the Houses of the Holy;*

William Echard, *Neil Young and the Poetics of Energy* (Bloomington: Indiana University Press, 2005).

8. John Miller Chernoff, *African Rhythm and African Sensibility: Aesthetics and Social Action in African Musical Idioms* (Chicago: University of Chicago Press, 1979).

9. Judith and Anton Becker, "Music as Icon: Power and Meaning in Javanese Gamelan Music," in *The Sign in Music and Literature*, ed. Wendy Steiner (Austin: University of Texas Press, 1981), 215.

10. Adorno, *Introduction to the Sociology of Music*, 25–27.

11. Ibid., 37–38.

12. Ibid., 28.

13. For example, see Richard Middleton, *Studying Popular Music* (Milton Keynes, UK: Open University Press, 1990), 34–63; Keith Negus, *Popular Music in Theory* (Hanover, N.H.: Wesleyan University Press, 1996), 8–12; Simon Frith, *Performing Rites: On the Value of Popular Music* (Cambridge, Mass.: Harvard University Press, 1996), 13.

14. Christopher Small, *Music of the Common Tongue: Survival and Celebration in African American Music* (1987; New York: Riverrun Press, 1998), 69; original emphasis.

15. Ibid., 70.

16. Ibid., 74.

17. Susan McClary, *Feminine Endings: Music, Gender, and Sexuality* (Minneapolis: University of Minnesota Press, 1991), 26.

18. Glenn T. Pillsbury, *Damage Incorporated: Metallica and the Production of Identity* (New York: Routledge, 2006); Michael Bannister, *White Boys, White Noise: Masculinities and 1980s Indie Guitar Rock* (Burlington, Vt.: Ashgate, 2006).

19. Peter Stearns, *American Cool: Constructing a Twentieth-Century Emotional Style* (New York: New York University Press, 1994), and *Battleground of Desire: The Struggle for Self-Control in Modern America* (New York: New York University Press, 1999).

20. Cheryl Harris, ed., *Theorizing Fandom: Fans, Subculture, and Identity* (Cresskill, N.J.: Hampton Press, 1998); Jonathan Gray, Cornel Sandvoss, and C. Lee Harrington, eds., *Fandom: Identities and Communities in a Mediated World* (New York: New York University Press, 2007); Matt Hills, *Fan Cultures* (New York: Routledge, 2002).

21. Simon Frith, *Performing Rites*; Lisa Lewis, *Gender Politics and MTV* (Philadelphia: Temple University Press, 1990); Bernard Gendron, *Between the Montmartre and the Mudd Club: Popular Music and the Avant-Garde* (Chicago: University of Chicago Press, 2002).

22. For example, Dwight Macdonald, *Against the American Grain* (New York: Da Capo, 1962); Joan Shelley Rubin, *The Making of Middle/Brow Culture* (Chapel Hill: University of North Carolina Press, 2006); Janice Radway, *A Feeling for Books: The Book-of-the-Month Club, Literary Taste, and Middle-Class Desire* (Chapel Hill: University of North Carolina Press, 1999).

23. For rare exceptions, see George Lipsitz, *Time Passages* (Minneapolis: University of Minnesota Press, 1990), or Edward Macan, *Rocking the Classics* (New York: Oxford University Press, 1997).·

24. Chris McDonald, "Exploring the Gendered Construction of a Rock Audience: The Case of Rush," paper presented at the Niagara Chapter of the Society for Ethnomusicology, Kent State University, 1998.

25. Burton Bledstein, "Introduction," in *The Middling Sorts: Explorations in the History of the American Middle Class,* ed. Burton Bledstein and Robert Johnston (New York: Routledge, 2001), 18.

26. Ibid., 18–19.

27. Arno J. Mayer, "The Lower Middle Class as Historical Problem," *Journal of Modern History* 47, no. 3 (1975): 422.

28. Bledstein, "Introduction," 18.

29. See, for example, Clifford G. Trott's astonishing admonition that "you, the 240 million middle-class Americans, are *an endangered species*" in *Middle-Class Americans: An Endangered Species* (New York: Vantage Press, 1994), 1; emphasis his.

30. Stuart Blumin, *The Emergence of the Middle Class: Social Experience in the American City, 1760–1900* (New York: Cambridge University Press, 1989), 9–10.

31. Mayer, "The Lower Middle Class as Historical Problem," 418; emphasis his.

32. Bledstein, "Introduction," 18.

33. Felski, "Nothing to Declare," 41.

34. Peter Bailey, "White Collars, Gray Lives? The Lower Middle Class Revisited," *Journal of British Studies* 38, no. 3 (1999): 274.

35. Lawrence Grossberg, "Another Boring Day in Paradise: Rock and Roll and the Empowerment of Everyday Life," *Popular Music* 4 (1984): 227.

36. Sean Albiez, "Know History! John Lydon, Cultural Capital, and the Prog/Punk Dialectic," *Popular Music* 22, no. 3 (2003): 358.

37. Blumin, *The Emergence of the Middle Class,* 4–5.

38. Ibid., 10.

39. Robert Bellah et al., *Habits of the Heart: Individualism and Commitment in American Life* (New York: Perennial Library, 1986); Burton Bledstein, *The Culture of Professionalism: The Middle Class and the Development of Higher Education in America* (New York: W. W. Norton, 1976); Pierre Bourdieu, *Distinction: A*

Critique of the Judgment of Taste (Cambridge, Mass.: Harvard University Press, 1984); Adrie Kusserow, *American Individualisms: Child Rearing and Social Class in Three Neighbourhoods* (New York: Palgrave Macmillan, 2004).

40. Lorraine Delia Kenny, *Daughters of Suburbia: Growing Up White, Middle-Class, and Female* (New Brunswick, N.J.: Rutgers University Press, 2000), 169.

1. "Anywhere But Here"

1. Discussed in Carol A. O'Connor, "Sorting Out the Suburbs: Patterns of Land Use, Class, and Culture," *American Quarterly* 37, no. 3 (1985): 382.

2. Ibid., 382–383.

3. Susan Saegert, "Masculine Cities and Feminine Suburbs: Polarized Ideas, Contradictory Realities," *Signs* 5, no. 3 (1980): S97.

4. Eric Avila, *Popular Culture in the Age of White Flight: Fear and Fantasy in Suburban Los Angeles* (Berkeley: University of California Press, 2004), 6.

5. Gary Burns and Jim Brown, dirs., *Radiant City* (DVD), 93 min.. National Film Board of Canada, 2006.

6. See, for example, Robert Fishman, *Bourgeois Utopias: The Rise and Fall of Suburbia* (New York: Basic Books, 1987); Barbara M. Kelly, *Suburbia Re-Examined* (New York: Greenwood Press, 1989); Joel Garreau, *Edge City: Life on the New Frontier* (New York: Doubleday, 1991); Rob Kling, Spencer Olin, and Mark Poster, *Postsuburban California* (Berkeley: University of California Press, 1991). See also Herbert Gans's *The Levittowners* (New York: Pantheon, 1967) for a foil against the "boring suburbs" myth; Gans disagrees that suburbanites are any more bored, alienated, or homogenous than the "middle Americans" who live in cities or small towns.

7. Loren Baritz, *The Good Life: The Meaning of Success for the American Middle Class* (New York: Harper and Row, 1990), 196.

8. Kenneth T. Jackson, *Crabgrass Frontier: The Suburbanization of the United States* (New York: Oxford University Press, 1985), 5–7.

9. Lawrence Grossberg, "Another Boring Day in Paradise: Rock and Roll and the Empowerment of Everyday Life," *Popular Music* 4 (1984): 229.

10. Lorraine Delia Kenny, *Daughters of Suburbia: Growing Up White, Middle-Class, and Female* (New Brunswick, N.J.: Rutgers University Press, 2000), 110.

11. Simon Frith, "The Magic That Can Set You Free," *Popular Music* 1 (1981): 167.

12. See Robert Walser, *Running with the Devil: Power, Gender, and Madness in Heavy Metal* (Hanover, N.H.: Wesleyan University Press, 1993); Harris M. Berger, *Metal, Rock, and Jazz: Perception and the Phenomenology of Musical*

Experience (Hanover, N.H.: Wesleyan University Press, 1999); and Deena Weinstein, *Heavy Metal: A Cultural Sociology* (New York: Macmillan, 1991).

13. Peter Trudgill, *On Dialect: Social and Geographical Perspectives* (New York: New York University Press, 1984), 144.

14. Neil Peart, "Rush: Presto," *The Rush Backstage Club Newsletter*, 1990.

15. Edward Macan, *Rocking the Classics* (New York: Oxford University Press, 1997), 112.

16. Kim Liv Selling, "Nature, Reason and the Legacy of Romanticism: Constructing Genre Fantasy" (Ph.D. diss., Centre for Medieval Studies, University of Sydney, 2005), 167–168.

17. Walser, *Running with the Devil*, 158–159.

18. Ibid., 157–160.

19. Susan Fast, *In the Houses of the Holy: Led Zeppelin and the Power of Rock Music* (New York: Oxford University Press, 2001), 67–69.

20. Paul M. Fournier, interview with the author, March 25, 2001.

21. William Johnston, interview with the author, November 14, 2001.

22. Quoted in George Aichele, "Literary Fantasy and Postmodern Theology," *Journal of the American Academy of Religion* 59, no. 2 (1991): 324.

23. Ibid., 323.

24. Ibid., 324.

25. Robert Bellah et al., *Habits of the Heart: Individualism and Commitment in American Life* (New York: Perennial Library, 1986), 143.

26. Robert Walser, "Deep Jazz: Notes on Interiority, Race, and Criticism," in *Inventing the Psychological: Toward a Cultural History of Emotional Life in America*, ed. Joel Pfister and Nancy Schnog (New Haven, Conn.: Yale University Press, 1997), 272.

27. Simon Frith, *Performing Rites: On the Value of Popular Music* (Cambridge, Mass.: Harvard University Press, 1996), 51.

28. Rita Felski, "Nothing to Declare: Identity, Shame, and the Lower Middle Class," *PMLA* 115 (2000): 40.

29. Ibid., 40.

30. Burton Bledstein, *The Culture of Professionalism: The Middle Class and the Development of Higher Education in America* (New York: W. W. Norton, 1976), 94.

31. Bellah et al., *Habits of the Heart*, 22, 23.

32. Ibid., 56–57, 62–63.

33. Larry Cotner, "Pink Floyd's 'Careful With That Axe, Eugene': Toward a Theory of Textural Rhythm in Progressive Rock," in *Progressive Rock Reconsidered*, ed. Kevin Holm-Hudson (New York: Routledge, 2002), 11.

34. Ibid., 88.

35. Macan, *Rocking the Classics*, 41.

36. See Charles Seeger, *Studies in Musicology, 1935–1975* (Berkeley: University of California Press, 1977), 222–235, John Guillory, "The Ordeal of Middlebrow Culture," *Transition* 67 (1995): 82–92.

37. Carl Dahlhaus, *The Idea of Absolute Music* (Chicago: University of Chicago Press, 1990), 80.

38. Mark Joseph, interview with the author, January 2, 2001.

39. Allen Kwan, interview with the author, September 2, 2001.

40. Bohdan Dziemidok, "Artistic Formalism: Its Achievements and Weaknesses," *Journal of Aesthetics and Art Criticism* 51, no. 2 (1993): 185.

41. Leo Treitler, *Music and the Historical Imagination* (Cambridge, Mass.: Harvard University Press, 1989), 12.

42. Walser, *Running with the Devil*, 127.

43. Pierre Bourdieu, *Distinction: A Critique of the Judgment of Taste* (Cambridge, Mass.: Harvard University Press, 1984), 54.

44. Ibid., 55–56.

45. Ibid., 376.

46. See Stuart Hall and Tony Jefferson, eds., *Resistance through Rituals: Youth Subcultures in Post-War Britain* (London: Hutchinson, 1976); Dick Hebdige, *Subculture: The Meaning of Style* (London: Routledge, 1979); John Fiske, *Understanding Popular Culture* (Boston: Unwin Hyman, 1989).

47. Hebdige, *Subculture*, 115.

48. Orrin Klapp, *Collective Search for Identity* (New York: Holt, Rinehart and Winston, 1969), 29–46.

49. Ibid., 34–35.

50. Felski, "Nothing to Declare," 43.

51. Peter Bailey, "White Collars, Gray Lives? The Lower Middle Class Revisited," *Journal of British Studies* 38, no. 3 (1999): 281.

52. Felski, "Nothing to Declare," 43.

53. Selling, "Nature, Reason, and the Legacy of Romanticism," 234.

54. Quoted in Chip Stern, "Neal [sic] Peart's Heady Metal," *Musician* no. 16 (June 1998): 89.

2. "Swimming Against the Stream"

1. Durrell Bowman, "Let Them All Make Their Own Music: Individualism, Rush, and the Progressive / Hard Rock Alloy," in *Progressive Rock Reconsidered*, ed. Kevin Holm-Hudson (New York: Routledge, 2002).

2. Examples include Barbara Ehrenreich, *Fear of Falling: The Inner Life of the Middle Class* (New York: Pantheon Books, 1989); Kevin Phillips, *Boiling*

Point: *Republicans, Democrats, and the Decline of Middle-Class Prosperity* (New York: Harper Collins, 1994); Trott, *Middle-Class Americans: An Endangered Species.*

3. Theodor Adorno, *Introduction to the Sociology of Music* (1962; New York: Continuum, 1976), 86.

4. Ibid., 87.

5. Robert Walser, *Running with the Devil: Power, Gender, and Madness in Heavy Metal* (Hanover, N.H.: Wesleyan University Press, 1993), 76–78.

6. Adrie Suzanne Kusserow, "De-Homogenizing American Individualism: Socializing Hard and Soft Individualism in Manhattan and Queens," *Ethos* 27, no. 2 (1999): 217.

7. Ibid., 220.

8. Ibid., 223.

9. Simon Frith, "The Magic That Can Set You Free: The Ideology of Folk and the Myth of the Rock Community," *Popular Music* 1 (1981): 165–66.

10. Robert Bellah et al., *Habits of the Heart: Individualism and Commitment in American Life* (New York: Perennial Library, 1986), 34.

11. Ibid., 27.

12. Ibid., 47.

13. Carol Selby Price and Robert M. Price, *Mystic Rhythms: The Philosophical Vision of Rush* (Berkeley Heights, N.J.: Wildside Press, 1999), 45.

14. This concept was theorized most fully by Louis Althusser, who explained that subjectivity and ideology engage in a very complicated dance of mutual recognition and reinforcement; certain ideological messages reflect back to us the relationship we believe we have to society, the State, our families, and so on. See *Lenin and Philosophy and Other Essays* (New York: Monthly Review Press, 1971), 162. It was adapted by Richard Middleton to help explain the process popular music plays in "interpellating" subjects and constructing identity (in *Studying Popular Music* [Milton Keynes, UK: Open University Press, 1990]: 249).

15. Mark W. Booth, *The Experience of Songs* (New Haven, Conn.: Yale University Press, 1981), 14.

16. Jennifer Hurtsfield, "'Internal' Colonialism: White, Black, and Chicano Self-Conceptions," *Ethnic and Racial Studies* 1, no. 1 (1978): 69.

17. Pamela Perry, *Shades of White: White Kids and Racial Identities in High School* (Durham, N.C.: Duke University Press, 2002), 78.

18. Ibid., 98. Going even further, George Lipsitz argues that liberal individualism in the United States not only fills in the "cognitive gap" regarding ethnicity that Perry describes, but actively works to sidestep any acknowledgment of the continued problem of white racism. The very ideas of systemic or institutional racism are negated in white middle-class discourse, says Lipsitz, because of "the

overdetermined inadequacy of liberal individualism to describe collective experience" (in "The Possessive Investment in Whiteness: Racialized Social Democracy and the 'White' Problem in American Studies," *American Quarterly* 47, no. 3 [1995]: 381).

19. Bellah et al., *Habits of the Heart*, 151–152.

20. Ibid., 152.

21. Tim Taylor, "Gaelicer than Thou," in *Celtic Modern: Music at the Global Fringe*, ed. Martin Henry Stokes and Philip Bohlman (Lanham, Md.: Scarecrow, 2003).

22. Price, *Mystic Rhythms*, 25.

23. Ibid., 26, italics hers.

24. I refer to the middle class as the one most dedicated to competition, because the capitalist upper class is not generally interested in evenhanded competition with anyone; they prefer using their political influence and business networks to freeze out upstart competitors and maintain market and status dominance.

25. Lawrence Grossberg, "Another Boring Day in Paradise: Rock and Roll and the Empowerment of Everyday Life," *Popular Music* 4 (1984): 234.

26. Allen Kwan, interview with the author, September 2, 2001.

27. William Johnston, interview with the author, November 14, 2001.

28. Bellah et al., *Habits of the Heart*, 82–83.

29. Ibid., 65.

30. Ibid., 84.

31. Victor Frankl, *Man's Search For Meaning* (1946; London: Hodder and Stoughton, 1987): 85.

32. See Adorno, *Introduction to the Sociology of Music*.

33. Anastasia Pantsios, "Canada's Power Trio Is Switched On Live," *Creem*, November 25, 1976.

34. Thatcher's quote appeared in an October 1987 issue of *Women's Own* magazine, quoted in Richard Osborne and Borin van Loon, *Sociology for Beginners* (Cambridge, UK: Icon Books, 1996), 6.

35. Roy MacGregor, "To Hell with Bob Dylan—Meet Rush, They're In It for the Money," *MacLean's*, January 23, 1978.

36. Barry Miles, "Rush: Is Everybody Feelin' all Right? (Geddit . . . ?)," *New Musical Express*, March 4, 1978.

37. The equating of fascism with Ayn Rand's philosophy has a history predating Miles's article. American conservative Whittaker Chambers published a scathing review of Rand's *Atlas Shrugged* in a 1957 issue of *National Review*, which lambasted Rand's individualism as a kind of tortured, Manichean extremism: "I can recall no other book in which a tone of overriding arrogance

was so implacably sustained. Its shrillness is without reprieve. Its dogmatism is without appeal" (595). In a famous and oft-quoted passage, Chambers stated, "From almost any page of *Atlas Shrugged*, a voice can be heard, from painful necessity, commanding: 'To the gas chambers—go'!" (595–596). I am not sure if Miles was aware of Chambers's review, but the similarities in their respective appraisals of Rand are striking.

38. Brian Harrigan, *Rush* (New York: Omnibus Press, 1981), 31.

39. Paul Stump, *The Music's All That Matters: A History of Progressive Rock* (London: Quartet Books, 1998), 257.

40. Ibid., 257–258.

41. Ibid., 258.

42. One exception is an article that appeared in *Creem* in 1981, written by John Kordosh. The author clearly had a personality conflict with Neil Peart, and Kordosh's brief interjection that Rand was a fascist lacked any context or content; it was simply another gibe in an article full of *ad hominem* insults.

43. The issue of class privilege, however, plays out in more than one way in England. It should be noted that Rush's middle-class sensibility, especially its merging of hard rock with elements of high literature and classical music, also garnered copious praise from a number of British reviewers, who admired Rush's gestures toward gentility. See, for example, reviews by Michael Oldfield, Steve Gett, Jon Gill, Brian Harrigan, and Derek Oliver.

44. Steve Lukes ("The Meanings of 'Individualism,'" *Journal of the History of Ideas* 32, no. 1 [1971]: 45–66), explains how the meanings of "individualism" differ in a number of Western countries, for historical and sociological reasons. The United States, of course, equates individualism with capitalism and liberal democracy (59), and its use in Britain carried positive meanings (industriousness, uprightness, and enterprising energy) in some political contexts, but the British left also associated it with false justifications of class privilege (63–64). Its meanings in France, intriguingly, are far more vexed, associated as it is with hubris and antisocial behavior (48), while in Germany it carried more ineffable, mysterious, and romanticized connotations, applied particularly to artistic genius (55).

45. Roger King and Neill Nugent, eds., *Respectable Rebels: Middle Class Campaigns in Britain in the 1970s* (Toronto: Hodder and Stoughton, 1979), 46.

46. Rita Felski, "Nothing to Declare: Identity, Shame, and the Lower Middle Class," *PMLA* 115 (2000): 40.

47. Sven Beckert, "Propertied of a Different Kind: Bourgeoisie and Lower Middle Class in the Nineteenth-Century United States," in *The Middling Sorts: Explorations in the History of the American Middle Class*, ed. Burton Bledstein and Robert Johnston (New York: Routledge, 2001), 292–93.

48. Peart, quoted in Scott Bullock, "A Rebel and a Drummer," *Liberty,* September 1997.

49. Stephen Blush, "Rush—Astronomicon," *Seconds* 25: 1994.

50. Ibid.

51. David Riesman, *The Lonely Crowd: A Study of the Changing American Character* (New York: Doubleday, 1953).

52. Ula Gehret, "To Be Totally Obsessed—That's the Only Way," *Aquarian Weekly,* March 9, 1994.

53. Quoted from the Canadian Governor-General's web site, www.gg.ca/honours/nat-ord/oc/index_e.asp.

54. See Bullock, "A Rebel and a Drummer."

3. "The Work of Gifted Hands"

1. This is not to say that Rush never exhibits an irreverent sense of humor in public; Lee's vocal performance in Dave Thomas's and Rick Moranis's novelty hit "Take Off to the Great White North" and Lifeson's appearance on an episode of *Trailer Park Boys* show a more relaxed, unguarded side to the band.

2. Sylvie Simmons, "The Moustache that Conquered the World: Guiding Genius Neil Peart Grapples With the Paradox," *Sounds,* April 5, 1980.

3. Danniels quoted in Roy MacGregor, "To Hell with Bob Dylan—Meet Rush, They're In It for the Money," *MacLean's,* January 23, 1978.

4. Malcolm Dome, "Interview with Neil," *Metal Hammer,* April 25, 1988.

5. Mary Turner, "Rush: Neil Peart," *Off the Record,* August 27, 1984.

6. Stephen Blush, "Rush—Astronomicon," *Seconds* 25: 1994.

7. Jon Stratton, "Capitalism and Romantic Ideology in the Record Business," *Popular Music* 3 (1983): 156.

8. Lisa Lewis, *Gender Politics and MTV* (Philadelphia: Temple University Press, 1990); Kembrew McLeod, "*1/2: A Critique of Rock Criticism in North America," *Popular Music* 20, no. 1 (2001): 47–60.

9. Simon Frith, *Performing Rites: On the Value of Popular Music* (Cambridge, Mass.: Harvard University Press, 1996).

10. William Weber, "The Muddle of the Middle Classes," *19th Century Music* 3, no. 2 (1979): 176.

11. Burton Bledstein, *The Culture of Professionalism: The Middle Class and the Development of Higher Education in America* (New York: W. W. Norton, 1976).

12. Scott Cohen Frost, "Geddy Lee, From Immigrants' Song to Rush's Lead Singer," *Circus,* October 27, 1977.

13. Nick Krewen, "Surviving With Rush—Drummer-Lyricist Neil Peart Looks Forward," *Canadian Composer,* April 1986.

14. See Simon Frith, "The Magic That Can Set You Free," *Popular Music* 1 (1981); Bernard Gendron, *From the Montmartre to the Mudd Club: Popular Music and the Avant-Garde* (Chicago: University of Chicago Press, 2002).

15. Keith Negus, *Popular Music in Theory* (Hanover: Wesleyan University Press, 1996), 49.

16. For further analysis, see also Keith Negus, *Music Genres and Corporate Cultures* (New York: Routledge, 1999).

17. Lewis, *Gender Politics and MTV*, 29, 32.

18. Glenn T. Pillsbury, *Damage Incorporated: Metallica and the Production of Identity* (New York: Routledge, 2006), 92–93.

19. Barbara Ehrenreich, *Fear of Falling: The Inner Life of the Middle Class* (New York: Pantheon Books, 1989), 157.

20. Ibid., 261.

21. Lifeson quoted in Ted Veneman, "Interview with Alex Lifeson," *Harmonix*, January 1983.

22. Stratton, "Capitalism and Romantic Ideology in the Record Business," 154.

23. Madonna provides a useful counterexample, an exception that proves the rule. Her recuperation and elevation by journalists and academics from a "fluffy" pop singer to an artist and a strong female role model turns at least partly on the fact that she seemed to have occupational autonomy. The ways she chose to present herself and her work seemed to be under her own control.

24. Michael Eraut, *Developing Professional Knowledge and Competence* (London: Routledge, 1994), 2.

25. Bledstein, *The Culture of Professionalism*, 4.

26. Peart quoted in Ula Gehret, "To Be Totally Obsessed—That's the Only Way," *Aquarian Weekly*, March 9, 1994.

27. Lee quoted in Greg Armbruster, "Geddy Lee of Rush," *Keyboard*, September 1984.

28. That is to say, acoustic guitars require more finger pressure on the neck than electric guitars, making quick passages on an acoustic guitar more difficult to execute.

29. Theo Cateforis, "How Alternative Turned Progressive: The Strange Case of Math Rock," in *Progressive Rock Reconsidered*, ed. Kevin Holm-Hudson (New York: Routledge, 2002), 257.

30. Ibid., 245.

31. Thanks to Nicole Biamonte and Durrell Bowman for helping me to identify this quote.

32. Steve Waksman, *Instruments of Desire: The Electric Guitar and the Shaping of Musical Experience* (Cambridge, Mass.: Harvard University Press, 1999), 266.

33. See Peart's comments in Dome, "Interview with Neil."

34. Robert Walser, *Running with the Devil: Power, Gender, and Madness in Heavy Metal* (Hanover, N.H.: Wesleyan University Press, 1993), 57–58.

35. Ibid., 99.

36. Bledstein, *The Culture of Professionalism*, 90.

37. Ibid., 94.

38. See John Stix, "Alex Lifeson," *Guitar for the Practicing Musician* 8, no. 7 (May 1991): 88.

39. H. P. Newquist, "The 50 Heaviest Riffs of All Time," *Guitar for the Practicing Musician* 12, no. 7 (May 1995): 167.

40. H. P. Newquist, "50 Albums That Shaped Rock Guitar," *Guitar For The Practicing Musician* 13, no. 4 (February 1996): 48.

41. Quartal harmony refers to chords built from stacked fourths, for example a chord made up of A, D, and G. Quartal chords are often described as suspended chords that do not resolve. In pop chord notation, my example could be named A7 suspended fourth, G suspended second, or D suspended fourth, depending on which note is taken as the root.

42. Mark Mitchell, "Show Don't Tell," *Rock School* 2, no. 3 (1990): 43.

43. Andy Aledort, "Performance Notes: Tom Sawyer," *Guitar for the Practicing Musician* (Winter 1989): 18.

44. In popular musicians' vernacular, "muso" refers to players who are obsessed with practicing musical technique and applying advanced concepts from music theory.

45. Lee quoted in Blush, "Rush—Astronomicon."

46. Ibid.

47. C. Wright Mills, *White Collar: The American Middle Classes* (New York: Oxford University Press, 1951), 240, 254.

48. For example, Charles M. Beach, *The "Vanishing" Middle Class? Evidence and Expectations*, Queen's Papers in Industrial Relations (Kingston, Ont.: Industrial Relations Centre, 1988); Trott, *Middle-Class Americans: An Endangered Species*; Phillips, *Boiling Point*.

49. Peart quoted in Bob Mack, "Confessions of a Rush Fan: Justifying His Love for Canada's Prog-Rock Pariahs," *Spin*, March 1992.

50. Perry Stern, "The Godfathers of Cyber-Tech Go Organic," *Network*, November 1993.

51. In my doctoral dissertation, I discuss a particularly long and angry thread on *The Rush Interactive Network* message board dealing with the Rock and Roll Hall of Fame's refusal to induct Rush; see Chris McDonald, "Grand Designs: A Musical, Social, and Ethnographic Study of Rush" (Ph.D. diss., York University, 2002), 92–93.

52. MacGregor, "To Hell with Bob Dylan—Meet Rush: They're In It for the Money."

53. See Philip Dawdy, "You Can't Hurry Change," *Bassics* 6, no. 2 (1996); Dan Hedges, "Rush Relives 18 Years of Wide-Screen Rock," *Circus*, April 30, 1992.

54. Negus, *Popular Music in Theory*, 155–156.

55. Lifeson quoted in Jim Schwartz, "Alex Lifeson: Rush's Kinetic Lead Guitarist," *Guitar Player*, June 1980.

56. Kurt Loder, "Grace Under Pressure Review," *Rolling Stone*, June 21, 1984.

57. David Fricke, "Power Windows," *Rolling Stone*, January 30, 1986.

58. Peart quoted in Mack, "Confessions of a Rush Fan."

59. Peart quoted in Frank Schulte, "Rush: Straight from the Heart," *Canadian Musician* 13, no. 5 (October 1991): 34.

60. Lee quoted in Carl Koryat, "Geddy Lee—Still Going," *Bass Player* (December 1993): 44.

61. Paul DiMaggio, "Classification in Art," *American Sociological Review* 52, no. 4 (1987): 440–455; Koen Van Eijck, "Social Differentiation in Musical Taste Patterns," *Social Forces* 79, no. 3 (2001): 1163–1185.

62. DiMaggio, "Classification in Art," 445.

63. Michael Emmison, "Social Class and Cultural Mobility: Reconfiguring the Cultural Omnivore Thesis," *Journal of Sociology* 39, no. 3 (2003): 215, 221.

64. Richard A. Peterson and Roger M. Kern, "Changing Highbrow Taste: From Snob to Omnivore," *American Sociological Review* 61, no. 5 (1996): 905–906.

65. Ibid., 906.

66. Allen Kwan, interview with the author, September 2, 2001.

67. On the other hand, their effacement of image put Rush in the middle of the AOR rock fashion of the early 1980s. As *Rolling Stone*'s Steve Pond wrote in his 1982 article "Faceless Bands," Rush, like colleagues in Styx, Foreigner, Journey, and REO Speedwagon, looked and dressed unremarkably. One industry insider, Cliff Burnstein, explained the "faceless band" phenomenon using familiar rhetoric: these bands sell based on musical quality, not image (see Steve Pond, "Faceless Bands," *Rolling Stone*, February 4, 1982, 38).

68. Peart quoted in Dome, "Interview with Neil."

4. "Experience to Extremes"

1. From Jacqueline Warwick, "Singing Style and White Masculinity," in *The Ashgate Research Companion to Popular Musicology*, ed. Derek B. Scott (Burlington, Vt.: Ashgate, 2009).

2. For more on modular forms in rock, see Glenn T. Pillsbury's work on Metallica in *Damage Incorporated: Metallica and the Production of Identity* (New York: Routledge, 2006), especially 18–27.

3. Neil Peart, "Creating the Drum Part," *Modern Drummer,* August 1988.

4. Quoted in Frank Schulte, "Rush: Straight from the Heart," *Canadian Musician* 13, no. 5 (October 1991): 34.

5. John Stix, "Alex Lifeson: Classical Precision, Blues Touch," *Guitar for the Practicing Musician* 5, no. 10 (August 1988): 16.

6. See, for example, Steve Weitzman's 1981 assessment of Rush's live show in *Circus* magazine: "Rush's two-hour Garden concert . . . proved to be one gigantic yawn. . . . They're not a true rock 'n' roll band, as their music is stiffly calculated and pre-planned. Each identical performance . . . holds all the excitement of a Howard Johnson's omelet." A similar sentiment was expressed by *Creem*'s John Kordosh in his 1981 article.

7. See Susan Fast, *In the Houses of the Holy: Led Zeppelin and the Power of Rock Music* (New York: Oxford University Press, 2001), 148–149, for further discussion of the meaning of static postures and restricted movement on the rock stage.

8. Ibid., 133.

9. Schulte, "Rush: Straight from the Heart," 37.

10. Ibid., 37–38.

11. This applies to Genesis's instrumentalists, not to singer Peter Gabriel, who dramatized many songs in costumes.

12. Edward Macan, *Rocking the Classics* (New York: Oxford University Press, 1997), 64.

13. Pillsbury, *Damage Incorporated,* 82.

14. Ibid., 93.

15. Ibid., 95.

16. Stix, "Alex Lifeson: Classical Precision, Blues Touch," 15.

17. Ibid., 15.

18. Pete Makowski, "Adrenaline Rush," *Sounds,* December 18, 1982.

19. John Stix, "Geddy Lee: It's a Groove Thing," *Guitar for the Practicing Musician* (December 1991): 82. Similar comments were made in Chris Welch, "Rush: Feeling Groovy," *Rock World* (November 1993), and Philip Dawdy, "You Can't Hurry Change," *Bassics* 6, no. 2 (1996).

20. Michael Bannister, *White Boys, White Noise: Masculinities and 1980s Indie Guitar Rock* (Burlington, Vt.: Ashgate, 2006), 46.

21. Ibid., 39.

22. Ibid., 55.

23. Peter Bailey, "White Collars, Gray Lives? The Lower Middle Class Revisited," *Journal of British Studies* 38, no. 3 (1999): 281.

24. Pillsbury, *Damage Incorporated*, 96.

25. Examples of such studies include Jennifer Hurtsfield, "'Internal' Colonialism: White, Black, and Chicano Self-Conceptions," *Ethnic and Racial Studies* 1, no. 1 (1978); George Lipsitz, "The Possessive Investment in Whiteness: Racialized Social Democracy and the 'White' Problem in American Studies," *American Quarterly* 47, no. 3 (1995); and Lorraine Delia Kenny, *Daughters of Suburbia: Growing Up White, Middle-Class, and Female* (New Brunswick, N.J.: Rutgers University Press, 2000).

26. Loren Baritz, *The Good Life: The Meaning of Success for the American Middle Class* (New York: Harper and Row, 1990), 199–201.

27. Ibid., 201.

28. Sherry B. Ortner, "Reading America: Preliminary Notes on Class and Culture," in *Recapturing Anthropology: Working in the Present*, ed. Richard G. Fox (Santa Fe: School of American Research Press, 1991), 164.

29. Kenny, *Daughters of Suburbia*, 25.

30. Peter Stearns, *American Cool: Constructing a Twentieth-Century Emotional Style* (New York: New York University Press, 1994), and *Battleground of Desire: The Struggle for Self-Control in Modern America* (New York: New York University Press, 1999).

31. Stearns, *American Cool*, 214–215.

32. Ibid., 268.

33. Ibid., 267.

34. Ibid., 280.

5. "Reflected in Another Pair of Eyes"

1. Vit Wagner, "What a Rush: Veteran Canadian Rock Trio Evokes Cult-Like Response from Fans," *Toronto Star*, May 11, 2002, J1.

2. Steve Pond, "Rush's Heavy Metal Sludge," *Rolling Stone*, May 15, 1980, 68; also Pond, "Faceless Bands," *Rolling Stone*, February 4, 1982, 37–38.

3. Durrell Bowman, "Permanent Change: Rush, Musicians' Rock and the Progressive Post-Counterculture" (Ph.D. diss., UCLA, 2003), 1.

4. Karl Coryat, "Geddy Lee—Still Going," *Bass Player* (December 1993): 43.

5. Pete Makowski, "Adrenaline Rush," *Sounds*, December 18, 1982.

6. Philip Bashe, "Rush's Simpler Signals," *Circus*, November 30, 1982.

7. Matt Hills, *Fan Cultures* (New York: Routlege, 2002), xiii.

8. As a good example of theorizing idiosyncratic, virtually invisible fandom, see Sue Wise, "Sexing Elvis," *Women's Studies International Forum* 7, no. 1 (1984): 13–17. Wise discusses her own atypical history as a fan with Elvis Presley, something she kept hidden as a teenager and as a professional woman. Her use of

Elvis as an object of comfort rather than desire was something unaccounted for in discussions of Elvis reception. My own Rush fandom is not particularly idiosyncratic, but ironically, if I were not the researcher, I would probably be nearly invisible ethnographically; I do not think I would be active on the internet, nor would I probably have attended Rush conventions.

9. Hills, *Fan Cultures,* 66–67.

10. Daniel Cavicchi, *Tramps Like Us: Music and Meaning among Springsteen Fans* (New York: Oxford University Press, 1998); Sara Cohen, *Rock Culture in Liverpool: Popular Music in the Making* (Oxford: Clarendon Press, 1991).

11. As defined in Cavicchi, *Tramps Like Us,* 41–51.

12. The web site, *Rush: A Test for Echoes,* was available at www.students .yorku.ca/~mcdonald from June 2000 to November 2006.

13. I extend my thanks to Ed Stenger at the *Rush Is a Band* blog for posting the questionnaire.

14. Bowman's questionnaire sample totaled 161.

15. Bowman, "Permanent Change," 73.

16. Ralph Whitehead Jr., "New Collars . . . Bright Collars," *Psychology Today* (1988): 44–49.

17. Instead of "bright collars," the lower middle class as discussed in Sven Beckert, "Propertied of a Different Kind," and Arno J. Mayer, "The Lower Middle Class as Historical Problem," could be substituted; similarly, Whitehead's bright collars map onto notions of a "new middle class" in the United States, discussed at length by C. Wright Mills in *White Collar* and by Arthur Vidich in *The New Middle Classes: Life-Styles, Status Claims, and Political Orientations* (New York: New York University Press, 1995). Whitehead's "new collars" correspond with the more generally used term "embourgeoised working class," as outlined in John H. Goldthorpe et al.'s "The Affluent Worker and the Thesis of Embourgeoisement: Some Preliminary Research Findings," *Sociology* 1, no. 1 (1967): 11–31, and Charles E. Hurst's *Social Inequality: Forms, Causes, and Consequences* (Upper Saddle River, N.J.: Prentice Hall, 2007).

18. Bowman, *Permanent Change,* 285.

19. Pond, "Rush's Heavy Metal Sludge," 68.

20. Keith Spera, "Marathon Concert a Real Rush," *New Orleans Times-Picayune,* December 11, 1996.

21. See Lee's comments in Pond, "Faceless Bands," 38; Peart's comments in Mack, "Confessions of a Rush Fan: Justifying His Love for Canada's Prog-Rock Pariahs," *Spin,* March 1992; and Peart's discussion of male-to-male identification in music in his *Masked Rider: Cycling in West Africa* (Lawrencetown Beach, Nova Scotia: Pottersfield Press, 1996), 118.

22. Wagner, "What a Rush," J1.

23. For more on broadcasting and narrowcasting, see Jonathan Gray, Cornel Sandvoss, and C. Lee Harrington, *Fandom: Identities and Communities in a Mediated World* (New York: New York University Press, 2007), 4.

24. Susan Fast, "Rethinking Issues of Gender and Sexuality in Led Zeppelin: A Woman's View of Pleasure and Power in Hard Rock," *American Music* 17, no. 3 (1999): 249–252.

25. Thomas R. Lindloff, Kelly Coyle, and Debra Grodin, "Is There a Text in This Audience?: Science Fiction and Interpretive Schism," in *Theorizing Fandom: Fans, Subculture, and Identity*, ed. Cheryl Harris (Cresskill, N.J.: Hampton Press, 1998), 219–220.

26. Robert Walser, *Running with the Devil: Power, Gender, and Madness in Heavy Metal* (Hanover, N.H.: Wesleyan University Press, 1993), 18.

27. Peart quoted in Malcolm Dome, "Interview with Neil," *Metal Hammer*, April 25, 1988.

28. Lee quoted in Robin Tolleson, "Geddy Lee: The Bass Is Still Key," *Bass Player*, November 1988.

29. Burton W. Peretti, *Jazz in American Culture* (Chicago: Ivan R. Dee, 1997), 37.

30. Examples of such interviews include those listed in the bibliography under Bashe (1982), Veneman (1983), Blush (1994), Gehret (1994), and Wagner (2002).

31. Lynn Van Matre, "Bucking the Trends, Rush Rides the Crest of 'Permanent Waves,'" *Chicago Tribune*, May 30, 1980.

32. Edward Macan, *Rocking the Classics* (New York: Oxford University Press, 1997), 156.

33. Challenges were manifested in the 1970s by all-girl punk groups like the Slits and mixed-gender groups like X-Ray Specs and Talking Heads. In the 1980s, all-girl pop-rock groups like the Bangles or the Go-Gos were highly visible through coverage on MTV. Jennifer Batten, an erstwhile side musician with Michael Jackson, was one of the few women to establish herself in the subculture of rock guitar "shredders," developing an incredible mastery of two-handed tapping, a technique made famous by Eddie Van Halen. In the 1990s, the return of the all-girl punk group flourished in the Riot Grrrls movement.

34. Michael Bannister, *White Boys, White Noise: Masculinities and 1980s Indie Guitar Rock* (Burlington, Vt.: Ashgate, 2006), xxiv.

35. Ibid., 72–73.

36. Sherry Turkle, "Computational Reticence: Why Women Fear the Intimate Machine," in *Technology and Women's Voices: Keeping In Touch*, ed. Cheris Kramarae (New York: Routledge and Kegan Paul, 1988), 43, 44.

37. From www.rushmessageboard.com, May 7, 2008.

was not

38. Perry Stern, "Rush: The Boys Focus on the Perfect Song," *Canadian Musician* 7, no. 6 (December 1985): 28.

39. Nick Carter, "Performance by 70s Band Brings Back Memories," *Milwaukee Journal*, November 2, 1996.

40. Bashe, "Rush's Simpler Signals."

41. See Frith, *Performing Rites*, 176–178.

42. See Michael Gray, *The Song and Dance Man: The Art of Bob Dylan* (London: Hart-Davis, McGibbon, 1972), or John Herdman, *Voice without Restraint: A Study of Dylan's Lyrics and Their Background* (New York: Delilah Books, 1981).

43. Keith Negus, *Popular Music in Theory* (Hanover, N.H.: Wesleyan University Press, 1996), 155.

44. Hills, *Fan Cultures*, 17–18.

45. Ibid., 18.

46. Robert Telleria, *Rush Tribute: Merely Players* (Kingston, Ont.: Quarry Music Publishers, 2001).

47. Carol Selby Price and Robert M. Price, *Mystic Rhythms: The Philosophical Vision of Rush* (Berkeley Heights, N.J.: Wildside Press, 1999), 8–9.

48. However, Carol Price credits her husband, theologian Robert M. Price, as a secondary writer.

49. Hills, *Fan Cultures*, 132–33.

50. See Mary Turner, "Rush: Neil Peart," *Off the Record*, August 27, 1984; Dome, "Interview with Neil."

51. See Nick Krewen, "Surviving With Rush—Drummer-Lyricist Neil Peart Looks Forward," *Canadian Composer*, April 1986; Frank Schulte, "Rush: Straight from the Heart," *Canadian Musician* 13, no. 5 (October 1991).

52. Bashe, "Rush's Simpler Signals."

53. Van Matre, "Bucking the Trends, Rush Rides the Crest of 'Permanent Waves.'"

54. *The Rush FAQ* was available in June 2008 at www.nimitz.net/rush/.

55. Derek Johnson, "Fan-tagonism: Factions, Institutions, and Constitutive Hegemonies of Fandom," in *Fandom: Identities and Communities in a Mediated World*, ed. Jonathan Gray, Cornel Sandvoss, and C. Lee Harrington (New York: New York University Press, 2007), 297.

56. See Lee's comments in Coryat, "Geddy Lee—Still Going," 43; Wagner, "What a Rush," J1.

57. This is extensively documented in Albert Ellis, *Is Objectivism a Religion?* (New York: Stuart, 1968), and Jeff Walker, *The Ayn Rand Cult* (Chicago: Open Court, 1999).

58. Hills, *Fan Cultures*, 143.

59. Ibid., 44.

60. Keith Negus provides a clear discussion of the concepts of "hardcore" and "softshell" music fans in *Music Genres and Corporate Cultures* (New York: Routledge, 1999), 107–110.

61. The term "insider-Other" has been theorized by Kenny in *Daughters of Suburbia* as a type of social actor whose deviant behavior within their own social group serves to rearticulate and reinforce what "normality" is for that group.

62. Mary Bucholtz, "The Whiteness of Nerds: Superstandard English and Racial Markedness," *Journal of Linguistic Anthropology* 11, no. 1 (2001): 86.

63. Ibid., 88.

64. See Christopher Kelty, "Geeks, Social Imaginaries, and Recursive Publics," *Cultural Anthropology* 20, no. 2 (2005): 185–214, for a study of geek culture among information technologists, where a taste for hard rock and interest in libertarian politics turned up as important commonalities in the culture. Individualism seems to play an important role in a number of geek-oriented subcultures.

6. "Scoffing at the Wise?"

1. Brian Harrigan, *Rush* (New York: Omnibus Press, 1981), 50; Bill Banasiewicz, *Visions: The Official Rush Biography* (New York: Omnibus Press, 1988), 3.

2. Max Thaler, "Recognition Is Only Half the Fun," *Circus* (November 1977): 35.

3. David Fricke, "Permanent Waves," *Rolling Stone*, May 1, 1980.

4. Bob Mack, "Test For Echo," *Rolling Stone*, December 17, 1996.

5. Peart quoted in Lynn Van Matre, "Bucking the Trends, Rush Rides the Crest of 'Permanent Waves,'" *Chicago Tribune*, May 30, 1980.

6. Alex Lifeson, interview with the author, December 7, 2001.

7. In 1981, Rush was considered for a cover spread in *Rolling Stone*. The magazine expected Rush, then on tour in the American Southwest, to drop everything and fly to New York for interviews and a photo shoot. The band refused to alter its touring schedule, but was willing to accommodate a photographer and reporter traveling with the band. The magazine editors were outraged at Rush's lack of deference, which seemed to open a rift between them.

8. See reviews in the magazine such as "Fly by Night," *Billboard*, March 1, 1975; "Hold Your Fire," *Billboard*, September 17, 1987.

9. To avoid misunderstandings, I underscore that this applies to the number of albums (not singles) awarded gold or platinum status; moreover, Rush's gross record sales nowhere near match those of the Beatles or Elvis Presley.

10. Bernard Gendron, *From the Montmartre to the Mudd Club: Popular Music and the Avant-Garde* (Chicago: University of Chicago Press, 2002), 5.

11. But scholarly work on popular music may have a mitigating effect, especially as academic attention gets lavished on non-canonical music like progressive rock, heavy metal, or 1960s girl groups.

12. Glenn T. Pillsbury, *Damage Incorporated: Metallica and the Production of Identity* (New York: Routledge, 2006), 141–142.

13. Keith Negus, *Popular Music in Theory* (Hanover, N.H.: Wesleyan University Press, 1996), 155.

14. Simon Frith, *Performing Rites: On the Value of Popular Music* (Cambridge, Mass.: Harvard University Press, 1996), 67.

15. Quoted in Mike Adams, "The Timeless Mystique of Hip," *Baltimore Sun,* September 29, 1996, 3B.

16. See Philip Tagg, "Open Letter: 'Black Music,' 'Afro-American Music' and 'European Music,'" *Popular Music* 8, no. 3 (1989): 294–295, for an eloquent critique of the white "projection" of spontaneity and bodily expression onto African Americans and their music, and the refusal to acknowledge the presence of the body in European-based music.

17. See Kembrew McLeod, "*½: A Critique of Rock Criticism in North America," *Popular Music* 20, no. 1 (2001): 54.

18. Simon Reynolds, *Blissed Out: The Raptures of Rock* (London: Serpent's Tail, 1990), 9–10.

19. Dave Marsh, "In Another Land—Rock's Icy Edge," *Rolling Stone,* February 24, 1977, 60.

20. Ibid., 61.

21. Bob Mack, "Where Angels Fear to Tread: Rush," *Village Voice,* November 5, 1985, 90.

22. Fricke, "Permanent Waves."

23. Jon Pareles, "Exit . . . Stage Left," *Rolling Stone,* February 4, 1982.

24. Michael Eck, "Rush's Music is Boring, Predictable," *Albany Times Union,* May 4, 1994.

25. Mikel Toombs, "Band's Intellectual Music Gets Lost in the Rush," *San Diego Union-Tribune,* February 5, 1996.

26. Jon Gill, "Permanent Raves," *Sounds,* March 14, 1981, 14.

27. Neil Peart, *The Masked Rider: Cycling in West Africa* (Lawrencetown Beach, Nova Scotia: Pottersfield Press, 1996); Peart, *Roadshow: Landscape With Drums* (Burlington, Mass.: Rounder, 2006).

28. Bart Testa, "Lumberjacks Aren't Sissies—Ask BTO," *Crawdaddy* (December 1976): 73.

29. Ibid.

30. John Lamont, "A Farewell to Kings: Rush," *Crawdaddy* (December 1977): 76.

31. Ibid.

32. Harrigan, *Rush,* 44.

33. John Rockwell, "Pop: Rush Plays at Palladium," *New York Times,* January 15, 1979.

34. Frith, *Performing Rites,* 65–66.

35. See Bill Martin, *Listening to the Future: The Time of Progressive Rock* (Chicago: Open Court Press, 1998), 89–90; Deena Weinstein, "Progressive Rock as Text: The Lyrics of Roger Waters," in *Progressive Rock Reconsidered,* ed. Kevin Holm-Hudson (New York: Routledge, 2002), 96.

36. Edward Macan, *Rocking the Classics* (New York: Oxford University Press, 1997), 177.

37. Martin, *Listening to the Future,* 89.

38. Ibid., 89–90.

39. Ibid., 90.

40. Weinstein, "Progressive Rock as Text," 106.

41. Martin, *Listening to the Future,* 14, 90.

42. Macan, *Rocking the Classics,* 171.

43. Kevin Holm-Hudson, "Introduction," in *Progressive Rock Reconsidered,* ed. Kevin Holm-Hudson (New York: Routledge, 2002), 10; John J. Sheinbaum, "Progressive Rock and the Inversion of Musical Values," in *Progressive Rock Reconsidered,* ed. Kevin Holm-Hudson (New York: Routledge, 2002), 28–29.

44. See Chuck Eddy, *The Accidental Evolution of Rock 'n' Roll* (Cambridge: Da Capo Press, 1997); Reynolds, *Blissed Out*; Richard Meltzer, *The Aesthetics of Rock* (New York: Da Capo Press, 1970); Greil Marcus, *Mystery Train: Images of America in Rock 'n' Roll Music* (New York: Dutton, 1982); Greil Marcus, *Lipstick Traces: A Secret History of the Twentieth Century* (Cambridge, Mass.: Harvard University Press, 1989).

45. Joan Shelley Rubin, *The Making of Middle/Brow Culture* (1992; Chapel Hill: University of North Carolina Press, 2006): xiv.

46. Dwight Macdonald, *Against the American Grain* (New York: Da Capo, 1962), 37.

47. Virginia Woolf, *The Death of the Moth* (New York: Harcourt, Brace, 1942).

48. Macdonald, *Against the American Grain,* 54.

49. James Gilbert, "Midcult, Middlebrow, Middle Class," *Reviews in American History* 20, no. 4 (1992): 548.

50. Robert Christgau, "A Farewell to Kings," *Village Voice,* 1977, reprinted in his *Rock Albums of the 70s: A Critical Guide* (New York: Da Capo Press, 1981), 388.

51. Gilbert, "Midcult, Middlebrow, Middle Class," 543.

52. Will Straw, "Characterizing Rock Music Culture: The Case of Heavy Metal," in *On Record: Rock, Pop, and the Written Word,* ed. Simon Frith and Andrew Goodwin (New York: Pantheon, 1990), 458–459.

53. Ibid., 456.

54. Gendron, *From the Montmartre to the Mudd Club,* 236.

55. Ibid., 321.

56. See Marcus, *Lipstick Traces.*

57. Reynolds, *Blissed Out,* 116–122.

58. See, for example, John Seabrook, *Nobrow: The Culture of Marketing, The Marketing of Culture* (London: Methuin, 2001), or Peter Swirski, *From Lowbrow to Nobrow* (Montreal: McGill-Queen's University Press, 2005).

WORKS CITED

Adams, Mike. "The Timeless Mystique of Hip." *Baltimore Sun,* September 29, 1996, 3B. http://www.fb10.uni-bremen.de/anglistic/kerkhoff/beatgeneration / Mailer.htm (accessed August 16, 2000).

Adorno, Theodor. *Introduction to the Sociology of Music.* 1962. Reprint, New York: Continuum, 1976.

————. "On Popular Music." *Studies in Philosophy and Social Sciences* 9 (1941): 17–48.

Aichele, George. "Literary Fantasy and Postmodern Theology." *Journal of the American Academy of Religion* 59, no. 2 (1991): 323–337.

Albiez, Sean. "Know History! John Lydon, Cultural Capital, and the Prog/Punk Dialectic." *Popular Music* 22, no. 3 (2003): 357–374.

Aledort, Andy. "Performance Notes: Tom Sawyer." *Guitar for the Practicing Musician* (Winter 1989): 18.

Althusser, Louis. *Lenin and Philosophy and Other Essays.* New York: Monthly Review Press, 1971.

Armbruster, Greg. "Geddy Lee of Rush." *Keyboard* (September 1984). http:// rushworld.net/nmsmirror.com (accessed May 25, 2000).

Avila, Eric. *Popular Culture in the Age of White Flight: Fear and Fantasy in Suburban Los Angeles.* Berkeley: University of California Press, 2004.

Bailey, Peter. "White Collars, Gray Lives? The Lower Middle Class Revisited." *Journal of British Studies* 38, no. 3 (1999): 273–290.

Banasiewicz, Bill. *Visions: The Official Biography of Rush.* New York: Omnibus Press, 1988.

Bannister, Matthew. *White Boys, White Noise: Masculinities and 1980s Indie Guitar Rock.* Burlington, Vt.: Ashgate, 2006.

Baritz, Loren. *The Good Life: The Meaning of Success for the American Middle Class.* New York: Harper and Row, 1990.

Bashe, Philip. "Rush's Simpler Signals." *Circus*, November 30, 1982. http://rushworld
.net/nmsmirror.com (accessed May 25, 2000).

Beach, Charles M. *The "Vanishing" Middle Class? Evidence and Expectations.*
Queen's Papers in Industrial Relations. Kingston: Industrial Relations Centre, 1988.

Becker, Alton, and Judith Becker. "Music as Icon: Power and Meaning in Javanese Gamelan Music." In *The Sign in Music and Literature*, ed. Wendy Steiner. Austin: University of Texas Press, 1981.

Beckert, Sven. "Propertied of a Different Kind: Bourgeoisie and Lower Middle Class in the Nineteenth-Century United States." In *The Middling Sorts: Explorations in the History of the American Middle Class*, ed. Burton Bledstein and Robert Johnston. New York: Routledge, 2001.

Bellah, Robert, Richard Madsen, William Sullivan, Ann Swidler, and Steven Tipton. *Habits of the Heart: Individualism and Commitment in American Life.* New York: Perennial Library, 1986.

Berger, Harris M. *Metal, Rock, and Jazz: Perception and the Phenomenology of Musical Experience.* Hanover, N.H.: Wesleyan University Press, 1999.

Bledstein, Burton J. *The Culture of Professionalism: The Middle Class and the Development of Higher Education in America.* New York: W. W. Norton, 1976.

Bledstein, Burton J., and Robert D. Johnston, eds. *The Middling Sorts: Explorations in the History of the American Middle Class.* New York: Routledge, 2001.

Blumin, Stuart M. *The Emergence of the Middle Class: Social Experience in the American City, 1760–1900.* New York: Cambridge University Press, 1989.

Blush, Steven. "Rush—Astronomicon." *Seconds* 25: 1994. http://rushworld.net/
nmsmirror.com (accessed May 25, 2000).

Booth, Mark W. *The Experience of Songs.* New Haven, Conn.: Yale University Press, 1981.

Bourdieu, Pierre. *Distinction: A Critique of the Judgment of Taste.* Cambridge, Mass.: Harvard University Press, 1984.

Bowman, Durrell. "Let Them All Make Their Own Music: Individualism, Rush, and the Progressive / Hard Rock Alloy." In *Progressive Rock Reconsidered*, ed. Kevin Holm-Hudson. New York: Routledge, 2002.

——. "Permanent Change: Rush, Musicians' Rock, and the Post-Counterculture." Ph.D. diss., UCLA, 2003.

Brackett, David. *Interpreting Popular Music.* 1995. Reprint, Berkeley: University of California Press, 2000.

Bucholtz, Mary. "The Whiteness of Nerds: Superstandard English and Racial Markedness." *Journal of Linguistic Anthropology* 11, no. 1 (2001): 84–100.

Bullock, Scott. "A Rebel and a Drummer." *Liberty* (September 1997). http://
rushworld.net/nmsmirror.com (accessed February 13, 2000).

Burns, Gary, and Jim Brown, dirs. *Radiant City*. DVD. 93 min. National Film Board of Canada, 2006.

Carter, Nick. "Performance by 70s Band Brings Back Memories." *Milwaukee Journal,* November 2, 1996. http://rushworld.net/nmsmirror.com (accessed July 10, 2000).

Cateforis, Theo. "How Alternative Turned Progressive: The Strange Case of Math Rock." In *Progressive Rock Reconsidered,* ed. Kevin Holm-Hudson. New York: Routledge, 2002.

Cavicchi, Daniel. *Tramps Like Us: Music and Meaning among Springsteen Fans.* New York: Oxford University Press, 1998.

Chambers, Whittaker. "Big Sister is Watching You." *National Review,* December 28, 1957, 594–596.

Chernoff, John Miller. *African Rhythm and African Sensibility: Aesthetics and Social Action in African Musical Idioms.* Chicago: University of Chicago Press, 1979.

Christgau, Robert. *Rock Albums of the 70s: A Critical Guide.* New York: Da Capo Press, 1981.

Cohen, Sara. *Rock Culture in Liverpool: Popular Music in the Making.* Oxford: Clarendon Press, 1991.

Coryat, Karl. "Geddy Lee—Still Going." *Bass Player* (December 1993): 40–48.

Cotner, Larry. "Pink Floyd's 'Careful With That Axe, Eugene': Toward a Theory of Textural Rhythm in Progressive Rock." In *Progressive Rock Reconsidered,* ed. Kevin Holm-Hudson. New York: Routledge, 2002.

Dahlhaus, Carl. *The Idea of Absolute Music.* Chicago: University of Chicago Press, 1990.

Davis, Stephen. *Hammer of the Gods.* New York: Ballantine Books, 1985.

Dawdy, Philip. "You Can't Hurry Change." *Bassics* 6, no. 2 (Fall): 1996. http://rushworld.net/nmsmirror.com (accessed May 25, 2000).

DiMaggio, Paul. "Classification in Art." *American Sociological Review* 52, no. 4 (1987): 440–455.

Dome, Malcolm. "Interview with Neil." *Metal Hammer,* April 25, 1988. http://www.geocities.com/SunsetStrip/Venue/9123/metal.html (accessed February 13, 2000).

Dziemidok, Bohdan. "Artistic Formalism: Its Achievements and Weaknesses." *Journal of Aesthetics and Art Criticism* 51, no. 2 (1993): 185–193.

Echard, William. *Neil Young and the Poetics of Energy.* Bloomington: Indiana University Press, 2005.

Eck, Michael. "Rush's Music is Boring, Predictable." *Albany Times Union,* May 4, 1994. http://rushworld.net/nmsmirror.com (accessed July 10, 2000).

Eddy, Chuck. *The Accidental Evolution of Rock 'n' Roll: A Misguided Tour through Popular Music.* Cambridge, Mass.: Da Capo Press, 1997.

Ehrenreich, Barbara. *Fear of Falling: The Inner Life of the Middle Class.* New York: Pantheon Books, 1989.

Ellis, Albert. *Is Objectivism a Religion?* New York: Stuart, 1968.

Emmison, Michael. "Social Class and Cultural Mobility: Reconfiguring the Cultural Omnivore Thesis." *Journal of Sociology* 39, no. 3 (2003): 211–230.

Eraut, Michael. *Developing Professional Knowledge and Competence.* London: Routledge, 1994.

Fast, Susan. *In The Houses of the Holy: Led Zeppelin and the Power of Rock Music.* New York: Oxford University Press, 2001.

———. "Rethinking Issues of Gender and Sexuality in Led Zeppelin: A Woman's View of Pleasure and Power in Hard Rock." *American Music* 17, no. 3 (1999): 245–299.

Feld, Steven. *Sound and Sentiment: Birds, Weeping, Poetics, and Song in Kaluli Expression.* 1982. Reprint, Philadelphia: University of Pennsylvania Press, 1990.

Felski, Rita. "Nothing to Declare: Identity, Shame, and the Lower Middle Class." *PMLA* 115 (2000): 33–45.

Finnegan, Ruth. *The Hidden Musicians: Music-Making in an English Town.* Cambridge: Cambridge University Press, 1989.

Fishman, Robert. *Bourgeois Utopias: The Rise and Fall of Suburbia.* New York: Basic Books, 1987.

Fiske, John. *Understanding Popular Culture.* Boston: Unwin Hyman, 1989.

Frankl, Viktor. *Man's Search For Meaning.* 1946. Reprint, London: Hodder and Stoughton, 1987.

Fricke, David. "Permanent Waves." *Rolling Stone,* May 1, 1980. http://www.rolling stone.com (accessed August 11, 2000).

———. "Power Windows." *Rolling Stone,* January 30, 1986. http://www.rollingstone .com (accessed August 11, 2000).

Frith, Simon. "The Magic That Can Set You Free: The Ideology of Folk and the Myth of the Rock Community." *Popular Music* 1 (1981): 159–168.

———. *Performing Rites: On the Value of Popular Music.* Cambridge, Mass.: Harvard University Press, 1996.

Frost, Scott Cohen. "Geddy Lee, From Immigrants' Song to Rush's Lead Singer." *Circus,* October 27, 1977. http://rushworld.net/nmsmirror.com (accessed May 25, 2000).

Gans, Herbert J. *The Levittowners: How People Live and Politic in Suburbia.* New York: Pantheon, 1967.

Garreau, Joel. *Edge City: Life on the New Frontier.* New York: Doubleday, 1991.

Gehret, Ula. "To Be Totally Obsessed—That's the Only Way." *Aquarian Weekly,* March 9, 1994. http://rushworld.net/nmsmirror.com (accessed February 13, 2000).

Gendron, Bernard. *Between the Montmartre and the Mudd Club: Popular Music and the Avant-Garde.* Chicago: University of Chicago Press, 2002.

Gett, Steve. "Permanent Waves." *Melody Maker,* February 2, 1980, 26.

———. *Rush: Success under Pressure.* Port Chester, N.Y.: Cherry Lane Books, 1984.

Gilbert, James. "Midcult, Middlebrow, Middle Class." *Reviews in American History* 20, no. 4 (1992): 543–548.

Gill, John. "Permanent Raves." *Sounds,* March 14, 1981, 12–14.

———. "Take That, You Loon Panted Bigots!" (review of *Moving Pictures*), *Sounds,* February 14, 1981, 37.

Goldthorpe, John H., David Lockwood, Frank Bechhofer, and Jennifer Platt. "The Affluent Worker and the Thesis of Embourgeoisement: Some Preliminary Research Findings." *Sociology* 1, no. 1 (1967): 11–31.

Gray, Jonathan, Cornel Sandvoss, and C. Lee Harrington, eds. *Fandom: Identities and Communities in a Mediated World.* New York: New York University Press, 1997.

Gray, Michael. *The Song and Dance Man: The Art of Bob Dylan.* London: Hart-Davis, McGibbon, 1972.

Grossberg, Lawrence. "Another Boring Day in Paradise: Rock and Roll and the Empowerment of Everyday Life." *Popular Music* 4 (1984): 225–258.

Guillory, John. "The Ordeal of Middlebrow Culture." *Transition* 67 (1995): 82–92.

Hall, Stuart, and Tony Jefferson, eds. *Resistance through Rituals: Youth Subcultures in Post-War Britain.* London: Hutchinson, 1976.

Harrigan, Brian. *Rush.* New York: Omnibus Press, 1981.

———. "Signals." *Melody Maker,* September 11, 1982, 20.

Hebdige, Dick. *Subculture: The Meaning of Style.* London: Routledge, 1979.

Hedges, Dan. "Rush Relives 18 Years of Wide-Screen Rock." *Circus* April 30, 1992. http://rushworld.net/nmsmirror.com (accessed May 25, 2000).

Herdman, John. *Voice without Restraint: A Study of Dylan's Lyrics and Their Background.* New York: Delilah Books, 1981.

Herring, Cedric. *Splitting the Middle: Political Alienation, Acquiescence, and Activism among America's Middle Layers.* New York: Praeger, 1989.

Hills, Matt. *Fan Cultures.* New York: Routledge, 2002.

Holm-Hudson, Kevin, ed. *Progressive Rock Reconsidered.* New York: Routledge, 2002.

Hurst, Charles E. *Social Inequality: Forms, Causes, and Consequences.* Upper Saddle River, N.J.: Prentice Hall, 2007.

Hurtsfield, Jennifer. "'Internal' Colonialism: White, Black, and Chicano Self-Conceptions." *Ethnic and Racial Studies* 1, no. 1 (1978): 60–79.

Jackson, Kenneth T. *Crabgrass Frontier: The Suburbanization of the United States.* New York: Oxford University Press, 1985.

Johnson, Derek. "Fan-tagonism: Factions, Institutions, and Constitutive Hegemonies of Fandom." In *Fandom: Identities and Communities in a Mediated World*, ed. Jonathan Gray, Cornel Sandvoss, and C. Lee Harrington. New York: New York University Press, 2007.

Keil, Charles. "Motion and Feeling through Music." *Journal of Aesthetics and Art Criticism* 24, no. 3 (1966): 337–349.

Kelly, Barbara M., ed. *Suburbia Re-Examined*. New York: Greenwood Press, 1989.

Kelty, Christopher. "Geeks, Social Imaginaries, and Recursive Publics." *Cultural Anthropology* 20, no. 2 (2005): 185–214.

Kenny, Lorraine Delia. *Daughters of Suburbia: Growing Up White, Middle-Class, and Female*. New Brunswick, N.J.: Rutgers University Press, 2000.

King, Roger, and Neill Nugent, eds. *Respectable Rebels: Middle Class Campaigns in Britain in the 1970s*. Toronto: Hodder and Stoughton, 1979.

Klapp, Orrin. *Collective Search for Identity*. New York: Holt, Rinehart and Winston, 1969.

Kling, Rob, Spencer Olin, and Mark Poster, eds. *Postsuburban California: The Transformation of Orange County since World War II*. Berkeley: University of California Press, 1991.

Kordosh, John. "Rush: But Why Are They in Such a Hurry?" *Creem*, June 1981. http://www.rush.dave-ward.com (accessed July 12, 2000).

Krewen, Nick. "Surviving With Rush—Drummer-Lyricist Neil Peart Looks Forward." *Canadian Composer*, April 1986. http://rushworld.net/nmsmirror.com (accessed May 25, 2000).

Krims, Adam. *Rap Music and the Poetics of Identity*. Cambridge: Cambridge University Press, 2000.

Kusserow, Adrie Suzanne. *American Individualisms: Child Rearing and Social Class in Three Neighbourhoods*. New York: Palgrave Macmillan, 2004.

———. "De-Homogenizing American Individualism: Socializing Hard and Soft Individualism in Manhattan and Queens." *Ethos* 27, no. 2 (1999): 210–234.

Lamont, John. "A Farewell to Kings: Rush." *Crawdaddy* (December 1977): 76.

Lewis, Lisa. *Gender Politics and MTV*. Philadelphia: Temple University Press, 1990.

Lindloff, Thomas R., Kelly Coyle, and Debra Grodin. "Is There a Text in This Audience? Science Fiction and Interpretive Schism." In *Theorizing Fandom: Fans, Subculture, and Identity*, ed. Cheryl Harris. Cresskill, N.J.: Hampton Press, 1998.

Lipsitz, George. "The Possessive Investment in Whiteness: Racialized Social Democracy and the 'White' Problem in American Studies." *American Quarterly* 47, no. 3 (1995): 369–387.

──────. *Time Passages: Collective Memory and American Popular Culture*. Minneapolis: University of Minnesota Press, 1990.

Loder, Kurt. "Grace Under Pressure Review." *Rolling Stone,* June 21, 1984. http://www.rush.dave-ward.com (accessed July 12, 2000).

Lukes, Steven. "The Meanings of 'Individualism.'" *Journal of the History of Ideas* 32, no. 1 (1971): 45–66.

Macan, Edward. *Rocking the Classics: English Progressive Rock and the Counterculture*. New York: Oxford University Press, 1997.

Macdonald, Dwight. *Against the American Grain*. New York: Da Capo, 1962.

MacGregor, Roy. "To Hell with Bob Dylan–Meet Rush, They're In It for the Money." *MacLean's,* January 23, 1978. http://rushworld.net/nmsmirror.com (accessed May 25, 2000).

Mack, Bob. "Confessions of a Rush Fan: Justifying His Love for Canada's Prog-Rock Pariahs." *Spin,* March 1992. http://rushworld.net/nmsmirror.com (accessed May 25, 2000).

──────. "Test For Echo." *Rolling Stone,* December 17, 1996. http://www.rollingstone .com.

──────. "Where Angels Fear to Tread: Rush." *Village Voice,* November 5, 1985, 79, 90.

Makowski, Pete. "Adrenaline Rush." *Sounds,* December 18, 1982. http://rushworld .net/nmsmirror.com (accessed May 25, 2000).

Marcus, Greil. *Lipstick Traces: A Secret History of the Twentieth Century*. Cambridge, Mass.: Harvard University Press, 1989.

──────. *Mystery Train: Images of America in Rock 'n' Roll Music*. New York: Dutton, 1982.

Marsh, Dave. "In Another Land—Rock's Icy Edge." *Rolling Stone,* February 24, 1977, 59–62.

Martin, Bill. *Listening to the Future: The Time of Progressive Rock, 1968–1978*. Chicago: Open Court Press, 1998.

Mayer, Arno J. "The Lower Middle Class as Historical Problem." *Journal of Modern History* 47, no. 3 (1975): 409–436.

McClary, Susan. *Feminine Endings: Music, Gender, and Sexuality*. Minneapolis: University of Minnesota Press, 1991.

McDonald, Chris. "Exploring the Gendered Construction of a Rock Audience: The Case of Rush." Paper presented at the Niagara Chapter of the Society for Ethnomusicology, Kent State University, March 14, 1998.

──────. "Grand Designs: A Musical, Social, and Ethnographic Study of Rush." Ph.D. diss., York University, 2002.

──────. "Making Arrows Out of Pointed Words: Critical Reception, Taste Publics, and Rush." *Journal of American and Comparative Cultures* 25, no. 3–4 (2002): 249–259.

McLeod, Kembrew. "*1/2: A Critique of Rock Criticism in North America." *Popular Music* 20, no. 1 (2001): 47–60.

Meltzer, Richard. *The Aesthetics of Rock.* New York: Da Capo Press, 1970.

Middleton, Richard. *Studying Popular Music.* Milton Keynes, UK: Open University Press, 1990.

Miles, Barry. "Rush: Is Everybody Feelin' all Right? (Geddit . . . ?)." *New Musical Express,* March 4, 1978. www.rocksbackpages.com/library/files/miles/00024 _miles_ rush.html (accessed March 17, 2001).

Mills, C. Wright. *White Collar: The American Middle Classes.* New York: Oxford University Press, 1951.

Mitchell, Mark. "Show Don't Tell." *Rock School* 2, no. 3 (1990): 43–54.

Moore, Allan F. *Rock: The Primary Text.* London: Open University Press, 1993.

Negus, Keith. *Music Genres and Corporate Cultures.* New York: Routledge, 1999.

———. *Popular Music in Theory: An Introduction.* Hanover, N.H.: Wesleyan University Press, 1996.

Newquist, H. P. "50 Albums That Shaped Rock Guitar." *Guitar for the Practicing Musician* 13, no. 4 (February 1996): 48.

———. "The 50 Heaviest Riffs of All Time." *Guitar for the Practicing Musician* 12, no. 7 (May 1995): 167.

O'Connor, Carol A. "Sorting Out the Suburbs: Patterns of Land Use, Class, and Culture." *American Quarterly* 37, no. 3 (1985): 382–394.

Oldfield, Michael. "Rush of Blood to the Heads." *Melody Maker,* February 25, 1978, 17.

———. "Rush: A Farewell to Kings." *Melody Maker,* November 5, 1977, 22.

Oliver, Derek. "Grace under Pressure." *Melody Maker,* April 21, 1984, 27.

Ortner, Sherry B. "Reading America: Preliminary Notes on Class and Culture." In *Recapturing Anthropology: Working in the Present,* ed. Richard G. Fox. Santa Fe: School of American Research Press, 1991.

Osbourne, Richard, and Borin van Loon. *Sociology for Beginners.* Cambridge, UK: Icon Books, 1996.

Pantsios, Anastasia. "Canada's Power Trio Is Switched On Live." *Creem,* November 25, 1976. http://rushworld.net/nmsmirror.com (accessed May 25, 2000).

Pareles, Jon. "Exit . . . Stage Left." *Rolling Stone,* February 4, 1982. http://www .rollingstone.com (accessed August 11, 2000).

Peart, Neil. "Creating the Drum Part." *Modern Drummer,* August 1988. http:// rushworld.net/nmsmirror.com (accessed May 25, 2000).

———. *The Masked Rider: Cycling in West Africa.* Lawrencetown Beach, Nova Scotia: Pottersfield Press, 1996.

———. *Roadshow: Landscape with Drums.* Burlington, Mass.: Rounder, 2006.

———. "Rush: Presto." *The Rush Backstage Club Newsletter,* March 1990. http:// rushworld.net/nmsmirror.com (accessed May 25, 2000).

Peretti, Burton W. *Jazz in American Culture.* Chicago: Ivan R. Dee, 1997.

Perry, Pamela. *Shades of White: White Kids and Racial Identities in High School.* Durham, N.C.: Duke University Press, 2002.

Peterson, Richard A. "The Rise and Fall of Highbrow Snobbery as a Status Marker." *Poetics* 25 (1997): 75–92.

Peterson, Richard A., and Roger M. Kern. "Changing Highbrow Taste: From Snob to Omnivore." *American Sociological Review* 61, no. 5 (1996): 900–907.

Phillips, Kevin. *Boiling Point: Republicans, Democrats, and the Decline of Middle-Class Prosperity.* New York: HarperCollins, 1994.

Pillsbury, Glenn T. *Damage Incorporated: Metallica and the Production of Identity.* New York: Routledge, 2006.

Pond, Steve. "Faceless Bands." *Rolling Stone,* February 4, 1982, 37–38.

———. "Rush's Heavy Metal Sludge." *Rolling Stone,* May 15, 1980, 68.

Popoff, Martin. *Contents under Pressure: 30 Years of Rush at Home and Away.* Toronto: ECW Press, 2004.

Price, Carol Selby, and Robert M. Price. *Mystic Rhythms: The Philosophical Vision of Rush.* Berkeley Heights, N.J.: Wildside Press, 1999.

Radway, Janice. *A Feeling for Books: The Book-of-the-Month Club, Literary Taste, and Middle-Class Desire.* Chapel Hill: University of North Carolina Press, 1999.

Rand, Ayn. *Anthem.* New York: Signet, 1938.

———. *Atlas Shrugged.* New York: Signet, 1957.

Reynolds, Simon. *Blissed Out: The Raptures of Rock.* London: Serpent's Tail, 1990.

Riesman, David. *The Lonely Crowd: A Study of the Changing American Character.* New York: Doubleday, 1953.

Roberto, Leonard. *A Simple Kind of Mirror: The Lyrical Vision of Rush.* Lincoln, Neb.: Writers Club Press, 2000.

Rockwell, John. "Pop: Rush Plays at Palladium." *New York Times,* January 15, 1979. http://www.rush.dave-ward.com (accessed July 12, 2000).

Rubin, Joan Shelley. *The Making of Middle/Brow Culture.* 1992. Reprint, Chapel Hill: University of North Carolina Press, 2006.

Saegert, Susan. "Masculine Cities and Feminine Suburbs: Polarized Ideas, Contradictory Realities." *Signs* 5, no. 3 (1980): S96–S111.

Schulte, Frank. "Rush: Straight From the Heart." *Canadian Musician* 13, no. 5 (October 1991): 32–39.

Schwartz, Jim. "Alex Lifeson: Rush's Kinetic Lead Guitarist." *Guitar Player* (June 1980). http://rushworld.net/nmsmirror.com (accessed May 25, 2000).

Scott, Derek B., ed. *The Ashgate Research Companion to Popular Musicology.* Burlington, Vt.: Ashgate, 2009.

Seabrook, John. *Nobrow: The Culture of Marketing, The Marketing of Culture.* London: Methuen, 2001.

Seeger, Charles. *Studies in Musicology, 1935–1975.* Berkeley: University of California Press, 1977.

Selling, Kim Liv. "Nature, Reason and the Legacy of Romanticism: Constructing Genre Fantasy." Ph.D. diss., Centre for Medieval Studies, University of Sydney, 2005.

Sharpe, William, and Leonard Wallock. "Bold New City or Built-Up 'Burb? Redefining Contemporary Suburbia." *American Quarterly* 46, no. 1 (1994): 1–30.

Sheinbaum, John J. "Progressive Rock and the Inversion of Musical Values." In *Progressive Rock Reconsidered,* ed. Kevin Holm-Hudson. New York: Routledge, 2002.

Shepherd, John. *Music as Social Text.* Cambridge: Polity Press, 1991.

Simmons, Sylvie. "The Moustache That Conquered the World: Guiding Genius Neil Peart Grapples with the Paradox." *Sounds,* April 5, 1980. http://rushworld .net/nmsmirror.com (accessed May 25, 2000).

Small, Christopher. *Music of the Common Tongue: Survival and Celebration in Afro-American Music.* 1987. Reprint, New York: Riverrun Press, 1998.

Spera, Keith. "Marathon Concert a Real Rush." *New Orleans Times-Picayune,* December 11, 1996. http://rushworld.net/nmsmirror.com (accessed July 10, 2000).

Stearns, Peter. *American Cool: Constructing a Twentieth-Century Emotional Style.* New York: New York University Press, 1994.

———. *Battleground of Desire: The Struggle for Self-Control in Modern America.* New York: New York University Press, 1999.

———. "The Middle Class: Toward a Precise Definition." *Comparative Studies in Society and History* 21, no. 3 (1979): 377–396.

Stern, Chip. "Neal [*sic*] Peart's Heady Metal." *Musician* no. 16, (June 1998): 89–92, 108.

Stern, Perry. "The Godfathers of Cyber-Tech Go Organic." *Network,* November 1993. http://rushworld.net/nmsmirror.com (accessed May 25, 2000).

———. "Rush: The Boys Focus on the Perfect Song." *Canadian Musician* 7, no. 6 (December 1985): 28–31.

———. "Rush: Real Life In A Rock 'n' Roll Band." *Canadian Musician* 10, no. 1 (February 1988): 36–43.

Stix, John. "Alex Lifeson." *Guitar for the Practicing Musician* 8, no. 7 (May 1991): 88–101.

————. "Alex Lifeson: Classical Precision, Blues Touch." *Guitar for the Practicing Musician* 5, no. 10 (August 1988): 14–22.

————. "Geddy Lee: It's a Groove Thing." *Guitar for the Practicing Musician* 9, no. 2 (December 1991): 81–84, 119.

Stratton, Jon. "Capitalism and Romantic Ideology in the Record Business." *Popular Music* 3 (1983): 143–156.

Straw, Will. "Characterizing Rock Music Culture: The Case of Heavy Metal." In *On Record: Rock, Pop, and the Written Word,* ed. Simon Frith and Andrew Goodwin. New York: Pantheon, 1990.

Stump, Paul. *The Music's All That Matters: A History of Progressive Rock.* London: Quartet Books, 1998.

Swirski, Peter. *From Lowbrow to Nobrow.* Montreal: McGill-Queen's University Press, 2005.

Tagg, Philip. "Open Letter: 'Black Music,' 'Afro-American Music' and 'European Music.'" *Popular Music* 8, no. 3 (October 1989): 285–298.

Taylor, Tim. "Gaelicer than Thou." In *Celtic Modern: Music at the Global Fringe,* ed. Martin Henry Stokes and Philip Bohlman. Lanham, Md.: Scarecrow, 2003.

Telleria, Robert. *Rush Tribute: Merely Players.* Kingston, Ont.: Quarry Music Publishers, 2001.

Testa, Bart. "Lumberjacks Aren't Sissies—Ask BTO" (review of *2112*). *Crawdaddy* (December 1976): 72–73.

Thaler, Max. "Recognition Is Only Half the Fun." *Circus* (November 1977): 35.

Tolleson, Robin. "Geddy Lee: The Bass Is Still Key." *Bass Player* (November 1988). http://rushworld.net/nmsmirror.com (accessed May 25, 2000).

Toombs, Mikel. "Band's Intellectual Music Gets Lost in the Rush." *San Diego Union-Tribune,* February 5, 1996. http://rushworld.net/nmsmirror.com (accessed July 10, 2000).

Treitler, Leo. *Music and the Historical Imagination.* Cambridge, Mass.: Harvard University Press, 1989.

Trott, Clifford G. *Middle-Class Americans: An Endangered Species.* New York: Vantage Press, 1994.

Trudgill, Peter. *On Dialect: Social and Geographical Perspectives.* New York: New York University Press, 1984.

Turkle, Sherry. "Computational Reticence: Why Women Fear the Intimate Machine." In *Technology and Women's Voices: Keeping In Touch,* ed. Cheris Kramarae. New York: Routledge and Kegan Paul, 1988.

Turner, Mary. "Rush: Neil Peart." *Off the Record,* August 27, 1984. http://www.geocities.com/SunsetStrip/Venue/9123/metal.html (accessed February 13, 2000).

Van Eijck, Koen. "Social Differentiation in Musical Taste Patterns." *Social Forces* 79, no. 3 (2001): 1163–1185.

Van Matre, Lynn. "Bucking the Trends, Rush Rides the Crest of 'Permanent Waves.'" *Chicago Tribune,* May 30, 1980. http://rushworld.net/nmsmirror.com (accessed July 10, 2000).

Veneman, Ted. "Interview with Alex Lifeson." *Harmonix* (January 1983). http://rushworld.net/nmsmirror.com (accessed May 25, 2000).

Vidich, Arthur J. *The New Middle Classes: Life-Styles, Status Claims, and Political Orientations.* New York: New York University Press, 1995.

Wagner, Vit. "What a Rush: Veteran Canadian Rock Trio Evokes Cult-Like Response from Fans." *Toronto Star,* May 11, 2002, J1, J8.

Waksman, Steve. *Instruments of Desire: The Electric Guitar and the Shaping of Musical Experience.* Cambridge, Mass.: Harvard University Press, 1999.

Walker, Jeff. *The Ayn Rand Cult.* Chicago: Open Court, 1999.

Walser, Robert. "Deep Jazz: Notes on Interiority, Race, and Criticism." In *Inventing the Psychological: Toward a Cultural History of Emotional Life in America,* ed. Joel Pfister and Nancy Schnog. New Haven, Conn.: Yale University Press, 1997.

———. *Running with the Devil: Power, Gender, and Madness in Heavy Metal.* Hanover, N.H.: Wesleyan University Press, 1993.

Weber, William. "The Muddle of the Middle Classes." *19th Century Music* 3, no. 2 (November 1979): 175–185.

Weinstein, Deena. *Heavy Metal: A Cultural Sociology.* New York: Macmillan, 1991.

———. "Progressive Rock as Text: The Lyrics of Roger Waters." In *Progressive Rock Reconsidered,* ed. Kevin Holm-Hudson. New York: Routledge, 2002.

Weitzman, Steve. "Rush Wrap Up Five-Month Tour." *Circus,* August 31, 1981. http://rushworld.net/nmsmirror.com (accessed May 25, 2000).

Welch, Chris. "Rush: Feeling Groovy." *Rock World* (November 1993). http://rushworld.net/nmsmirror.com (accessed May 25, 2000).

Whitehead, Ralph Jr. "New Collars . . . Bright Collars." *Psychology Today* (October 1988): 44–49.

Wise, Sue. "Sexing Elvis." *Women's Studies International Forum* 7, no. 1 (January 1984): 13–17.

Woolf, Virginia. *The Death of the Moth.* New York: Harcourt Brace, 1942.

SELECTED
DISCOGRAPHY

"Not Fade Away/You Can't Fight It" (single). Moon Records. 1973.
Rush. Anthem Records ANR-1-601. 1974.
Fly by Night. Anthem Records ANR-1-602. 1975.
Caress of Steel. Anthem Records ANR-1-603. 1975.
2112. Anthem Records ANR-1-1001. 1976.
All the World's a Stage (live), Anthem Records ANR-2-1005. 1976.
A Farewell to Kings. Anthem Records ANR-1-1010. 1977.
Archives (compilation). Anthem Records ANR-3-1013. 1978.
Hemispheres. Anthem Records ANR-1-1014. 1978.
Permanent Waves. Anthem Records ANR-1-1021. 1980.
Moving Pictures. Anthem Records ANR-1-1030. 1981.
Exit . . . Stage Left (live). Anthem Records ANR-4-1035. 1981.
Signals. Anthem Records ANR-1-1038. 1982.
Grace Under Pressure. Anthem Records ANR-1-1045. 1984.
Power Windows. Anthem Records ANR-1-1049. 1985.
Hold Your Fire. Anthem Records ANR-1-1051. 1987.
A Show of Hands (live). Anthem Records A1-1055. 1989.
Presto. Anthem Records ANK-1059. 1989.
Chronicles (compilation). Anthem Records AN2K-1060. 1990.
Roll the Bones. Anthem Records ANK-1064. 1991.
Counterparts. Anthem Records ANK-1067. 1993.
Test for Echo. Anthem Records ANSD-1073. 1996.
Different Stages (live). Anthem Records AND3-1092. 1998.
Vapor Trails. Anthem Records 6682510962. 2002.
Snakes and Arrows. Anthem Records 6682520122. 2007.

INDEX

CHRIS MCDONALD, an ethnomusicologist for fifteen years, a musician for twenty, and a Rush fan for twenty-five, obtained his Ph.D. at York University in Toronto. Specializing in popular music studies, he has taught at the University of Western Ontario, York University, and Ryerson University, and currently teaches at Cape Breton University in Sydney, Nova Scotia.